James Leasor was educated at
Oriel College, Oxford. In Wor
into the Royal Berkshire Re
Lincolns in Burma and India,
half years. His experiences ther
both past and present, and in

G000070555

as *Boarding Party* (filmed as *The Sea Wolves*). He is a former
feature writer and foreign correspondent at the *Daily Express*.
There he wrote *The One that Got Away*, the story of the sole
German POW to escape from Allied hands. As well as non-
fiction, Leasor has written novels, including the Dr Jason Love
series, which have been published in 19 countries. *Passport to
Oblivion* was filmed as *Where the Spies Are* with David Niven.

BY THE SAME AUTHOR
ALL PUBLISHED BY HOUSE OF STRATUS

JAMES LEASOR

The Plague
and the Fire

HOUSE OF
STRATUS

This edition published in 2001 by House of Stratus, an imprint of
Stratus Books Ltd., 21 Beeching Park, Kelly Bray,
Cornwall, PL17 8QS, UK.

www.houseofstratus.com

Typeset, printed and bound by House of Stratus.

A catalogue record for this book is available from the British Library
and the Library of Congress.

ISBN 0-7551-0040-9

CONTENTS

CHAPTER ONE

The Squalor in the City

On every night in that cold, clear week before Christmas 1664, the thick white candles had burned late in the Palace of Whitehall. Their dim trembling glow cast gentle shadows on the tapestried walls and was reflected in the smooth silent waters of the wintry river outside.

Lord Sandwich, the Admiral commanding in Portsmouth, had reported that from the West Country a strange new star had been sighted. News of this star had also come from places as far apart as Spain and Danzig.

King Charles II, superstitious, fascinated by the occult, by signs and portents, moved by the utterances of astrologers and soothsayers, and only recently restored to his throne after the end of Cromwell's dictatorship, decided to see this for himself. A comet was not seen unless great and moving events were due; it was conceivable that these might affect him. Thus, each evening he had waited patiently in the huge ground-floor withdrawing room, hung with tapestries for warmth and effect, heated by a fire crackling in a metal grate large enough to hold logs as long as a man.

He waited in no discomfort for its appearance: his Palace had a frontage of nearly half a mile along the river bank, and was unquestionably the greatest house in his Kingdom, and also much more than a King's Palace; it was his home, his office, a meeting place for scientists and courtiers, a centre of royalty and intrigue, a city within a city. The Palace was surrounded by gardens, and it was the King's custom to walk in them every morning and check the accuracy of his watch by a sundial.

King Charles was fascinated by time and how it was measured. Beyond the great room where he awaited a sight of the new star, a small staircase led to his Closet, possibly the only room where he could be himself, without bothering with the pretence of Royalty; where his collection of clocks with moving figures, gilded pendulums, strangely wrought hands and figures chimed and ticked away the hours of waiting.

It was hot near the fire, but elsewhere in the high-ceilinged room the dark velvet curtains that hung across the doorways moved and trembled under the fingers of the wind. Beyond this withdrawing-room was the King's bedchamber, overlooking the Thames, with the fishing boats, the barges and all the traffic of the river.

The King's fiddlers and musicians played endlessly, softly, impersonal as eunuchs in the background, and then suddenly came the news they expected. The music stopped, and the King crossed to the windows of thick cloudy glass and opened them. Stars glittered like a thousand eyes above him in the freezing sky; and then across the frozen arch of heaven he saw a strange star moving.

It seemed larger and yet less bright than the others and for a comet was disappointing; it had no tail and no one could be positive where it had originated or where it went, for abruptly it melted away in the infinite darkness. King Charles was left in the suddenly silent room with the cold wind from the river blowing on his face.

In the City of London, about two miles to the east of the Palace, thousands of the King's subjects also sat up to see the passage of what they called 'The Comet'. They stood on higher ground than the Palace, and many swore that it almost touched the rooftops; an exaggeration, but an indication of their alarm and dread at the unknown. It had been visible on several nights, and with each sight of it the feeling grew that this must surely herald some event of immense importance to London. If not, then why had it come so close?

Samuel Pepys, the Secretary to the Admiralty, went out with his porter at two o'clock on the morning of Christmas Eve to see this star for himself. Lord Sandwich, who had first reported it, was a relation and had nominated him to a clerkship in the Admiralty. Pepys made it his business to see and note all occurrences of interest. The arrival of a comet naturally aroused his curiosity.

Someone told him that it could best be seen from Tower Hill. The night was bright and cold, with nearly a full moon, and the ruts in the road left by carriage wheels had frozen and glittered silver with frost as they climbed. Pepys saw the comet very clearly, noting that it passed 'so very near the houses' that many people considered 'this imported something very peculiar to the City alone'.

And what a small, strange City, lying under the hard mantle of frost, did the faint and flickering trail of that comet illuminate! The City of London stickled with short twisted chimneys, thick as the bristles on a brush, with its 109 church spires, and the houses of lath and tar and plaster; with huts and hovels where thousands crowded together for warmth and necessity, had more in common with the Middle East and the Middle Ages than any Western city since.

It was a city of unbelievable contrasts; a nobleman's house could contain sixty servants, from Steward, Gentleman Usher, Gentleman of the House, to scullions; yet there would be no proper lavatory, apart from a stinking 'house of easement'. Although Sir John Harington had invented the water-closet seventy years earlier, and Queen Elizabeth had copied his design for Richmond Palace and Queen Anne had installed a WC in Windsor Castle, most people still considered this an unnecessary affectation. Servants were so cheap – a good maid cost barely thirty shillings a year – that there was no lack of labour to clear away filth. Bathrooms were similarly rare; a man was old at forty and senile at fifty; yet if he were rich he lived on a scale virtually impossible today. Breakfast for the wealthy consisted of oysters, anchovies, tongue, wine and Northdown ale. And this was only a preparation for the main meal at noon.

Here in the large houses in Covent Garden and Whitehall they ate huge quantities of soups, roast mutton and fish served with pungent sauces; tarts, pies and cheese. Salads contained such strange and exotic ingredients as rosemary, borage flowers, even violet buds. They ate until the sweat streamed down their faces: huge steaming joints of pork, beef or venison, capon, teal, pheasant, snipe, pigeons and larks.

The poor did not fare so well: they lived on bread and roots stolen from farms, on any small animals they could snare, or what the rich men left them.

In London, then as now, rich and poor lived close together; in one street would stand a mass of garrets and filthy tenements swarming like hives with people; across the way could be the town house of a nobleman costing £50,000.

Physically, the City was tiny. It covered barely 448 acres, two-thirds the size of the present-day borough of Chelsea, one-sixth the size of London Airport, about half the total of Hyde Park and Kensington Gardens put together.

Superimposed upon a modern map of Greater London, its river boundary extended for barely a mile, a curving stretch of water from the fifteenth-century Baynard's Castle at Blackfriars to the Tower.

A stout city wall, more than thirty feet high, and nearly as thick, a relic of days when armed bands would ride in from the country round about to loot and rape, ran north from Blackfriars to the first of the City gates – Ludgate, a short distance east of what is now Ludgate Circus. From there the wall enclosed the site of the present Old Bailey, and continued on to Newgate, another of the main City gates with which was combined one of London's chief prisons. On to Aldersgate, the wall turned north to Cripplegate, then east along London Wall to Moorgate and Bishopsgate. Finally, it bore south to Aldgate and the Tower.

On a map of the present-day London Underground system, the extent of the old City, commemorated by the names of its gates, forms only a small loop at the eastern end of the Circle Line. Yet this tiny area was the richest, most important city in north Europe. In this small, cramped area, roughly half a million people lived and worked; and here in the summer and autumn of the year 1665 nearly one in every four died of the Great Plague.

Londoners were very parochial in attitude and outlook; to all of them Knightsbridge and Kensington were remote villages on the Bath Road, dangerous to reach and seldom visited. Nearly a hundred years later, this road west to Kensington was still described by Lord Hervey, then Lord Privy Seal, as 'a great impassable gulf of mud'. In 1665 it was far worse: a river of liquid mud and manure in wet weather; a dusty, rutted, indefinite lane through fields in summer.

The small hills around London, which slowed down the unsprung coaches and carriages and the farm carts drawn by teams of shaggy Shire horses, were thick with highwaymen, footpads and gangs of thieves; with Army and Navy deserters, desperate for food and afraid to venture into town. Such men would hold up any coach and kill for a few coppers. If caught, they were strung up on a gibbet above the road they had terrorized, for birds to pick; the body of one such criminal swung from a tree on top of Shooter's Hill on the Dover Road all through that year. Most of them escaped this rough justice; they bribed coachmen to bog their coaches in the mud so that they could ambush them more easily, and paid postillions to drop the reins.

Professional highwaymen had their own beats, their own limits. On Finchley Common some would hide behind a large oak tree in wait for unsuspecting, unaccompanied riders. This tree regularly received a fusillade of bullets from zealous guards on passing coaches, in the hope of hitting at least one highwayman.

If a journey beyond the City walls, out west through the marshes of Uxbridge and Hillingdon, or south-west to Dover, was dangerous in summer and virtually impossible in any other season, it was also enormously expensive. The coach from Aldersgate, highwaymen permitting, took three days to reach Salisbury; a seat on it cost twenty shillings. For £2 – more than the annual salary for a good woman servant – a man could travel twice the distance to Exeter.

Travel within the City also had its peculiar hazards, although from the south bank of the Thames the City certainly presented a noble view.

Dominated by St Paul's Cathedral, the skyline was castellated by slim church spires. At the eastern end, old London Bridge threw its nineteen arches across the Thames, not unlike the Ponte Vecchio in Florence. Inside the City, however, the scene was distinctly less ethereal and more earthy. Streets were tortuous and narrow, paved with cobbles, slippery with dung and urine; timber-framed Tudor houses leaned across them from either side, like old crones whispering secrets to each other.

The Restoration of Charles II to the throne had brought with it a wave of optimism in the future; rich and poor had flocked to London in the confident expectation of a settled reign and a new prosperity.

Overcrowding was fantastic; twenty, thirty, forty people would live crammed together in a three-roomed house, sleeping and eating by rota. The stinking side-streets wound meaninglessly and without plan into squares and yards and still more streets. Open drains trickled down their centres, buzzing with dark swarms of flies in summer, and dangerous roaring rivers of sewage after rain. Most houses lacked gutters and so rainwater streamed in cascades from their eaves. Into these drains also went all kitchen waste and garbage. The next downpour of rain would carry away along the crude culverts everything the scavenging dogs, cats, pigs and beggars could not remove. Pedestrians had to pick their way through these streaming streets, and at the same time avoid buckets of night soil or faeces that householders emptied out of upper windows with no word of warning or thought for those beneath. Many wore pattens, odd-shaped metal platforms which fitted beneath their shoes, and which could be removed before entering a house, to keep their feet out of the muck.

The City Corporation employed 'rakers' and scavengers to clear away the worst of the filth, but the work was foul and most people, even in the poverty of that time, considered hunger or crime preferable to shovelling away these crawling streams of putrefaction. Refuse and excreta would accumulate until the whole city reeked like a giant privy: the stench was oriental.

The scavengers had, in any case, no effective means of disposing of what they had collected. Piles of decomposing matter were merely heaped in pyramids, known as 'lay-stalls', around the outskirts of the City. There they rotted, fouling the air with their stench. Sometimes they were dumped into the river; then they polluted the water and killed the fish.

Courtiers and ladies of fashion carried scented handkerchiefs or held posies of flowers to their noses to filter the air they breathed. When the Plague began, the stench of the dead and dying increased the foulness of the atmosphere, so that much reliance was placed on 'pomanders' and 'pouncet-boxes' – collections of pungent or sweet-smelling herbs that people carried or wore in an attempt to sweeten the air they breathed. Some even went so far as to plug their nostrils with pellets of wormwood and rue and breathed through their mouths.

Seventeenth-century England was not a fastidious country, but even Londoners born in the City and accustomed to these conditions since childhood, found them intolerable. There were frequent complaints to the Lord Mayor about the rivers of liquid manure that coursed through the streets; about alley-ways and side-streets almost knee-deep in mud; about half-paved thoroughfares overflowing with water because there were no drains, and rows of gutterless houses where filthy water showered down on passers-by long after a storm.

The City Fathers had made some half-hearted attempts to remedy the worst of the horrors. The Town Ditch, an open sewer, was being filled in, but below Ludgate the Fleet River contained the bloated bodies of dead animals and even unwanted babies. Some farmers drove their pigs into its stinking slime in order to fatten them more quickly.

Short of rebuilding the entire City, there seemed little chance of substantial improvements; and when the Fire finally gave the City Fathers this opportunity, they were too dilatory to make use of it.

The only access from the suburbs to the old walled City, the centre of commerce and industry, was through one or other of the City gates, or across London Bridge. Several of the gates, including Aldgate, Aldersgate, Newgate and Cripplegate, had been rebuilt and widened since 1630, but without any thought or regard to the fact that the population of both City and suburbs would more than double in thirty years, and that industries within the walls would also develop enormously, with a consequent increase in traffic.

Many of London's necessities and the raw material for these industries – such as coal – arrived in barges, but an ever-increasing amount came in on horses and carts. This meant chaos at the City gates. Long lines of carts pulled by teams of heavy horses, plus beautifully painted and accoutred coaches, and hackney carriages, frequently queued for hours for admission. Travellers suffered what one of them called 'intolerable stops and embarrasses'. Sometimes the drivers fought each other for the right to go through first. Little barefoot boys nipped between the coaches and stole anything removable. In rainy weather, with steaming weary horses, soaked passengers, cursing coachmen and horses falling down in the mud, delays were infinitely worse.

On London Bridge congestion was even more severe. It had been built in the thirteenth century, during the reign of King John. It extended for about 400 yards, nineteen arches of masonry supporting it twenty yards above the river. Apart from a drawbridge at the centre, raised to let through high-masted vessels, the bridge was lined on both sides by decrepit, overhanging houses, so that its full width was barely thirty feet. This meant almost continual traffic jams in the narrow thoroughfare.

To add to the confusion, half-hearted attempts had been going on for twenty years to repair serious damage which the bridge had suffered in a fire thirty-three years earlier, when in eight hours more than forty houses at the northern end were completely gutted. The fire-fighters' efforts had been hampered by the fact that the Thames was frozen over and they could not break the ice to draw water. The blaze began because of 'the carelessness of a needlemaker's servant near St Magnus' Church, leaving a tub of hot ashes under a pair of stairs'. Its effects were still being felt, for little had been done in the meantime to restore the damage, apart from nailing up a row of planks to stop drunks from falling into the Thames.

Once inside the City, the confusion and congestion was as bad as at the gates. No pavements or sidewalks existed, and the roadways extended, often without interruption, from wall to wall of the houses facing each other across every street. Frequently these roads were so narrow that the gables of facing houses almost met above the heads of passers-by, shutting out the light. Only after the Great Fire had virtually destroyed the City did the King authorize an Act which stipulated that the more important roads should have a minimum width of fourteen feet.

The unhappy pedestrian, unprotected by raised footways, walked in far greater fear of injury than at any time since. Licensed hackney carriages had been plying for trade for the past thirty years, and the huge carriages of the rich had multiplied with the return of the Monarchy. In these wooden-wheeled vehicles, as large as a small room, the well-to-do trundled through the stinking streets, spraying less fortunate pedestrians with mud and filth from their gigantic wheels.

In some streets foot passengers could leap from under the pounding hooves of horses and hold on to thick wooden posts, known as 'massy' posts, and originally intended as a kind of bumper to prevent damage to houses from passing carts and drays.

Sedan chairs had also become a fashionable mode of conveyance since Charles I had brought three back from his travels in Spain. They provided not only a novel but frequently a quicker method of travel than the coach in these congested streets: they had become the seventeenth-century equivalent of the bubble-car. Thus, the pedestrian taking shelter behind the 'massy' posts was quite likely to escape being trodden down by the foam-flecked horses of the rich, only to be knocked unceremoniously aside by sweating chairmen rushing some highly born burden to a lunch with his mistress.

Another cause of confusion arose from the fearful smoke pollution. Nearly all the manufacturers – the iron smelters, the makers of soap, the brewers and others who day and night burned great quantities of coal – had their factories within the City walls. Dense, choking clouds of thick black smoke hung over the rooftops, making the air foul and adding to the grime. The smoke became so thick (for even the chimney stacks of the furnaces were no higher than the roofs) that people could scarcely see one another in the streets, and stumbled about coughing and spluttering, as though walking in a never-lifting fog.

With 15,000 houses also using coal for heating their rooms and boiling their water, it was not surprising that John Evelyn, a middle-aged Government official with a habit of making notes on all he saw, should write a pamphlet on the subject.

'This horrid smoke obscures our churches and makes our palaces look old,' he wrote. 'It fouls our clothes and corrupts the waters, so that the very rain and refreshing dews that fall in the several seasons precipitate this impure vapour, which with its black and tenacious quality, spots and contaminates whatever is exposed to it.'

King Charles immediately commanded Evelyn to prepare a Bill incorporating reforms which could be placed before Parliament. But, of course, before the matter reached the Commons, the Plague and Fire had effected reforms far more dramatic.

Many noble families and some rich merchants had already abandoned the crowded City and set the fashion of moving westwards. They built fine, spacious houses along the river towards Westminster, at Whitehall, at Knight's Bridge, across the low-lying ground divided by a stream known as West Bourne; and at the village of Paddington. Farther west, the villages of Brompton, Chelsea (already famous for its buns) and Battersea had also started to grow.

Along what is now Victoria Embankment stood several great houses: Arundel House, Somerset House and Northumberland House among them. Around Hyde Park, Bays Watering and Mary-le-Bone new houses were also being built. Soho Fields, Pall Mall and St James's were the choice of those with a taste for solitude, and the Haymarket, which served the function its name implies, contained only one house.

In neighbouring Piccadilly not even one house was built: here the ground rose to command an uninterrupted view over lawns, woods and the park of St James's Palace towards Westminster and the river.

Tremendous business was done round the clock in upwards of a thousand taverns within the City limits. These included many 'dives' or cellars that specialized in bawdy and depraved entertainments; men, women, boys, even animals were among the performers. Pornographic spectacles were not uncommon, even in public; a great fair, which was held on a site near Piccadilly each May, was suppressed several times because of the crude excesses perpetrated there, although it managed to survive, in a censored form, until 1809.

Venereal disease was a scourge of the times, and two lock-hospitals [1] at Southwark and Kingsland were maintained to treat the sufferers. Hundreds, probably thousands, died from

11

this disease every year, although the causes of death were often disguised in parish registers as 'ulcers', 'sores', and other more respectable ailments. According to one account, only the parish clerks in St Giles-in-the-Fields and St Martin-in-the-Fields honestly recorded the true number of deaths from 'the Pox', and these probably only because they had to. Their two parishes contained 'most of the vilest and most miserable Houses of Uncleanness' to be found.

Drink was another London weakness, and often fatal; no less than 3,986 people are officially admitted to have died of dropsy caused by alcohol between 1657 and 1665; this figure was again probably only a fraction of the real total.

The Court also treasured a well-deserved reputation for licentiousness and debauchery. Anthony à Wood, an Oxford scholar in his thirties at the time of the Plague, made some outspoken comments in his private journals about the Royal circle, which moved to Oxford to escape the epidemic. The chief courtiers, noted Wood bitterly, were 'high, proud, insolent and looked upon Scolars no more than Pedants... Very nasty and beastly, leaving at their departure their excrements in every corner, in chimneys, studies, colehouses, cellers'. They were, in the main, 'rude, rough, whoremongers, vaine, empty, carelesse'.

Despite the wealth of London, the main buildings were not notably impressive and generally in poor repair. St Paul's Cathedral was one of these. In 1630 the renowned architect Inigo Jones had been commissioned to restore this Cathedral, which had been in a semi-ruined state since being severely damaged by lightning half a century before. Jones rebuilt the nave in Portland stone and transformed the west front into a magnificent near-replica of a Roman temple. To the Puritans during the Commonwealth his grand design savoured of Popery; their soldiers used the cathedral as stabling for their horses, tore down the ancient carving for woodwork, and showed their final contempt by playing ninepins in the splendid portico.

Nor did the Restoration change the public attitude towards the Cathedral. Itinerant vendors still used the aisle as a place of barter, young bloods and 'swaggering roisterers' would call there for assignments, for prostitutes found it a popular promenade. Now, a dilapidated mixture of Gothic and Renaissance, the City's first place of worship was surrounded by a mass of grimy, tottering timber houses which had crept up to its walls.

The Tower, a steel-grey fortress standing guard over the river, was in little better condition. Around it ran an evil-smelling ditch, soggy with sewage and the decomposing bodies of cats and dogs. On the far bank stood huddles of decayed houses. Even the ancient Guildhall was hidden from view by a maze of streets and jumbled rooftops and lacked any open approach from which a visitor could admire it.

Such was London in the year the Plague broke out, a city of contrasts: hunger and prodigality, filth and luxury; a boudoir next to a dung hill.

London had known at least three serious epidemics of plague in the previous sixty years. In the first of these outbreaks, in 1603, more than 30,000 people died. Queen Elizabeth, who had retreated to Windsor in the face of an earlier plague epidemic forty years before, had been so alarmed that she set up gallows in the market place to hang anyone who dared to enter Windsor from the capital in case they brought the plague with them. Twenty-two years later, another epidemic killed 35,000 Londoners; indeed, until the City was stricken again in 1665, this was known as 'The Great Plague'. In 1636, too, 10,400 people died of plague out of a total death roll for the year of 23,000. Indeed, in only four separate years since 1603 had London been completely free from plague.

When the strange new comet soared through the winter sky at Christmas 1664, severe onslaughts of the Black Death,[2] as the plague was popularly called, had been raging on the Continent, particularly in Holland, for some time; but since Holland was a week's journey away and Britain was on the point of war with the Dutch, London was neither much concerned nor perturbed.

Twenty-eight years previously, the College of Physicians had defined a number of 'annoyances' which they considered were likely to encourage epidemics of the plague. These included fouled sewers and drains, pools of filthy water left lying in the streets, refuse discarded near houses, churchyards filled to overflowing with corpses buried after previous plagues and tainted food, which was almost staple diet among the poor. But when the full horror of the greatest plague of all engulfed the City, virtually no measures had been taken against any of these things. The foul atmosphere, the unsavoury streets, the rat-infested, rickety houses, often only restrained from falling on to each other by props and bars, remained as they had been.

Yet if living conditions within the City walls were disturbing, the situation in the 'Liberties' and 'out-parishes' immediately bordering the City were far worse.

The Restoration had brought vast numbers of wretchedly paid, ambitious craftsmen and tradespeople into London. The City was quite incapable of absorbing them, and this had resulted in the rapid growth of out-parishes, or suburbs, which spread in a rash of wooden shanties outwards from the City walls into the green fields that had formerly ringed in the capital.

It was calculated that more than a quarter of a million people lived in these parishes, far more densely packed together than in the City. In addition to those from the country and provinces who hoped to make their fortunes in London, refugees had settled there to escape religious persecution on the Continent. Most were Protestant weavers existing in hovels built of plaster and wattle or boards. One contemporary estimate thought that they numbered a hundred thousand, but although this was probably an exaggeration, these immigrants formed large communities in Shoreditch, Stepney, Whitechapel and Bishopsgate.

In an effort to protect London from the chronic diseases which afflicted these outside parishes, and to prevent the swallowing up of all fields and open land outside the City walls, several Acts had been passed to stop further haphazard development. These were largely ignored, and so the shanty towns grew, virtually unaccompanied by sanitation or drainage. It was thus no wonder that when plague struck, these were the areas most seriously affected.

One in every fourteen people in Britain lived in London, and probably three-fifths of all Londoners lived in the crammed Liberties and nearer out-parishes, which included Holborn, St Bartholomew, St Bridget, Bridewell, Aldersgate, Aldgate, Bishopsgate, St Dunstan-in-the-West, Cripplegate, St Sepulchre's, the Minories, Whitechapel and Southwark. The rest lived in the farther suburbs, such as St Giles-in-the-Fields, Stepney, Redriff, Newington, Lambeth, Islington, Hackney, Westminster, St Martin-in-the-Fields, Clerkenwell, Bermondsey, Shoreditch and Rotherhithe.

Thus possibly 276,000 Londoners lived herded together in a narrow belt of parishes clustered about the City walls. Several of these parishes stood on the edge of polluted streams, such as the River Fleet.

Within this decaying arc around the City, thousands of mean dwellings were built back to back, their shaky timber frames filled in with wattle or planks, waterproofed with pitch, or at best with laths and roughcast plaster: building with brick and stone was still only for the well-to-do. Thousands more lived in tenements converted from noblemen's town houses. Many of the Royalist families who returned with Charles II found that their houses had been commandeered by homeless families during the Commonwealth. Dozens of such families would occupy a single great house. The splendours of town houses owned by the Earl of Arundel, Lord Rivers and the Dean of St Paul's all disappeared in this way, as did the ruined Palace of the Bishop of London near St Paul's. The destructive habits of the occupants, who tore out doors and banisters for firewood, and a complete lack of repair and any maintenance, soon transformed these buildings into rat-infested slums, containing an almost unbelievable number of people living in squalor and wretchedness.

Shortly before the plague began, John Graunt, a Fellow of the Royal Society, made the first detailed study of London's population and death rates from various diseases. He was a professional statistician, an unusual profession at that time, who carried on business at the sign of the Seven Stars in the City. Earlier, he had been apprenticed to a haberdasher, and despite his humble beginnings, Charles II personally recommended that he be elected to the Royal Society, adding 'if there found any more such tradesmen, they should be sure to admit them all, without any more adoe'. His so-called 'Bills of Mortality' are probably the most reliable guide to the population of the day and the diseases that were most prevalent.

Graunt declared that 'London, the Metropolis of England, is perhaps a Head too big for the Body... Our parishes are now grown madly disproportionable... The old streets are unfit for the present frequency of coaches.' He estimated the total population of the City of London, the Liberties, Westminster and the farther out-parishes at 460,000 – about as large as those of Edinburgh or Bristol today.

The French Ambassador, Count Cominges, who reported to his king that London was 'a great and wealthy city', added that the population occupied houses only two storeys high – but compensated for this 'by the existence under them of cellars so full of people...that it would be difficult to try to give their exact numbers'. He considered that London contained 600,000 people.

Graunt based his calculations upon his 'Bills of Mortality', which were published every week, recording, among other things, the number of deaths, and their causes, in each of more than 130 parishes. These Bills were available to anyone who cared to subscribe four shillings a year for the privilege of reading them. They were not always accurate as regards the causes of death, for information about deaths was brought to the clerk of each parish by 'searchers of the dead'. These were ignorant, impoverished and often venal old women, who either by age or physical or mental infirmity were capable of no other work, and who did this job simply to avoid becoming a charge upon their parish.

'When any one dieth,' wrote Graunt, 'either the Tolling or Ringing of the Bell, or the bespeaking of a Grave, intimateth to the Searchers (who keep a strict Correspondence with the Sexton), and thereupon the Ancient Matrons sworn to that Office, repair to the Place where the dead Corps lieth, and upon their own View, and others' Examination, make a Judgment by what Disease or Casualty the Corps died; which Judgment they report to the Parish Clerk...'

For each death they reported the 'searchers' were entitled to a small fee, generally about fourpence. Any examination by others more expert in medical matters was seldom made, so the cause of death was generally left entirely for them. Hungry, cold, wretched and lonely, forced to live by the deaths of others, many of them were thankful to augment their tiny incomes by taking a bribe to disguise the cause of death. The fact that they had taken solemn oaths 'diligently to search the corps' and report the cause of death 'faithfully, honestly, unfeignedly and impartially', was not so important as their next meal.

People could scarcely be condemned for trying to conceal any plague deaths which occurred in their own households, for disclosure meant that the whole family, or even several families, would immediately be shut up in the infected house for forty days' quarantine. Thus to admit that someone had died of plague was tantamount to signing their own death warrants; frequently every member of the family died because of these inhumane regulations.

Dr Thomas Vincent, a divine who remained in London throughout both Plague and Fire, noted that: 'It was very Dismal to behold the Red Crosses, and read in great letters "Lord Have Mercy Upon Us" on the doors, and Watchmen standing beside them with Halberts, and such a solitude about those places, and people passing by them so gingerly and with such fearful looks,

17

as if they had been lined with enemies in ambush that waited to destroy them.'

The more enlightened medical men of the time were unanimous in condemning their practice of close confinement, which only increased infection and the death rolls; but this did not have any effect on those responsible for the law. It was thus infinitely safer to conceal any Plague deaths. This was not difficult to do, for medical science in England had made little progress since the Middle Ages; thus, some entries in the Bills made strange reading.

When the cause of death was clearly violent or accidental the searchers were able to make more confident claims. Thus, in 1665 one man is known to have died as a result of being 'scalded in a brewer's mash, at St Giles, Cripplegate'; a woman 'poysoned herself at St Anne, Blackfryers'; another 'starved herself at St Leonards, Fosterland'; a middle-aged man was 'Murdered at St Martin-in-the-Fields', yet another 'died with the fall of a house at St Mary, Whitechapel'.

But when the fatality resulted from disease diagnosis was more difficult. A typical list includes as causes of death: 'French Pox', 'Frighted', 'Griping in the Guts', 'Lethargy', 'Planet' (supposed to be the malign influence of the stars), 'Rising of the Lights', and, in sheer despair, 'Suddenly'. According to the reports of the searchers, 'Teeth', 'Tiffick', 'Winde' and 'Worms' also accounted for large numbers of the population. In cases where the corpse was 'very lean and worn away' the searchers invariably diagnosed consumption.

'After the mist of a Cup of Ale, and the Bribe of a Two-Groat fee instead of one given them,' wrote one contemporary, the poor old women could not tell whether the emaciation was from 'a Phthisis', a 'Hectick Fever' or 'The Pox'. Anyone over sixty who died without obvious injury or ailment was simply said to have been 'Aged'.

Shortly before Christmas each year an annual summary of the Bills was issued to the subscribers, and, in time of plague or other epidemic, the rich based their decision whether to remain in London or retreat to their country houses upon these annual death totals. Even if they avoided plague, however, they would probably succumb to some other illness fairly soon. Of every hundred babies who survived birth, thirty-six died before they were six; twenty-four more before their sixteenth birthday and another fifteen by the age of twenty-six. Thus, only a quarter of the population survived to reach full maturity.

Such was the City of London on the eve of 1665, when the blazing comet suddenly appeared to fascinate and perturb King and commoners alike.

1. The word comes from Loke, meaning a house for lepers; as leprosy declined as a disease, VD patients increased, and presumably moved into the building in their place.
2. The Black Death took its name from the black spots which covered the body of the person attacked. It was a contagious fever which, like the pestilence in the reign of Justinian, entered Europe from the East, and made terrible ravages. In Germany during the mid-fourteenth century more than 1,000,000 people died of it, while in England possibly one half of the population was affected. The pestilence had also been especially severe in Florence, in Italy.

   Under the terror of this visitation, religious penitents, seeking to turn away what they felt was Divine displeasure by unusual penances, went about in procession, lacerating themselves with whips. They were called flagellants; this religious frenzy had its most remarkable manifestations in Germany.

CHAPTER TWO

The Signs

On the morning after the Comet was first seen, John Allin, an unlicensed physician who was practising in London, wrote to a friend in the country: 'Ye chief discourse is of a blazing starr – ye city was last night setting up to see it.'

Why it should have so suddenly appeared, and what this appearance meant, was the subject of what Pepys called 'mighty talk' in almost every tavern and coffee house. Fellows of the Royal Society even conducted experiments and read papers to each other in an endeavour to explain its significance. No one was much comforted or convinced by their belief that it had no significance whatever.

John Milton, the blind poet, who was then fifty-seven and living in Artillery Walk, Bunhill Fields, with his third wife, thirty-three years his junior, whom he had never seen, probably referred to this star when he wrote of:

> a Comet
> That Fires the Length of Ophiucus huge
> In th'Artick Sky, and from his horrid hair
> Shakes Pestilence and Warr.

Britain was already at war with Holland, and the Bills of Mortality had already recorded three cases of death by 'Pestilence', one of them in the out-parish of St Giles-in-the-Fields [1] during December.

20

This caused little concern, for London was rarely entirely free from plague, and an occasional case among the thousands of deaths from other diseases set out in the Bills could pass almost unnoticed. It was no more remarkable than a case of diphtheria would be today.

During the whole of 1664 only five cases had been recorded, three in Whitechapel, one at Cripplegate and one at Aldgate: Portsmouth, seventy miles away, had also reported several plague deaths. But throughout London many people must have been dying from plague during those last two weeks in December, and relatives effectively concealed the real cause of death.

Dr Nathaniel Hodges, a physician and a physician's son, who practised in Watling Street, and who stayed in London throughout the Great Plague, recalled that 'in the middle of the Christmas Holy-Days I was called to a young man in a Fever, who after two days Course of alexiterial Medicines, had two Risings about the bigness of a Nytmeg broke out, one on each Thigh'.

From the black, soft appearance of these swellings, and the ominous inflamed circle around them, the doctor rightly diagnosed them as 'plague tokens'. Under his care, however, the patient recovered, and no report was made: indeed, if the patient recovered a doctor was not called to make one.

Another factor helped to conceal the existence of plague; the cruel weather. London lay in the grip of one of the most severe winters in memory; even the Thames froze over. From November 1664 until March 1665 there was almost continuous black frost and, as earlier experience had already proved, cold weather always held the Black Death in check.

The summer had been unusually hot and oppressive, remarkable for swarms of flies and small flying insects.

William Boghurst, an apothecary whose shop was near the White Hart Inn, in St Giles-in-the-Fields, probably near where Denmark Street now is, recalled afterwards: 'There was such a multitude of flyes that they lined the insides of houses, and if any threads or strings did hang downe in any place, it was presently thicke set with flyes like a rope of onions, and swarm of Ants covered the highways that you might have taken up a handful at a tyme, both winged and creeping Ants.'

In the foul ditches on either side of the parched roads of cracked mud, he discovered 'such a multitude of croaking froggs that you might have heard them before you saw them'.

Boghurst was thirty-four, with a young family. Frequently he practised unofficially as physician, as did many apothecaries, and he was alarmed that smallpox, an endemic disease in England, had been very prevalent at the time of the plague of insects. It 'was soe rife in our parish that betwixt the Church and the Pound in St Giles, which is not above six score paces, about forty familyes had the Small Pox'.

Boghurst also knew that cases of plague had occurred in his parish, and also in the parishes of St Clement's, St Paul's Cripplegate and St Martin's; these cases had all been successfully concealed from the authorities. But since such deceptions were commonplace, there seemed nothing particularly sinister about this, and certainly no reason why he should make himself unpopular by taking the matter farther. He did not know that while London was not concerned with the prospect of an epidemic but with the arrival of the new comet, many thousands on the Continent had already died from plague. Holland had been badly affected, and at least 10,000 died in Amsterdam alone.

As plague spread rapidly to The Hague and Leyden, merchant ships from Spain, Portugal, France and England refused to call in at Dutch ports, lest their crews fell ill.

By August – when flying insects were annoying the citizens of London – Antwerp was already riddled with plague and a spokesman of the burghers of a nation almost entirely reliant upon its maritime trade reported despairingly: 'We can very hardly find men to serve us – at our wits end what to do, either with our persons or our estates.'

That month, Edinburgh and London banned trade with Dutch ships, and King Charles forbade any further traffic with

Holland until the following December. The Dutch Ambassador bitterly complained that this move was a mere pretence, an unfair stroke in the trade battle that had already run on between the two nations for many years. In reply, Charles declared his 'affliction' for the suffering of Holland, but emphasized the need to protect his own people.

The Dutch naturally tried to minimize the full horror of their own situation, but with a thousand people dying every week in Amsterdam alone this soon became difficult to do. Their trade was slowly being strangled, 'a plague', as one recorded, 'scarce inferior to the other'. Then, with the arrival of cooler autumn weather, casualties from the plague in Holland decreased, but the threat of war with England became much greater.

Such a prospect found plenty of popular support in London, for there had been much friction between England and Holland over mercantile expansion in the East Indies, in North America and West Africa; and for the past two years sporadic naval engagements had been fought over disputed Dutch possessions on the African coast. In addition, the Dutch were at war with England's old ally, Portugal, and England had seized the Dutch settlement of New Amsterdam in America and changed its name to New York, in honour of the King's brother, the Duke of York.

Periodic reports of these happenings, and of the spread of the Dutch plague to Germany, Belgium and France, appeared in the *Publick Intelligencer*, a twice-weekly news sheet published in London by one Roger L'Estrange. He was a loyal supporter of the monarchy, and as such had more than once been in fear of his life during Oliver Cromwell's Commonwealth regime. As a reward for his loyalty, King Charles, on his restoration to the throne, gave L'Estrange the congenial task of advising on newspapers. L'Estrange was not the most obvious choice for the post; he believed that newspapers printing too much news could be dangerous to authority, for 'that makes the multitude too familiar with the actions and counsels of their superiors'.

Since L'Estrange was entirely dependent for his livelihood upon the favour of the Court, he was naturally careful not to publish anything which could conceivably embarrass them or make their social inferiors too familiar with their actions. Thus L'Estrange, as with some editors since, tried to publish news his superiors would want to read – or what he thought they wanted to read. The throne was so recently re-established that news of a possible plague outbreak was not likely to be popular – especially since some people felt that plague was a divine visitation on the capital for the sins of the King and his Court.

Graunt, in his work *Natural and Political Observations*, carefully remarked in his dedication to Lord Roberts, the Lord Privy Seal, 'that the opinion of Plague accompanying the Entrance of Kings is false and seditious'.

Disgruntled Puritans, incensed at the return of the monarchy, had been at some pains to promote the theory that the accession of a Stuart King was a signal for disaster. They pointed out that the calamitous plagues of 1603 and 1625 had both coincided with the enthronement of Kings of that ill-fated line – James I and Charles I.

L'Estrange ignored such controversial matters; it was safer and more prudent to do so. Early in May he announced that 'His Sacred Majesty, having declared it his Royal will and purpose to continue the healing of his people for the Evil during the month of May and then to give over till Michaelmas next, I am commanded to give notice thereof that the people may not come up to Town in the Interim and lose their labour.'

Such a report could give nothing but pleasure to his King; and what pleased Charles naturally pleased him. For months after the terrible scourge of the Black Death began to empty London's streets, the *Intelligencer* still pretended that nothing very much out of the ordinary had taken place.

Thus most Londoners remained quite unmoved by odd reports and rumours from travellers who visited the capital from the Continent. Those able to read for themselves could find no corroboration of such things in the few newspapers of the day;

those who could not read did not greatly care. 'Let the foreigner suffer, particularly as we expect to be waging a victorious war against him any day now,' was a typical reaction.

Foreigners were distrusted and disliked; in a community so insular that a man from the next village, two miles away, was considered a foreigner, a visitor from another country, wearing strange clothes, not even speaking English, was as alien then as a Martian would be today.

When a 'prodigious rain' fell upon the devastated cities of Haarlem and Amsterdam, 'which, dropping upon the Trees, was in a moment turn'd to Ice, to the bigness of a man's Arme, tearing up some with the weight, and splitting others', the taproom philosophers in London interpreted this as a judgement upon the proud Dutch for their notorious vanity about the luxuriance of their plants. It was only what such foreigners deserved; and when war was declared on Holland in February 1665, there was general approval that the foreigners would be taught 'a notable lesson'. But what this would be few cared to say.

The Government maintained a more cautious attitude towards the news of plague in Holland. Some realized that plague was contagious, as had been proved by its spread from country to country. There was concern lest impoverished fishing towns like Great Yarmouth, on the east coast, might be tempted 'to hazard themselves for a present advantage' by trading with the Dutch fishing fleet, unless restrained by threats of severe penalty. In fact, several houses in Yarmouth were boarded up and their occupants quarantined because of illicit meetings with Dutch sailors. Even so, only one man died of plague, and the disease did not spread.

A letter from a Government official at Yarmouth, dated November 30th, 1665, mentioned that local searchers of the dead had reported that plague was spreading, but the writer added reassuringly: 'They are drunken persons and very poor, and may make false returns because of the large allowance they have for this work.'

Nevertheless, a close watch was kept upon ports, and Navy officials began to insist upon proper inspection of shipping, certificates of clearance, and strict quarantine of all suspect vessels. But of these things the public knew nothing and cared less; for the overwhelming majority their chief concern was simply to find work and enough to eat. Such matters of policy were above their heads and beyond their understanding.

So in an atmosphere of total unpreparedness the year of 1665 began, with ground like concrete in the severe frost. Most areas around the capital were suffering from a drought, unbroken since October, when the instalment of London's new Lord Mayor, Sir John Lawrence, in the presence of the King and Queen and in unprecedented grandeur, had been marred by heavy rain.

In March the frost broke and a second comet, bigger and brighter than the first, swept its trail across the heavens. This further omen in the sky heaped fuel upon the fires of superstition, and caused widespread trepidation. What did this portend? No one knew, but equally no one liked to appear ignorant. Thus, in their anxiety to find an answer, hundreds sought the opinion of fortune-tellers and astrologers.

'This folly,' wrote Defoe, 'presently made the town swarm with a wicked generation of pretenders to magic, to the Black Art as they called it.' These 'pretenders' practised their trade openly – as fortune-tellers still do in fairgrounds and seaside booths – and their signs and inscriptions were usually exhibited above their doors. 'Friar Bacon's Brazen Head', or a silhouette of Merlin, the legendary wizard at the Court of King Arthur, were popular insignia.

Defoe was forthright in his scorn of such people – and also in his contempt for those who believed the future could be foretold: 'If but a grave fellow in a velvet jacket, a band, and a black cloak, which was the habit those quack conjurers generally went in, was but seen in the street,' he wrote, ' the people would follow them in crowds and ask them questions as they went along.'

26

The grave fellows in the velvet jackets were naturally not slow to capitalize on this public interest. They realized that bad news obviously seemed more important to their clients than good – perhaps because it seemed so much more likely to happen – and accordingly they laced their almanacs liberally with gloomy prophecies. Hawkers cried these pamphlets through the packed streets, but the dismal predictions in their pages were usually so ambiguous that readers could place upon them almost any interpretation they wished, whether national or personal, or both. Readers of some present-day astronomical predictions will observe that this deliberate ambiguity still survives.

The pedlars of nostrums and other meretricious remedies also increased their sales of charms, philtres, exorcisms, signs of the zodiac and amulets, which they claimed would protect the purchasers from calamity. Even coffee, which had been drunk widely in London for seventeen years, was held to be a remedy for such afflictions as 'the King's Evil', for gout, dropsy and scurvy.

'It so incloseth the orifices of the stomach, and fortifies the heat within, that it is very good to help digestion,' announced one pamphlet for a coffee house. 'It much quickens the spirits and makes the heart lightsome.'

'It is incredible and scarce to be imagined,' wrote Defoe, 'how the Posts of Houses and Corners of Street were plastered over with Doctors' Bills, and Papers of Ignorant Fellows; quacking and tampering with Physick, and inviting the People to come to them for Remedies; which was generally set off with such flourishes as these, viz. INFALLIBLE preventive Pills against the Plague.

'NEVER-FAILING Preservatives against the Infection. SOVEREIGN Cordials against the Corruption of the Air. EXACT Regulations for the Conduct of the Body, in case of an Infection. Anti-pestilential Pills. INCOMPARABLE Drink against the Plague never found out before. AN UNIVERSAL Remedy for the Plague. The ONLY-TRUE Plague-Water. The ROYAL ANTIDOTE against all Kinds of Infection; and such a number more that I cannot reckon up; and if I could would fill a Book of themselves...'

The first plague casualties coincided with advertisements for its cure.

'An Italian Gentlewoman, just arrive from NAPLES, having a choice Secret to prevent Infection, which she found out by her great Experience, and did wonderful Cures with it in the late Plague there; wherein there died 20,000 in one day...'

'An eminent HIGH-DUTCH Physician, newly come over from HOLLAND, where he resided during all the Time of the great Plague, last year in AMSTERDAM; and cured Multitudes of People that actually had the Plague upon them...'

'An antient Gentlewoman having practised with great Success, in the last plague in this city, ANNO 1636, gives her advice only to the Female Sex...'

For the plague (and for almost every other disease) 'powdered unicorn's horn' was a very popular panacea, and even an educated man like Allin, who had been Vicar of Rye in Sussex, wrote about a plant called 'nostock' which he claimed was 'permeated by a magic substance derived from fallen stars'; and which also contained the 'universal spirit'. Nostock had to be gathered before sunrise; after this early hour it withered and lost its supernatural power. This accounted for the fact that it was hard to find: searchers for it in the dark hours before dawn couldn't see where it was growing.

Not only did the illiterate poor take an extraordinary interest in such superstitions; the rich were almost equally gullible. They followed the advice of the more respected astrologers, who peppered their almanacs with Latin phrases. A physician of standing, Dr George Thomson, who remained in the City throughout the Great Plague and courageously dissected a plague corpse in the furtherance of medical science, admitted the influence of the stars.

In his *Loimotomia, or Pest Anatomized* he wrote: 'That Comets, or Blazing Stars, do portend some Evil to come upon Mortals, is confirmed by long observation and sad experience, as likewise Phenomena of...new Stars, Battles Fought and Coffins carried through the Air, Howlings, Screechings and Groans heard about Churchyards, also raining of Blood...' Such manifestations, being outside nature, were in his opinion both 'portentous and prodigious'. With this latter suggestion few would disagree.

There were plenty of people credulous enough to report such sights, having read about them first. Mr Allin wrote of a cistern of water 'turning to blood' in January 1665, and in February he described a mysterious army that appeared overnight at 'a greate towne' (which he did not name) and miraculously disappeared again into the air.

During the three months leading up to the Plague, he also declared without contradiction that the gate of Northampton Castle opened without the aid of human hands, and a voice declaimed: 'War, war, war, such as never yet was.' He also claimed to have had a vision in which sheets of flame 'were throwne from Whitehall to St James, and thence back againe to Whitehall'. Since Allin, who had earlier been relieved of his living at Rye because of a dispute with the Established Church, had no love for authority, the siting of this latter incident in the vicinity of the Royal Palace may have been due to wishful thinking.

One of the most respected almanacs of the time was published annually by William Lilly, an astrologer of wide repute, and also of other distinctions; he had three wives and only one eye. Lilly published his almanac every year from 1644 until his death in 1681, at the surprising age of seventy-nine.

In his *Astrological Judgments* for 1665, he placed considerable importance on the eclipse of the moon in January. The effects of this, he prophesied, would include 'the Sword, Famine, Pestilence and Mortality or Plague'. He risked a little more particularization when he continued that 'strange Feavers even unto Madness and Frensies, Pestilence, or Plague, unwholsome Airs, pestiferous winds' would predominate in Europe. Plague was, of course, already on the Continent at the time he wrote.

William Andrews, another astrologer, foretold in his almanac for 1665 that the position of Saturn in the sky meant 'A Mortality which will destroy and bring many to their Graves'.

Various other forecasters saw in the conjunction of Mars and Saturn late in 1664, a warning of imminent political upheavals. Lilly added that in June 1665, the sun, moving into Cancer, would set off many catastrophes; 'for where, and in what country, Providence hath designed a Plague, or Pestilence, it will be a Smart or destructive one, a World of Miserable People perishing therein'.

Lilly's associate, Richard Edlin, made one of the most accurate predictions when he foretold, in his *Prae-Nuncius Syderus*, two years before the Plague, 'an eminent Plague or Pestilent Disease to afflict us' especially in the years 1665 and 1666. He added piously: 'And pray God divert it!'

A similar, and equally forlorn, hope was expressed by Thomas Trigge in his Calendarium Astrologicum, published in June 1665. He feared 'a sickly season in earnest; from which evill God of his Mercy protect this great and populous City'.

Others read cabalistic significance into the three sixes which occurred in the year 1666, and many were the references to Revelations, Chapter 13, verse 18: 'Let him that hath understanding count the number of the beast, for it is the number of a man, and his number is Six hundred, three score and six.'

John Gadbury, another well-known astrologer, went farther; realizing the need for topicality, he published a pamphlet in which he maintained that comets and eclipses had been invariable forerunners of the epidemic. He cited the Black Death of the Middle Ages, in which a third of the nation was said to have perished, and also five other plague attacks in 1527, 1593, 1603, 1625 and 1636. Either a comet or an eclipse had been seen before each of these epidemics, so he claimed. To cover himself, however, he added cautiously: 'If the Pestilence be not an effect of the before-mentioned causes, it must be an effect of some other causes, more powerful than they.'

From his reading of the latest comets, Gadbury feared that even worse evils than plague might follow. He recorded that he was 'visited' with plague at Christmas 1664, but his friend and surgeon Josias Westwood saved him. Westwood told him 'that many of his patients were afflicted with the same Distemper, and yet obtained a Cure against it, the Air being then so friendly to nature, and an enemy unto the Pestilence'. Gadbury was referring, of course, to the prolonged frost, and he added that since few, if any, died of plague in that freezing weather, it was 'but prudence' for those who caught it to conceal the fact.

Theories about the cause of plague were almost numberless. On the assumption that plague was an 'Infection of the Earth', many held that a sure sign of a coming epidemic was when subterranean creatures, such as moles, foxes, serpents and rabbits, left their burrows and were seen in large numbers above ground. Others considered that plague was contained in 'pestilential effluviums' carried in the air. Therefore, any sudden and widespread sickness in cattle and other farm animals living in the open, was a certain omen of the Black Death.

A third opinion inclined to the view that an increase in toads, frogs, mice and flies presaged the plague; at least their presence was a sign of unhealthy and insanitary conditions. The movements of birds, if at all unusual, were also suspect, and it was even held that a scarcity of swallows in the early summer might be dangerous. Phenomenal weather from extreme drought to excessive damp, was also blamed, and even cloudy weather unaccompanied by rain, prevailing south or west winds and abnormal tides. Indeed, any unusual sight or occurrence, any departure from an accepted norm, was afterwards viewed with suspicion.

Plague omens relating to human beings were no less eccentric. Widespread affliction of the populace with 'boils and blains' or such abnormalities as preceded the plague of the first-born in Egypt; outbreaks of smallpox, spotted fever or measles, chronic diseases among the aged (for valetudinarians were more-sensible of approaching 'disorder' than the strong and healthy) – all were afterwards said to have been portents of the plague. So, incredibly enough, were 'children in sport fancying and aping out funerals', and any 'general sadness and sense of foreboding' among the people.

In the prevalence of so many signs of certain plague, it seems strange that nothing whatever was done on any national or City scale to prepare London for the horrors ahead. In fact, another two centuries passed before it was established beyond question that the disease was carried by fleas living in the fur of rats. In the meantime, some could take consolation in Gadbury's remark: 'He that hath powerful Stars, is not onely shot-free, but Plague-free!'

In the midst of such a welter of superstition and fantasy, Hodges noted drily that: 'The Mischief was much more in the Predictions of the Star-gazers than in the Stars themselves.' The 'mean sort' of people, who were frightened out of their wits by the prophets of doom, merely 'Precipitated their own Destruction'.

Long before public panic had provided a rich field for the bogus physicians and fortune-tellers, and the comets had set the astrologers poring over their complicated charts of the planets, Puritan preachers had warned their congregations about Gehenna and the New Babylon, about Sodom and Gomorrah. According to an individual point of view, a good sermon was accepted either as a necessary part of the Sabbath, or simply as a regular Sunday entertainment. Huge congregations flocked to the City churches – three times as many churches as the City has today – to hear what their preachers thought about the future, and the significance of this new star.

Openly and in private meetings – for the Royalists forbade religious gatherings of more than five adults unless they conformed to the established Liturgy – Puritan divines warned of a coming judgement upon the capital for its sins. Many claimed to have had visions of an all-consuming fire which would purge London of its venery. Literal interpretation of the Bible was, of course, invariable.

One celebrated Quaker, Humphrey Smith, published a pamphlet about *A Vision* he had seen concerning the City. In this he described his passage through a burning London in a great fire whose origins none knew, with all the buildings falling, and the streets emptied of the citizens. 'And the fire continued, for, though all the lofty part was brought down, yet there was much old stuffe, and parts of broken down desolate walls, which the fire continued burning against... And the Vision thereof remained in me as a thing that was showed me of the Lord.'

Another divine, Daniel Baker, declared that 'the evil ways of the city shall be punished by a consuming fire...a great and large slaughter'.

The ruin of the City with those in high places being subsequently cut down to size was a favourite theme, as it has been among preachers for centuries, and still is. But perhaps the most remarkable prophet of all was a powerful preacher and pamphleteer, Thomas Reeve, who forecast the two calamities of plague and fire in considerable detail eight years before the event. In his pamphlet *God's Plea for Nineveh*, published in 1657, he wrote: 'Methinks I see you bringing pick-axes to dig downe your owne walls, and kindling sparks that will set all in a flame from one end of the City to the other.

'What inventions shall ye then be put to...when your sins shall have shut up all the conduits of the city, when ye shall see no men of your incorporation, but the mangled citizen; nor hear no noise in your streets but the crys, the shrieks, the yells and pangs of gasping, dying men; when among the throngs of associates not a man will own you or come near you?'

The only music heard would be doleful knells; in the centres of commerce no wares would be carried, but corpses. Overnight, mansions would become pest-houses for the sick and dying;

congregations would find their way 'rather into churchyards than churches'. The markets would be so empty that 'scarce nessaries will be brought in'.

Many who had heard Reeve's words remembered them in later years. 'Can sin and the City's safety, can impenitence and impurity stand long together?' he asked his congregation rhetorically from his pulpit during a famous sermon. 'Fear you not some plague, some coal blown with the breath of the Almighty, that may sparkle and kindle, and burn you to such cinders that not a wall or pillar may be left to testify the remembrance of the City?'

If they didn't, with all these signs and prophecies and portents, they certainly should have done.

1. The parish was roughly centred upon what is now known as St Giles Circus, at the present junction of Oxford Street, Charing Cross Road and Tottenham Court Road.

CHAPTER THREE

The Great Plague Strikes

The Great Plague, which the Company of Parish Clerks called 'London's Dreadful Visitation' in their weekly Bills of Mortality, began quietly enough with a few isolated cases during the hard winter of 1664–5.

Accounts of how the plague actually started are conflicting. The first reported deaths were not, in fact, the first deaths. Dr Hodges, who had studied medicine at Oxford and Cambridge, was convinced that the plague arrived contagiously from the Netherlands. He also believed that the first fatalities occurred in December, when 'Two or three Persons died suddenly in one family at Westminster, attended with like Symptoms, that manifestly declared their origin'. As a result, 'some Timorous Neighbours, removed into the City of London', carrying with them 'the pestilential Taint'.

Because the first victims were not confined to their rooms, so Hodges believed, the plague spread eastwards to the City. This may well have been the case, and as soon as the news became public, there was widespread alarm for 'it was a received Notion among the common People, that the Plague visited England once in twenty years'.

Plague had last occurred eighteen years previously, in 1647, when the official death roll was 3,597. But not since 1636 had London experienced a severe epidemic.

William Boghurst, the apothecary, was already treating patients for plague in November. He courageously treated up to sixty plague patients a day all through the following summer, with the additional responsibilities of a wife and six children, as well as his normal custom in his shop, and still found time to spend half an hour every day writing his own account of local happenings.

The fact that he was treating plague cases so early surprised him; for he felt that his parish enjoyed the advantages of being on possibly the highest ground near the City, and also had 'the best Aire'. Boghurst believed that the prevailing West wind had carried the germs east to the City. The plague did not start in one place and spread by degrees, but 'fell upon several places of the City and Suburbs like raine, even at the first at St Giles', St Martin's, Chancery Lane, Southwark, Houndsditch and some places within the City, as at Proctor's House'.

At the time the Great Plague struck, Daniel Defoe, though he lived in London, was only five or six years old. His *Journal of the Plague Year* was thus not written in that year at all, but about fifty years later, when plague was again topical because of an outbreak in Marseilles. Defoe had the advantage of family recollections, plus interviews with people who had survived the catastrophe, and the use of such official records as had been published.

From the weight of this opinion, he advanced a third theory. Two Frenchmen, so he claimed, who were lodging at Long Acre at one end of that troublesome parish of St Giles-in-the-Fields, died of plague in the first or second week of December 1664 – a week for which Bills of Mortality do not survive. Their hosts, terrified of the almost certain consequences to themselves if they admitted the presence of plague, tried to conceal the real cause of their deaths; but their attempts at concealment were crude and clumsy, and only served to arouse suspicion. Rumours of the truth reached the Secretaries of State (Sir Henry Bennett, later Lord Arlington, and Sir William Morice). Two physicians and a surgeon were sent to inspect the house.

'The people showed great concern at this, and began to be alarmed all over the Town,' said Defoe. According to this story, another man in the same house died from the disease at the end of the month, and this could be one of the three plague deaths reported at St Giles, in the Bill for the week ending December 27th.

One fact on which these three people agree is that the plague began in the West and moved East.

No further plague deaths were recorded in the Bills until February 14th, when one more case was admitted, again in the parish of St Giles. Two more in this parish also died from plague in late April. Although only these four plague deaths appear in the Bills for the first four months of the year, the deaths, supposedly from other diseases, increased enormously and without any reason. No doubt many of these victims died of plague and not from 'dropsy' or 'griping of the guts', or 'falling down in a fit', and other strange and unlikely causes listed in the Bill.

It was not very difficult to conceal the fact that plague had been the cause of death. In the unusual cold of those winter months before the epidemic began, the tell-tale signs of plague – round marks, like moles – appeared only rarely. Dr Thomson admitted afterwards how easy it had been for a physician to confuse the symptoms of plague with 'scorbute' (scurvy) and other diseases. His own brother, he reported, 'had the Pest twice' with a fever and various bodily sensations peculiar to the plague, yet was 'neither Botch, Carbuncle, Blane, Vesicle, Pimple or Spot apparent in his whole Body'. Happily, Thomson's brother was saved; he must have suffered from a mild form of the disease, for the plague 'tokens' were so deadly that Boghurst called them 'the fore-horses of Death's Chariot'.

When these round blotches appeared, varying in colour from purple and black to scarlet, and usually surrounded by livid inflammation, death was rarely far behind. They were impossible to mistake, yet the old women, the searchers of the dead, were consistently and constantly failing to identify them. This was either through their own ignorance, for spotted fever, consumption, pox or plague, were all alike to them – or because a bottle of gin or a shilling in their hand persuaded them to forget whatever they might have seen.

If the sick man or woman died quickly, the 'tokens' and other outward signs, mostly rising in the groin and armpits, or swellings behind the ear or under the chin, did not always appear. Death could thus be safely ascribed to anything from fever to 'great stomach-ache'. The searchers, upon whom authority was still to rely for another seventy years, had the right of entry into any houses where a death had occurred, but even in the dual unlikelihood of these old women proving skilled in their diagnosis and incorruptible, there remained other methods of concealing outward signs before they ever saw the corpse.

Many mourners held soaking cloths, or chips of ice hacked from waterbutts, to the faces of their dead as soon as life had left them, for the chill tended to disguise any inflammatory signs already on the body, and to prevent others appearing.

Hundreds, probably thousands of deaths, were never reported to the parish clerks to record in their ledgers, for families of a number of religious persuasions – Anabaptists, Quakers and Jews among them – would have nothing to do with an established Church, which, in their view, violated their beliefs. They refused to have their children christened, and they buried their own dead. Not until the Registration Act of 1836 – 171 years later – was there any statutory compulsion in such matters. Many thus came into the world and left it again without any record of their lives being made. There was no income tax to pay, and no registration for voting, census or military service; so far as government records were concerned, they had never existed.

Some parish clerks failed to mention early plague cases in their returns for the Bills of Mortality, because they realized that they would only cause panic in their own districts. Other villages would ostracize them, with a consequent effect on local trade and poverty.

Thus, as a guide to the actual numbers of bodies that were heaped upon the dead-carts in that terrible year, the figures in the Bills of Mortality stand very strongly on the side of optimism.

Their pages contained news of 97,306 deaths, of which 68,596 – roughly two out of every three – were admitted to be caused by plague.

In an average year, about 17,000 people died in London. In the December week when the first known fatality from plague occurred, only 291 people died in all of London's 130 parishes; about two in each. Only sixty of these deaths occurred in the ninety-seven parishes enclosed within the City walls. As the months passed, those figures were to be multiplied five, ten, twenty, even thirty times. There can be no doubt that these huge increases were due to plague, no matter what supposed causes of death might be reported.

The proportion of the population that actually caught plague can never be calculated, for only deaths were recorded. Most of those who survived considered it miraculous that they had escaped infection when surrounded for months by fearful evidence of the disease.

So the spring passed and then, after that week in April when two plague deaths were admitted in St Giles, the weekly death rate in London suddenly increased to 398. After some minor fluctuations, it began to climb, first in tens, then hundreds, then thousands. The plague had begun; only time and the cold weather of the following winter would abate it.

As the plague took hold of the City, Lord Clarendon (then Lord Chancellor) wrote that the 'ancient men, who well remember'd in what manner the last great plague first broke out, and the progress it afterwards made, foretold a terrible summer, and many of them removed their families out of the city'. These prudent people were laughed at by their neighbours who, being younger, could not remember the earlier outbreaks. But they soon had cause to regret their own lack of foresight, for when they eventually decided to leave London, they were caught up in the panic of a mass exodus into a countryside that did not want them. In many cases country towns and villages refused them entry so that they were driven into the fields and forests to eat roots and the raw flesh of any animals they could snare.

By the end of April, those close to authority knew that the government feared a serious epidemic. During that month an official warrant empowered three Justices of the Peace in the City and Westminster to acquire ground on which to build new 'pesthouses', as the crude hospitals of the day were called, and to open up suitable roads to reach them. The City and Westminster already possessed a pesthouse each, and three more were eventually built in Marylebone, in Soho Fields, and in Stepney. The largest could not accommodate a hundred cases; and to fit in this number meant that patients lay so close together that their beds were touching. The crowding was so great that it was easier to cross a ward by walking on the beds than to attempt to thread a way between them and the buckets of vomit and faeces that littered the floor.

During that same month, Parliament expressed itself ready to be prorogued by the King until September, when it was hoped that the worst of the epidemic would be over. As an additional insurance, Members arranged that they should only be recalled by Royal Proclamation and not by any political emergency, 'so that they might not hazard themselves'.

Rumours that sickness was rife in the Fleet at Southampton, Portsmouth and other seaports were widespread in London and added to the alarm, for the Navy was the nation's first line of defence and attack in the war against the Dutch.

In fact, the Fleet had so far escaped, but sickness in one of the smaller ships was suspected to be plague, and while the vessels were in port, no amount of discipline, however strict – and Naval discipline included the lash and being keel-hauled – could prevent the crews from going ashore to the taverns and the prostitutes. Before the end of the month, His Majesty's ships were out at sea under the command of the Duke of York, His Majesty's brother, and so were safe from the plague, if in some danger from the enemy.

In the first week of May, only four parishes – St Mary Woolchurch, St Andrew's, Holborn, St Giles-in-the-Fields and St Clement Danes – were infected, with a total of nine deaths between them; all but one stood outside the City walls. In the next week the death roll dropped to three. The observant noticed a sharp and quite unexplained rise in deaths attributed to other causes, and kept their counsel about this ominous fact.

Within the City everyone was anxious, and the atmosphere grew tense. Pepys noted: 'Great fears of the sickness...it being said that two or three houses are already shut up. God preserve us all!'

The optimists still attempted to console themselves with the thought that plague had so far been confined to the squalid back alleys and ramshackle houses of the poor in the western suburbs, but their confidence declined with publication of the Bill for the second week in May. Fourteen new plague deaths were admitted and the parish of St Dunstan-in-the-West was among those infected. Complacency vanished altogether in the following week, when seventeen cases were listed, with two further parishes – St Botolph's, Bishopsgate, and St Olave's, Southwark – now being included.

At this time, wrote Defoe, there were 'terrible apprehensions among the people, especially the weather now being changed and the summer being at hand'. Those rich enough and wise enough began to make plans to leave their London houses and retreat to their country houses, or at least to the houses of friends in the country.

Visiting a coffee house on May 24th, Pepys found that, apart from news of Dutch movements at sea, all the conversation was of 'plague and the remedies against it – some saying one thing and some another'. By the end of May most said one thing: there was no hope whatever of this epidemic subsiding, as other, earlier epidemics had done. Instead of declining in ferocity, the plague increased in horror. That strange star had not appeared in vain; it lit the way to a year of horror when people, Defoe noted, 'searched the houses and found that the plague was really spread every way, and that many died of it every day'.

To make matters worse, the weather grew oppressively warm and humid. If the past winter had been the coldest in living memory, this summer would be one of the hottest. The only wind, as June began, was a warm westerly breeze. Apart from what one man recalled as 'a slight sprinkling of rain in April', there had been a drought lasting for almost six months. Richard Baxter, a cleric who lived in Acton, wrote that it was 'the driest Winter, Spring and Summer that ever Man alive knew, or our Forefathers mention of late Ages'. The grazing land where cattle should have fed was 'burnt like the High-ways'; the grass was so brown and poor that a meadow near his home 'bare but four Loads of Hay, which before bare forty'.

Under such conditions the plague was almost certain to spread, and every effort was made by the authorities to minimize the swiftly growing peril, in case of public panic. Roger L'Estrange therefore waited until June 5th before reluctantly printing in his *Intelligencer* a few paragraphs about the most important and the deadliest news in the country.

'There are such Reports Spread abroad of the multitudes that dye weekly of the Plague in this Town, that for better information I shall briefly deliver the Truth of the matter,' he began disparagingly. 'There have died three, and nine, and fourteen and seventeen in these four last weeks, forty-three in all, and none of these within the walls, and but five Parishes infected of 130.'

L'Estrange's figures were only slightly inaccurate when compared with the published Bills for May, but anyone who could read knew what a false picture they presented.[1] In fact, nearly 1,500 people had died in London that May, and of these only forty-five had been attributed to Plague. Yet no one advanced any reason for the sudden increase in other mortal illnesses.

A few days after L'Estrange's report, a further Bill was published listing forty-three plague deaths for the first week in June, thirty-one of them in St Giles-in-the-Fields. It was widely rumoured that at least another fifty people had died from plague in that parish during the week; but their deaths had been ascribed to other causes.

The *Intelligencer* suggested that riders from the provinces who said that towns were also suffering from plague were activated by malice 'to spoil our Markets and Fairs and to hinder our Commerce'.

Less than a week later, a printed order was distributed forbidding the great Barnwell Fair, near Cambridge, which was to have taken place later in June, and guaranteeing some recompense to those who would lose money by this decision. Nine days later, St James's Fair at Bristol was banned for the same reason, barely forty-eight hours before it was due to open.

The plague was certainly in the provinces, but it attacked them with nothing like the ferocity with which it visited London. News could only travel as fast as a horse and rider; it rarely lost anything on its journey.

The Lord Mayor of Leicester and the local Justices of the Peace actually issued a disclaimer of reports that their city had been visited, because of the serious damage to trade which had followed upon these 'lying rumours'. At Stevenage, in Hertfordshire, local inns lost almost all their business overnight when another rumour was circulated that a man infected with plague had stopped at one of them on his way out of London, bound for the north country. A notice was hurriedly inserted in the *Intelligencer* containing an assurance 'from persons of good credit upon the place, fully informed' that The Swan, Stevenage, was not infected, nor, indeed, was any other inn in the town.

The towns that were infected kept quiet about their troubles; the news was bad enough without passing it on. Yarmouth was already badly affected, and thirty died in the town by June 16th. A correspondent there, Richard Bower, wrote that 'it will increase until there are cleansing houses, which the people do not like to build, on account of the charge. Infected families are put all together; and then after the month (of quarantine) return to the town'.

The Yarmouth poor, who comprised most of the population, were also in great trouble because most of their employers had fled and so they had no money to buy bread. Part of the Fleet, anchored in Southwold Bay, had hurriedly set sail for other ports because relatives of serving men from Yarmouth flocked on board the ships to beg for food there rather than starve on shore. Visitors fromYarmouth had already been banned for fear of plague crippling the Navy, but many still passed the guards on the gangways by pretending they were from other towns.

Portsmouth was also infected, and a single plague death at Cambridge threw the university city into consternation, although the disease did not spread.

Back in London, Pepys received a shock early in June, on the 'hottest day that ever I felt in my life', when he walked up Drury Lane and saw the first houses marked with the sign of plague upon their doors; a crude red cross daubed on the dirty woodwork.

On the next day, the Mortality Bill for May 30th–June 6th was released, showing that the plague toll had almost tripled in a week, and seven parishes were now affected instead of five. While Londoners were still trying to digest the ominous significance of this, Pepys recorded a more personal tragedy: 'June 10th. In the evening, home to supper; and there, to my great trouble, hear that Plague is come unto the City, that is to say, right inside the City Walls. But where should it begin but in my good friend and neighbour's, Dr Burnett, in Fenchurch; which, in both points, troubles me mightily.'

As the preacher Dr Vincent remarked, 'Few that had any note for goodness or profession, were visited at the first,' but Pepys' doctor, Alexander Burnett, was one of the exceptions. He lived near St Gabriel's Church in Fenchurch Street, a conscientious man of simple tastes who shut up his house the moment he diagnosed the symptoms of the plague – much to the relief of his neighbours, who feared they might also catch the disease. Not one of those he had helped in their illnesses or troubles came to offer him aid or comfort in his. Pepys noted that the doctor's action had 'gained great goodwill among his neighbours', adding his own opinion that Burnett's self-sacrifice was 'very handsome'. Pepys' curiosity, however, eventually overcame his trepidation sufficiently to allow him to go out and have a morbid look at the door of the doctor's house, behind which his friend lay ill.

In fact, Dr Burnett recovered, although his house was shut up for a total of nearly two months, and one of his servants, William Passon, died of plague. The doctor recovered to face not the congratulations of his patients that he had survived, but a malicious and damaging rumour that he had killed his servant. There was no truth whatever in this allegation, but it was so widely believed that his practice was gravely harmed, and finally he had to ask for a certificate from Nathaniel Upton, the Master of the City Pesthouse, which proved that Passon had died from plague, 'with buboes visible in his right groin and two spots on his right thigh'. Dr Burnett had a copy of this certificate hung at the Royal Exchange, and published a denial of the rumour in the advertisement columns of the *Intelligencer*.

In August, when plague was striking down thousands every week, Dr Burnett forgave all those who had abandoned him in his illness and who had passed on the false story about Passon, and resumed his practice. He did not shirk treating plague cases, with the result that he became infected again and died on August 25th. 'Poor unfortunate man,' wrote Pepys.

The lives of the chemists and doctors who bravely remained in London during the Great Plague were arduous and dangerous. A typical apothecary was William Boghurst, born at Ditton in Kent, and thirty-four years old when the plague began. He was a keen scholar and also a skilled lute player. He risked his life and the lives of his wife and six children by his heroic work among the sick.

Boghurst condemned the general unreasoning terror which made people 'egregiously fearfull and consequently soe uncharitable, superstitious and cruel' to each other. Many people believed that plague was 'like a Basiliske or Salamander, which kill all they see or touch', but Boghurst believed that with proper care and hygiene plague could spare as many as it took.

45

Every day he worked until ten o'clock in the evening, going from house to house to treat the plague victims, 'out of one house into another, dressing soares and being allwaies in their breath and sweate, without catching the disease of any, through God's protection'.

At first the variations of the pestilence baffled him, but soon he became able to diagnose individual cases after one or two visits to the sufferers. He endured great personal danger in order to make detailed observations of their symptoms, explaining that he realized he could learn nothing by being 'nice and fearfull'. He commonly dressed forty sores a day, and would take the pulse of a fever-ridden patient for as long as ten minutes 'to give judgment and inform myself of the various tricks of it'.

Boghurst helped to hold victims upright in their bed when they were almost choking from the disease, and assisted their respiration, even though they vomited in his face. 'I eate and dranke with them, especially those that had soares, sate down by their bedd sides and upon their bedds discoursing with them an hour together, if I had tyme,' he wrote afterwards, for he was unusually conscious of the need to bolster up the confidence of the sufferers.

He closed the eyes and mouths of those who died, 'for they died with the mouths and eyes very much open and staring', and if help in the house was scarce, then Boghurst would lay out the corpse and wrap it in a shroud or a blanket, Sometimes, out of pity for the relatives, who were not allowed to leave their homes, he even accompanied the body to the grave, and was the only mourner.

That Boghurst was not in practice for the financial return is clear from an advertisement he published in the *Intelligencer* on July 31st.

'Whereas William Boghurst, Apothecary at the White Hart in St Giles, in the Fields,' it announced, 'hath administered a long time to such as have been infected with the Plague; to the number of forty, fifty or sixty patients a day, with wonderful success, by God's blessing upon certain excellent medicines which he hath, as a Water, a Lozenge, etc.

'Also an Electuary Antidote, of but 8d the ounce price. This is to notify that the said Boghurst is willing to attend any person informed and desiring his attendance, either in City, Suburbs or Country, upon reasonable terms, and that the remedies above mentioned are to be had at his house or shop, at the White Hart aforesaid.'

The apothecary's prices were cheap compared with those asked for completely useless specifics.

When he died years afterwards, he was buried at Ditton, his birthplace. His epitaph stated that he was 'honest and just, skilled in his profession and in the Greek and Latin languages, and a student of antiquity'. His most abiding memorial lies in the great and selfless work he did.

Dr Nathaniel Hodges, two years older than Boghurst, born in Kensington, the son of a doctor, and educated at both Oxford and Cambridge, wrote two learned works on the plague; the first he called *An Account of the first Rise, Progress, Symptoms and Cure of the Plague, being the Substance of a Letter from Dr Hodges to a Person of Quality*. This was published in 1666, and he followed it with the second and larger work, *Loimologia, or an Historical Account of the Plague in London in 1665*, published six years later.

Despite his selfless and heroic work, in the plague, Hodges' story ended in personal tragedy. When he was in his early fifties, his practice suddenly began to dwindle, and then fell away altogether. Finally, he was arrested as a debtor, and committed to Ludgate Prison, where he died, a broken man, in 1688.

During the summer of 1665, Hodges rose early every day during the epidemic, and before he began work, took what he called 'the Quantity of a Nutmeg of the Anti-Pestilential Electuary'... 'After the Dispatch of private Concerns in my Family,' he wrote later, 'I ventured into a large Room where Crowds of Citizens used to be in waiting for me.'

In this surgery he generally spent two or three hours every morning. 'Some ulcers yet uncured, and others to be advised under the first Symptoms of Seizure; all of which I endeavoured to dispatch with all possible Care to their various Exigencies.'

Not until every patient had been dealt with would the doctor eat his breakfast. He never missed this rather heavy meal of the time, 'judging it not proper to go out fasting'. Afterwards, he visited the sick in their homes until the afternoon.

'Entring their Houses, I immediately had burnt some proper Thing upon Coals, and also kept in my mouth some Lozenges all the while I was examining them... I took Care not to go into Rooms of the Sick when I sweated, or were short-breathed with Walking; and kept my Mind as composed as possible, being sufficiently warned by such who had greviously suffered by Uneasiness in that Respect.'

After hours of visiting, Hodges walked home. Before dinner each evening he drank a glass of sack 'to warm the Stomach, refresh the Spirits and dissipate any beginning Lodgment of the Infection'. He watched his diet carefully, only eating foods which he considered were nourishing, fresh and easily digested.

After dinner, his work began again. People flocked to him for advice, and he rarely finished before nine o'clock in the evening. 'I then concluded the Evening at Home, by drinking Chearfulness of my old favourite Liquor, which encouraged Sleep, and an easier Breathing through the Pores all Night.'

Twice Hodges sickened with plague symptoms, but on both occasions he cured himself before any of the dangerous tokens appeared. He firmly believed in the therapeutic qualities of sack – a drink rather like sherry. Hodges thought it tasted best when 'middleaged, neat, fine, bright, racy and of a Walnut Flavour', and considered it particularly effective in cases of nervous disorders. Hodges even advised people intent on visiting sick friends that they should drink half a pint of sack before doing so. 'But,' he added practically, 'if you be very fearfull 'tis best to stay away and save your life though you lose a legacy.'

The next Mortality Bill, for the second week in June, admitted that 112 had died in twelve different parishes. Worse still, three of the infected parishes and four of the deaths were within the City walls, one each at St Albans, Wood Street and St Gabriel's, Fenchurch Street (the death of Dr Burnett's servant); and two at St Michael's, Crooked Lane. In the parish of St-Giles-in-the-Fields 120 people died in that one week, yet apparently only sixty-eight were victims of the plague. Clearly, many who were said to have died 'afrighted' or 'of a great pain', or of 'a guts-acke', died from the plague.

Regarding this sudden increase in deaths, Dr Vincent wrote: 'Now secure sinners begin to be startled... Now a consternation seizeth upon most persons... The Plague is so deadly; it kills where it comes without mercy – suddenly the arrow is shot which woundeth unto the heart...'

Those with money were now using it to buy their immediate escape from London. Those without had to stay where they were. Men who depended upon their own labours for their livelihood knew they had little chance of finding work in the insular rural communities. All countrymen distrusted Londoners who, in healthier times, looked down on them as 'gulls' or idiots. For the rich, the decision to move meant little. They habitually spent much time on their great country estates; the plague simply persuaded them to leave London a little early that year. True, they faced an uncomfortable journey in a coach with wooden wheels, leather curtains and dubious springs, rocking alarmingly on the rutted roads already packed with carts, carriages, sedan chairs, even wheelbarrows laden with other people escaping. But this was more a matter of concern to their coachmen and grooms and postillions; somehow these fellows would bribe, shout or whip a way through the crowds for them; after all, that was what they were paid for. Other servants could be trusted to guard their empty houses in Covent Garden and Soho until they decided to return. They were left behind for this purpose, for, as servants, they were expendable.

The rich therefore did not delay their departure an hour longer than it took their men to prepare their gilded coaches and victual their horses.

'The great Orbs begin first to move,' wrote Vincent sourly. 'The Lords and Gentry retire into their Countries; their remote houses are prepared, goods removed, and London is quickly upon their backs; few ruffling Gallants walk the streets: few spotted Ladies to be seen at Windows; and great forsaking there was of the indecent places where the Plague did first rage.'

Defoe, whose description of the exodus was probably derived from his father, then a butcher in St Giles, Cripplegate, described the scene in the broad main street of Whitechapel, thronged with the rich, their wives, their families and servants.

'Nothing was to be seen but wagons and carts, with goods, women, servants, children, coaches filled with people of the better sort, and horsemen attending them, and all hurrying away; then empty wagons and carts appeared and spare horses with servants, who it was apparent were returning or sent from the country to fetch more people; besides innumerable numbers of men on horseback, some alone, others with servants, and, generally speaking, all loaded with baggage and fitted out for travelling.'

Soon the roads out of London, in all directions, like the spokes of a great wheel with the City at the centre, were thick with traffic. It moved slowly with much creaking of axles and leather harnesses; then, as now on the narrow English roads, there was little room for the faster carriages to pass the slow unsprung carts. Beggars with crutches, poor families with their belongings bundled on their backs in blanket, servants for whom there was no room in the carriages; all these clogged the roads on either side of the coaches. Sometimes someone, already ill with plague or struck with weariness or age, fell in the dust. No one stopped to succour such unfortunates. They were pushed to one side into the thick, dry, speary grass to die or to recover. If anyone thought they had anything valuable on them

– a ring, a purse, a coin – they were stripped and robbed and left naked to the sky.

There were not many heroes in London during that spring, summer and autumn: the urge for self-preservation, for survival in a city of the dying and the dead, stripped away the thin shells of conscience and kindness. Everyone was for themselves; to stay alive was all that mattered; how they did so was their own affair. Clergy abandoned their parishes without a thought, doctors their patients, landlords their tenants, and the rich their dependants.

Edward Cotes, printer of *London's Dreadful Visitation*, expressed in his preface the hope that 'neither the Physicians of our Souls or Bodies may hereafter in such great numbers forsake us'.

Many wealthy families decided to leave their London homes locked and bolted, with all windows shuttered, during their absence. In these circumstances they could see no point in continuing to pay servants who had nothing to do. They therefore dismissed them at the moment their own carriages started to move. Those who were discarded in this way followed the coach for a little way either begging their masters to reconsider their decision, or cursing them, according to age, sex and temperament. They had no chance of finding any other employment at such a time. They were literally left in the street outside the locked houses, without refuge, without food, without hope, facing the alternatives of starving to death or dying of plague.

It was from these wretched and abandoned creatures that parishes found some to drive the two- and four-wheeled carts – the 'dead-carts' – to collect the corpses of plague victims. Others roamed the streets looking for empty houses to loot or lonely pedestrians to rob. Since many London households contained between thirty and fifty servants, these desperate characters became a serious and constant problem during that year and for some time afterwards.

'The town grows very sickly,' Pepys noted on June 15th, and a couple of days later, as he was being driven down Holborn from the Lord Treasurer's Office, he saw just how sickly it had become. His coachman suddenly began to drive more and more slowly, until finally the horses stopped altogether, and the man almost fell from his box. He staggered round to Pepys, and, thrusting his head in at the open window, gasped that he was 'suddenly struck very sick' and almost blind. Clearly he had suffered a seizure of some kind; but now all sicknesses were suspect; all symptoms were only signs of plague.

Pepys hurriedly climbed out and hailed another carriage, in which he was whisked away, making no attempt to help the stricken coachman or to summon assistance. Afterwards he wrote rather shamefacedly that he had 'a sad heart for the poor man', but he added, 'And for myself also, lest he should have been struck with plague'.

Pepys may be criticized from this present safety of years, but he was no worse than his fellow citizens, whose dread of plague so overwhelmed their humanitarian instincts that hundreds and possibly thousands of sufferers, who would probably have recovered with even the minimum of care and attention, were abandoned to the agonies of a fearful and solitary death. Many who were not ill of plague at all, but who showed symptoms of other illnesses that seemed suspicious were also left to die. Every person complaining of a headache, a sickness, or a fever and with any rash or spot whatever, was thought to be a plague victim and was treated accordingly.

Meanwhile, the mass departures from London increased. The noblemen led the way, and then came the merchants and the rich tradesmen. There was no need for them to stay on in London, they claimed, for their best clients had gone. Most of the clergy also left, ostensibly for their normal summer vacations in the country, or with the same excuse as the tradesmen. So many of their parishioners had fled that they had no choice but to follow them to the country themselves, and save their souls there.

Vincent was scathing about these ministers of religion who left 'the greater part of their Flock without Food or Physick in time of their greatest Need'. He added that possibly they thought that 'God was now preaching to the City, so what need of their preaching?'

The lawyers, with customary prudence, were not far behind. In the middle of June the Benchers of the Inner Temple, Middle Temple, Lincoln's Inn and Gray's Inn issued orders suspending all activities of the Inns of Court. By the end of the month, the Inns were deserted except for a handful of flunkeys left to watch over the chambers of barristers and students who had hastily departed for the country.

The poorer tradesmen decided to follow their example, although one contemporary declared that many of these gentlemen had 'scarce the wherewithal to bring them back'. Their impecuniosity may in part be explained by a letter from Sir Edmund Berry Godfrey, a magistrate, who wrote that when some of the courtiers, nobility and gentry fled, they forgot their debts as well as their charity'.

Now in the dust and the hot weather, the narrow gates in the City wall, which were usually blocked with carriages and carts trying to enter London, were jammed with those in agonies to leave. Overloaded carts and coaches became locked together as their drivers tried to overtake each other; terrified horses leapt up, kicking and foaming at the mouth. Axles broke under three times the load they were designed to bear; thieves and barefoot boys, emboldened with hunger and opportunity, slashed the ropes and thongs that held the burdens of luggage and made off with all they could.

In the sweat and heat and fear of this strange, terrible summer, coachmen raged and cursed each other as they charged the narrow gates together. Some tried to fight a way through with whips or teams of servants. Others sat more patiently, holding the reins with grim faces, waiting their turn. Behind the leather curtains rolled down over the open windows, women wept and little children screamed. Many mothers with no homes in the country had used their savings to buy a seat in a coach or cart on the promise that accommodation would be found 'at the other end'. They had no idea where they were going or whether they would find somewhere to set up a makeshift home, but the urge to save their children overcame their common sense. They grieved for the homes and the husbands they had been forced to leave. The children sobbed simply because they were too young to understand.

Until June, anyone could pack up and leave London, for officially no emergency existed; but in the second week of June it was announced that no one would be allowed out of London on any of the roads without a certificate of health signed by the Lord Mayor, Sir John Lawrence. He was also Alderman for Queenhithe Ward, and lived in Great St Helen's, Bishopsgate. For weeks after this pronouncement was made his door was besieged by would-be refugees clamouring for the scraps of paper without which none could expect to be allowed to pass through the town gates and toll-gates outside the City, nor to be accommodated at inns along the escape roads. He and his clerks scribbled away with their quill pens while those desperate to leave shouted their names at them. Thousands of certificates were issued; many changed hands at fantastic sums; others were pirated and copied and forged; and still the narrow, dusty highways were throttled with passengers and goods.

'London doth empty itself into the Countrey,' wrote Vincent, and Hodges thought the City 'had quite gone out of itself, like the hurry of a sudden conflagration; all Doors and Passages are thronged for escape'.

There was one bright spot in the otherwise gloomy capital at this time. News came in of a big sea victory over the Dutch, and June 20th was appointed as a Thanksgiving Day. This prompted a fanatic, Arise Evans, to write to Lord Arlington, Secretary of State, declaring that the victory was achieved only because the King believed in the Bible, whereas the Plague was a sign of God's anger at the widespread questioning of the Holy Book.

Crowds went along to the popular pleasure gardens at Vauxhall to celebrate the Dutch defeat, with drinking and sideshows of monsters and dwarfs and idiot children and the like. This welcome release from tension prompted some to hope that the City would be granted a reprieve from the plague. Such optimism was ill-founded. London was soon to lose many more in a single week of the Black Death than the 2,000 men lost by the Dutch Admiral Opdam in the fierce engagement off Lowestoft.

The celebration was indeed quickly forgotten, and plague became once more the main topic of conversation. Quarantined houses with guards standing outside were in King Street, Westminster, near the Palace; in the parish of St Clements; along London Wall; in Long Lane; at Pall Mall. Every day the area fouled by the Plague grew larger; every day the feeling of fear and hopelessness and the inevitability of death grew greater and more widespread.

Pepys, who, as early as May 28th reported that Lady Sandwich had told him she was 'resolved to be gone into the country' because of her fear of the sickness, was still gloomily considering – three weeks later – what to do with his own family. He lived with his pretty twenty-five-year-old wife, whom he had married when she was fifteen, and his mother, in a little house in Seething Lane, which looked over the gardens of the Navy Office. Sometimes retreat seemed the only course; and then to stay seemed best. He was still undecided on June 22nd, when he wrote: 'In great pain whether to send my mother into the country or no.'

After much anxious debate with himself, he suggested to her that she would be wiser to leave, but this she was 'to the last unwilling to go'. Mother and son seemed to have shared a capacity for shilly-shallying, with the unhappy result that when she finally decided to go she lost her seat in the coach to Cambridgeshire and had to ride 'in the waggon part' instead – a far less comfortable journey.

A couple of weeks afterwards, Pepys saw his wife leave for Woolwich, then a riverside town ten miles out of London in the country, where he had taken lodgings for her. He was 'sorry to part with her', and 'worse by much without her'.

The Queen Mother, Henrietta Maria, who was suffering from consumption, gave this illness as her reason for leaving the City; all was soon being packed for her departure at Somerset House. She left for France towards the end of June, ostensibly for a cure, and was escorted to the coast by her son, King Charles. She never returned to England.

Many public officials also found pressing business out of London, or other unexpected reasons for leaving the capital. Among them was Sir Robert Long, one of the Exchequer auditors. In July he wrote the following instructions to his clerk about the care of his town house: 'Lett noe body stirre out, nor any suitors come into the house or office.

'Lett every one take every morning a little London treacle, or the kernel of a walnutt, with five leaves of rue and a grayne of salt beaten together and roasted in a figg, and soe eaten; and never stirre out fasting.

'Lett not the porter come into the house; take all course you can agaynst the ratts, and take care of the catts; the little ones that will not stirre out may be kept, the great ones must be killed or sent away.'

No one had suggested that rats could be directly responsible for carrying the plague – as indeed they were – and at the beginning of the epidemic an Order was published by the Lord Mayor and Justices of the Peace declaring that all dogs and cats should be immediately killed. Official exterminators were employed, who were paid about twopence for each one they killed. In these circumstances, no pet dog was safe, for this fee represented two days' wages to an ordinary labourer. Defoe calculated that probably 40,000 dogs, and possibly five times that number of cats, were destroyed. An item still surviving in the City accounts of the time shows that £36 10s 0d was paid to the Common Hunt alone 'for killing of Dogges in the beginning of the Plague'. At twopence each this represented the deaths of 4,380 dogs.

The dogs and cats were cornered in the streets and killed by one man, while another followed with a wheelbarrow to pick up their bodies. Many more were fed poisoned meat – or the poisoned carcases of other dogs. Frequently the corpses of these animals that had crawled away to die were left lying in the street or thrown into the Thames or the Fleet River to add to those streams of putrefaction. Such was the stench, that, on July 5th, the Court of Aldermen had to make a special additional Order for these carcases to be cleared from the streets by the 'rakers'. Like most anti-plague measures, the Order to kill dogs and cats had been very ill-advised. As Boghurst scornfully remarked: 'Sure, the rat killers will have a sweeping trade next year, the Arsenick and Ratbane being all spent, and the cats killed.'

Meanwhile more and more people of consequence and authority, whose presence in London could have been of value, decided to leave. The Royal Society, which numbered Sir Christopher Wren among its members, dispersed early to evade the epidemic, and the Faculty of the College of Surgeons, led by their President, Sir Edward Alston, also moved to the country. The fact that they did so was no bar to some of their number later writing learned treatises about a disaster which they had conveniently left many miles away.

Before they drove out of London, however, the President was pleased to announce, that, by order of a Privy Council Committee, appointed by the King himself, they had nominated an official apothecary, one William Johnson, to deliver doses of 'a peculiar and proper medicine' which they had devised for both cure and prevention of the plague. This was to be given free to 'every infected house, or Family, which at this present are Poor and Necessitous'. Quick to seize a sound business opportunity at the same time, they added that everyone in London might also make use of their 'Spiritus Antiloimoides, or Antidote against the Plague' which could be bought from Johnson's shop at Amen Corner, next to the College buildings. The efficacy of this preparation can be judged by the fact that the Surgeons did not stay to take it themselves; and that William Johnson, who did, died a few weeks afterwards.

Also on Privy Council instructions, the College issued a book of *Directions for Cure of the Plague*. This booklet was sold by the King's printers in Blackfriars, but apart from purely commonsense measures, which had little to do with medicine, it contained nothing of value.

On June 29th, Whitehall was filled by wagons and coaches beautifully varnished and glittering with polished brass fittings, with leatherwork as soft as a doe's nose; they had been ordered up by their owners, the courtiers, to take them out of London. Passers-by heard from servants and footmen and postillions as they rushed busily in and out of the great and noble houses with boxes and trunks, that the King and Queen were joining the general exodus, and planned to establish themselves at Hampton Court, about ten miles out of London.

Before Charles left, he took the precaution of issuing a Proclamation ordering all disbanded officers and soldiers from 'the Armies of any of the late Usurped Powers' to leave London and its suburbs by the end of June – in fact, within twenty-four hours, and not to return within twenty miles of London until after November 1st. This was in case of general insurrection; a determined body of troops could have controlled the City within hours; and from controlling the capital it could have been but a step to control the whole Kingdom. Troops with homes in the capital were granted access to them, but all were forbidden, on pain of severe penalties, to wear arms.

The abandonment of London by its main merchants and tradesmen had already brought the commercial life of the City virtually to a standstill. Now that the Court had also gone the fear grew that the capital was being abandoned by everyone who could leave. Those who could not, without money, without work – for all depended directly or indirectly on the rich – faced the future without hope or promise.

Beggars roamed the streets, to rob or steal if no one would give them alms; hunger, poverty and despair prepared the way for the worst onset of the plague.

Sir Ralph Verney, up from the country and staying in Chancery Lane, was of the opinion that ' 'tis an ill time to put out money, for fear of the Plague makes many willing to take their Estates out of the Goldsmiths' hands, and the King's great want of money makes many very unwilling to lend any money to these that advance greate summs for him'.

Coal, said Verney, was not only 'excessive deare' but also difficult to find at any price, because coasters from Newcastle were afraid to put in at the Port of London. This also helped to cripple the industrial and manufacturing concerns in the City, and to spread the effects of poverty and unemployment even more widely.

Those left in London were too nervous to speak to one another in the streets for fear of somehow catching infection. Soon few dared even to venture out into the town at all without their pomanders of aromatic herbs – rue, wormwood, zedoary (a type of ginger), myrrh and others. Charlatans brave enough to remain, compounded their absurd potions and elixirs from anything that they could find – roots, pepper, sour milk, urine, salt; the result generally tasted and smelled so atrocious that simple folk declared sincerely that they 'felt it was doing them good'. The only ones to whom these mixtures did any good were the men who sold them, who were soon among the richest left in London. And all the time the death totals grew steadily like the swellings of the disease they represented. In the second week of June, 168 died from plague; 267 in the following week; 470 the next; 725 in the week after.

By the middle of July it was officially admitted for the first time that over 1,000 had perished of the plague within one single week.

Soon the cries of the shopkeepers and hawkers, who would walk the street wheeling barrows of oysters or cherries or cats' meat, calling outside the big houses for people to come and buy their wares, were heard no more. The rattling of the busy coaches and hackneys over the cobbles was a sound that died with them. Grass and weeds sprouted in the wheel tracks; the corpses of dogs, cats, even pigs and horses, swelled in the summer sun and then burst, buzzing with swarms of black flies, mountains of putrefaction, crawling with worms. No one bothered to bury them; the living could not cope with their own dead; there was no time to attend to animals.

Gradually an uneasy and ominous silence fell over the City, even at noon when it had been busiest. This silence was broken only by cries and screams from the suffering, by the mournful almost unending tolling of church bells for the dead; by the rumble of the dead-carts' wooden tyres, and the hoarse, thick shouts of the drivers as they passed house after house marked with the red cross of plague: 'Bring out your dead! Bring out your dead!'

1. Allen, writing to a friend on May 26th, was convinced that 'treble the number' reported in the Bills had actually died in the Plague.

CHAPTER FOUR

Rigorous Measures

Those stricken with bubonic plague in London during that summer expected no mercy, and were not disappointed. Shunned by almost everybody with whom they usually came into contact – for blood ties and kinship meant nothing at such a time – locked in their homes by armed guards, visited only by ignorant 'plague nurses' whose chief concern was to enrich themselves as quickly as possible, they died in agony and by the thousand. Only the valiant efforts of a few doctors and apothecaries, such as Hodges and Boghurst, lightened and redeemed the fearful selfishness that engulfed the capital.

Measures to limit the suffering were archaic and only reflected the panic which plague always induced in the official mind. Since 1574, for example, anyone whose house had contained a plague victim was forbidden 'to come abroad into any streete, markete, shoppe, or open place of resort' until twenty days after plague had left their home, unless they carried 'one white rodde' at least two feet long.

This was an echo of the clapper bell, the yellow flag and the 'unclean' call of the leper. Anyone seen on the streets with visible plague sores was liable to forty days in jail or a £5 fine; prominent crosses had to be nailed or painted on the doors of all infected houses until the premises had been free from infection for at least a month.

The extent of the Great Plague demanded more rigorous measures. Everyone in an infected house, for example – father, mother, children, lodgers and servants – were locked in until forty days after the sufferer had either been cured or carried out dead. To enforce this, watchmen armed with sharpened halberds stood guard at the front door, one by day and another by night. Their orders were to prevent anyone inside having any contact with people outside. If a fresh plague case broke out before the end of the quarantine period – and under these conditions this naturally occurred very frequently – another forty days' quarantine was added to the first. Some families were thus imprisoned for the whole of the epidemic, until all had died.

As early as April, when only a few cases were being admitted, the College of Physicians advised the Privy Council that this course was necessary, and the Privy Council ordered the Lord Chief Justice to pass these instructions to all magistrates. The first plague houses were shut up in St Giles-in-the-Fields before the end of the month. A riot followed immediately, and neighbours of those afflicted ripped down the crosses and plague notices nailed on the doors and released the families. Constables quickly suppressed the demonstration, and local magistrates dealt severely with the ringleaders. Later, fear alone was enough to inhibit such neighbourly relations; there were no more demonstrations.

Conditions inside the locked houses during that hot, oppressive summer, with the dying, the dead, with terrified children and dwindling supplies of food, were almost indescribable. An anonymous pamphlet, *The Shutting Up Infected Houses*, published as a protest against the practice, referred to 'this dismal likeness of Hell, contrived by the College of Physicians'.

Several more enlightened doctors also protested against the stupidity and injustice of the measures; their voices were soon overwhelmed by the terror which the plague induced in everyone as it spread. Even a humanitarian like Dr Hodges was powerless in the face of such prejudice and ignorance, although he recorded that 'the tedious confinement of sick and well together' often ended in the death of both. It was, he said,

'Abhorrent to Religion and Humanity, even in the Opinion of a Mahometan'; those shut up quickly became 'an Easier Prey to the devouring Enemy'.

The red cross of plague which stigmatized their doors cut them off completely from the help they so desperately needed. 'I verily believe,' wrote Hodges, 'that many who were lost might now be alive, had not the tragical Mark upon their Door driven proper Assistance from them.'

The watchmen were allowed to buy bread for their charges, provided always that the sick families had any money, which was seldom. If they had no savings inside the house with them, they either starved or handed whatever few possessions they did have through the windows and trusted the watchmen to sell them for what they would fetch. Frequently the watchmen swindled them, and as frequently their pathetic household goods – a few cooking pots, a rush mat, a candle in its holder – found no buyers. During the plague money increased its value but possessions lost theirs. Before such transactions could begin, the watchmen nailed up the doors and windows in case the plague victims escaped during their absence.

Relief from parish funds was beggarly, and so the most miserable poverty resulted, which, as Dr Thomson noted, 'hath always an Equipage and Train of Sad Calamities attending upon it'. Nor was this worthy physician blind to the psychological implications of such close confinement. It led to acute depression, while what he called 'magnanimity and undauntedness of spirit' would undoubtedly have helped many sufferers to recover from 'this Pestilential Poison'.

Indeed, as early as May it had been suggested to Lord Arlington, the Secretary of State, that if every infected person could receive medical attendance and payment for loss of time, people would not conceal the sickness, and that 'forty houses thus provided might prevent the infection of 10,000'. Like most sensible proposals at that time, this suggestion came to nothing, although more thoughtful people realized that the answer to the rising tide of plague was to segregate those still healthy from those infected.

Boghurst was incensed at the unnecessary waste of life. His word for the confinement of as many as two dozen healthy people with a single plague sufferer was direct enough; he called it murder. This system of imprisonment at home, born of fear and fostered in ignorance and selfishness, helped to spread the Black Death rapidly throughout the capital and into the country round about London. It invited anyone who suspected plague in his family to go to any lengths to conceal it; or, failing concealment, to escape before their plight was discovered.

Some people, having failed to bribe the searchers to make a false report on a plague death in their house, fled from their homes before the watchmen arrived. This usually meant that they had to abandon all their belongings, apart from what they could bundle on their backs or push in a wheelbarrow. They thus became, in a night, a family of wanderers, with no food, no work, no home. Others persuaded the watchmen to go off on some pretext, and then escaped with spare door keys or hammered off the lock and were away. Such escapes, happening scores of times every day, decided the authorities to issue watchmen with padlocks and bolts, so that they could secure the doors and shutters from the outside. Then, without light, with little air and cornered like captive beasts, the victims frequently went mad.

Fathers could not bear to watch their families die one by one in the stinking atmosphere of a shuttered, darkened house, foul with blackened corpses of plague victims, the air heavy with the smell of vomit, excreta and death. They would creep up to attics with weighted ropes and nooses and drop these stealthily over the heads of their guards beneath. If the guard still refused to unlock the door, they would pull on the rope until he changed his mind or was strangled. At least a score of the guards were reported killed by people incarcerated in houses tainted by plague. The actual total is probably far more. In several cases the crimes were ingeniously concealed by wrapping the bodies in shrouds, so that they were taken for plague victims, and tossed into the dead-carts and carried away.

One distracted householder made a bombshell with gun-powder he kept in his house for fireworks, and blew up the watchman at his door. As the man writhed on the ground in agony from his fearful burns, the whole family jumped out of a first-floor window – all doors were bolted – and fled, leaving him to die. Other families hacked holes in their walls (which were mostly of thin plaster and wooden laths) at the back of their houses and slipped silently away over the backyards of their neighbours. Others threw messages, wrapped around tiles or wooden blocks to friends in the street. They bought hemlock or some less drastic sleep inducer at the apothecary's shop and mixed this in a glass of ale which they offered the guard. Then, as he dozed, they would steal his keys, open the padlocks, and help the family to escape. Other families tunnelled their way to freedom under the foundations of their house.

Those with more scruples – or less courage and imagination – were forced to pace their narrow, shuttered rooms for days and weeks, compelled to watch the agonizing deaths of one after another of their family, waiting for death to come for them. The desperate, often demented screams of grief-stricken parents, mingled with the cries of their terrified and dying children, echoing along the narrow streets and alleys, struck fear into the hearts of those who hurried by, trying not to look at the blood-red crosses and pitiful inscriptions, 'Lord Have Mercy Upon Us', chalked on so many front doors.

With doctors warning that 'the melancholy' was frequently a prelude to the plague, it was not surprising that the Bills of Mortality began to include a surprising number of cases of people who had been 'Frighted' to death.

So the weeks passed, and the plague grew worse. Its rapid growth during the early summer was as much due to the lack of effective medical services as to the official blunders which exacerbated the deplorable conditions in the capital.

The College of Physicians recommended twenty-seven measures to curb it in their *Certain necessary Directions for the Prevention and Cure of the Plague in 1665*. The main one was a proposal that four or six doctors should be appointed to take special responsibility for plague victims; each would be a salaried official, and would have two apothecaries and three 'chirurgeons' to serve him. The College noted sombrely that during plague epidemics 'in Paris, Venice and Padua and many other places', people died like flies when no one was appointed to attend them.

Half a dozen doctors to care for a plague-struck city of nearly half a million may seem inadequate today, yet the basic idea of salaried officials being employed for such a public service was in itself revolutionary. The further suggestion was even made that the widow of any doctor dying in such service should receive a pension, a rare favour at that time.

A small committee of Alderman and Sheriffs was set up, and their first appointments were those of Dr Hodges, then practising in Walbrook, and Dr Thomas Witherley of Hatton Garden, who became joint chiefs of the service. At their request, Dr Edward Harman, of Finch Lane, and Dr Thomas Gray, of Temple Bar, were subsequently appointed. Their salary was £30 on appointment, with a further £30 at Michaelmas, and a final £40 at Christmas if, as the proclamation gloomily stated, 'they or either of them shall then be living'. At the time of their appointment that likelihood seemed slight.

These four men would have been left to fight the plague alone if the matter had been left to the civic authorities, but fortunately seven more doctors with a true sense of vocation came forward to offer their services, without fee. Not all of them survived the epidemic, and they practised in the most primitive manner, without hospitals or staff. Yet their efforts were better than nothing, and they earned a further distinction: they were among the very few in London who acted selflessly and with mercy.

Because it was felt that no reliance could be placed upon the searchers to report plague deaths, these doctors and surgeons were also directed to examine all suspected cases themselves. They would receive a shilling for each plague case certified, but by the time this additional burden was placed upon them, the task was already impossible for hundreds were dying every day all over London. These few brave doctors did what they could to limit the spread of the Great Plague, and to alleviate the sufferings of those infected, but most of their efforts were defeated by ignorance, superstition and the neglect of centuries.

It was of little use for the College of Physicians to recommend sluicing the streets, removing slaughter-houses from the congested Liberties, and burying victims outside the City in deep graves with quicklime, once the plague had already begun. Their advice came too late, for not only did the deaths and the fear of infection make reform impossible; it disrupted what few primitive sanitary arrangements the City possessed. Before long all City churchyards were full, and mass burials were being made in huge holes gouged out of the earth on any open space. These were known as plague pits.

In the absence of any proper medical service, plague sufferers were generally given over to the care of 'plague nurses', old corrupt women, hitherto unemployed and unemployable, even as searchers of the dead. They were nurses only in name and not by qualification, inclination or experience; parishes hired them at a wage as low as 5s a week. Most of these 'ugly, unwholesome bags', as one contemporary described them, only took the job to avoid starvation. They had no intention of risking their lives for a parish pittance, but saw this epidemic as an unbelievable opportunity to grow rich, one that would probably never come their way again. They thus lost no opportunity of plundering the sick, and even of smothering those who did not die as quickly as they hoped. They ran little risk of discovery, for the sight of corpses piled high on the dead-carts was becoming a common-place.

'What greatly contributed to the loss of the people shut up was the wicked Practices of Nurses,' wrote Dr Hodges. 'These Wretches, out of Greediness to Plunder the Dead, would strangle their Patients, and charge it to the Distemper in their Throats; others would secretly convey the pestilential Taint from Sores of the Infected to those who were well.' Nothing, declared Hodges, deterred these 'abandoned miscreants' from their avaricious purposes, for their deeds were usually done without any witnesses. He hoped that some kind of Divine vengeance would punish their barbarity, and warned against anyone trusting such people should the City ever be ravaged by another epidemic.

No afflicted household could refuse to admit the plague nurse sent by the parish, but their evil reputation preceded them, so that many became more afraid of the nurses than they were of the plague. 'Who can express the misery of being exposed to their rapine, that have nothing of the woman left but shape?' asked the unknown author of *The Shutting Up Infected Houses*.

It was with relish that Hodges recounted the story of a plague nurse 'struck down from Heaven' in the middle of looting a shop, whose owner she had been sent to nurse. Staggering from the place, carrying a great sack filled with every ornament and candlestick she could find, she had a stroke and fell down dead under her heavy burden. Another old woman had actually begun to strip her patient, thinking him dead and intending to sell his clothes, when he revived again and 'came a second Time into the World naked'.

In Houndsditch, constables entered a house (to see what they could loot before locking it up) and found a father and his daughter, both dead and naked on the floor. The nurse had carried off their nightclothes and bedclothing to sell elsewhere.

Elsewhere, a 'young gentlewoman' was smothered while in a fainting fit; in another case the nurse held a wet cloth tightly over a man's mouth and nose as he lay delirious until he suffocated and died. Such accounts magnified the panic of those left in the City as they read of the mounting death totals in the Mortality Bills.

A few of these old women were caught and publicly whipped in the market places, but most escaped. Some even invested the money they made and grew rich. Defoe cited the case of one nurse who, on her death bed years after the Great Plague, confessed with contrite tears the many robberies of plague sufferers that had made her a wealthy woman.

Once the plague spread to the parishes outside the City walls, its progress accelerated more and more rapidly with every week that passed. The Bills recorded 1,006 deaths from all causes in the week ending July 4th; of these 470 – less than half – were said to be due to plague. In the next week, 1,268 deaths were admitted, 725 of plague. In the week following there were 1,761 deaths, 1,089 from plague; then 2,785, of which 1,843 were due to plague; and then, for the week ending August 1st, no less than 3,014 deaths were recorded – more than ten times the average – with 2,020 from plague. And even these figures fell far short of the truth.

Pepys recorded how about this time he met by chance a Mr Hadley, the parish clerk of St Olave's, Hart Street, who told him that plague was growing worse in his parish every day, and added: 'There died nine this week, though I have returned only six.'

'It is a very ill practice,' commented Pepys afterwards, 'and makes me think it is so in other places; and therefore the plague much greater than people take it to be.'

As Pepys looked about him, he was struck by the change in the attitude and outlook of everyone he met. 'Lord,' he wrote in amazement later on, 'how everybody's looks and discourse in the street, is of death, and lothing else; and few people going up and down, that the town is like a place distressed and forsaken.'

The *Intelligencer* made another attempt to allay the City's alarm, and L'Estrange wrote testily that only twenty-three of the 470 who had died 'during the past week' had died in the City.

He did not add that only three of the nearer out-parishes remained plague-free, and that the whole of Westminster was suffering severely. His vague reassurances appear incongruous alongside the advertisements of 'approved Antidotes or Pectorals against the Plague' which every issue of his newspaper contained.

One advertiser praised the virtues of 'Aurum Volans, sive Potabile, being the true Philosophical Preparation of Potable Gold', which at 5s an ounce was a 'universal specific' that would cure 'all pestilential and contagious distempers', including the 'Scorbutick and Venereal Evils'.

Pepys found some consolation when he went to St Michael's Church, Cornhill, to act as godfather to a friend's child, for Parson Meriton and his clerk assured him that in their parish, 'one of the middlemost parishes, and a great one of the town, there hath, notwithstanding this sickliness, been buried of any disease, man, woman or child, not one for thirteen months past'. Unhappily, Mr Meriton's claim did not last long. Plague soon struck St Michael's, Cornhill, but much to his credit he remained with his people, one of the relatively few Established clergy who did not put his own safety before the needs of his parishioners.

By August 1st, all thirty-three parishes outside the City walls were infected by plague, and forty of the ninety-seven within – a total of forty-three parishes newly involved in only four weeks.

The hasty flight of most of the administration and Established clergy gave dissenting preachers a chance of emerging again into the limelight, and this they were quick to take. With 'pulpits to let', as one put it, they returned to churches from which many of them had been forcibly ejected only a few months previously, and began once more to conduct services. They were unanimous that the plague was a judgement upon the sins of the City, for it had begun 'indeed in those parts of the Town where Uncleanness kept her Courts, and Venus hath too many Altars and Votaries'. This was the view of Dr Thomas Gumble, chaplain and friend of the Duke of Albermarle, by whose side he stayed throughout the Plague.

The City authorities also felt that the Plague might be a manifestation of divine displeasure. The Court of Aldermen therefore ordered that churchwardens, constables and other officials should enforce strict observance of the Sabbath Day by preventing 'tippling, disorderly conduct, indecency, gaming, rowing on the Thames and labouring'. Ministers like Vincent, James Janeway, Edward Chester, Edward Turner, John Grimes and Robert Franklin, 'exceeded themselves in lively, fervent preaching', and the people crowded constantly to hear them. Ironically enough, these sincere dissenting preachers whose sermons the pious flocked to hear, indirectly added to the death rolls.

Vincent, who had earlier been dismissed from his living at St Mary Magdalene, Milk Street, and compelled to earn his keep by teaching in Islington, went from church to church in the City, where what one member of his congregation called his 'moving, pathetic and searching' sermons made him famous within a few days. Multitudes followed him wherever he preached, filling the aisles of every church, even though as Baxter noted sadly, those who heard him one day were very often 'sick the next and quickly dyed'.

'Every Sermon was unto them as if they were preaching their last,' wrote Vincent afterwards. 'Grim Death seems to stand at the side of the Pulpit with its sharp Arrow, saying "Do thou shoot God's Arrows, and I will shoot mine"'.

At times the congregations were so great that ministers could not 'come near the Pulpit door for the press, but are forced to climb over the Pews to them'. Congregations had 'such open ears, such greedy attention, seldom seen in London before', and among those 'drowning in their fear' many conversions were made. These crowded churches caused considerable controversy. Medical men argued that such huge congregations, packed close together, were dangerous to health, and bound to pass on any infection. Dissenters maintained that lack of worship was dangerous to people's souls. The King, to whom the open defiance of these preachers was represented 'very odiously', thought the risk of sedition thinly disguised as preaching was dangerous to the Monarchy.

He was not sufficiently concerned himself to risk a return to London, however, and from his retreat in the country informed Lord Arlington of his feelings in the matter. Arlington sent a stiff letter to the Bishop of London, asking him to put a stop to these swollen congregations. The Bishop protested feebly that he had 'heard nothing of it', but admitted most of his own incumbents had left for the country, although the 'sober clergy' remained. He promised to refuse livings to any suspected of sedition, but this was not hard to do for very few clergymen of the Established Church wanted livings in London.

Later that year, in October, when the danger from plague was lessening, Parliament passed the Five Mile Act against the dissenters. By this statute, any clergyman refusing to take an oath to the effect that it was unlawful to bear arms against the King or to try and change the government of Church or State, was forbidden to come within five miles of any town with a Corporation unless when travelling. This meant virtual exile and certain privation for most dissenters, but while the plague continued to rage no one stopped them preaching.

Boghurst, like the preachers, thought the plague was a judgement upon such transgressions as 'Lust, Pride and whoredom, wantonness and prophaneness'. He advised his patients to avoid all wordly indulgence – 'profit, pleasure, usury, feasts and plays, censure, blasphemy and hypocrisy'. Since he considered that excessive 'venereal exercise' could be dangerous to those unused to it, the apothecary thought couples ill-advised to marry during the plague. This he declared applied particularly to men – as witnessed by the large number of women left as widows.

While Dr Hodges would not go so far as to declare that sexual over-indulgence, drunkenness or 'passions of the mind' actually caused plague, he wholeheartedly agreed that 'such practices' could increase susceptibility to it. He underlined his personal belief that plague 'tainted the breath' by recounting a story of 'that Woman, who with her Importunities, drew her unhappy Husband into her Embraces, which ended his Life with hers'.

The unexpected emphasis upon sex in an age when even venereal disease was dignified by the title of 'The King's Evil', is more understandable when it is realized that some symptoms of plague were likened by physicians of the period to 'an Ague at the beginning and the Lues Gallica (venereal disease) at the end'.

Whether the Plague was a judgement upon sins or not, the more thoughtful among the community were obliged to admit that the hand of the avenging angel was certainly impartial. 'The Good and Bad fared all alike, and if any fared worse I thinke it was the Good,' admitted Boghurst. He noted particularly that 'all the common hackneyed prostitutes' of Lukener's Lane, Dog Yard, Cross Lane, Balwin's Gardens, Hatton Garden and other localities where they lived and worked were 'still alive and scarce one dead', yet these 'unclean beasts' were full of 'old sores, itch, scabs and such like'.

The 'impudent, drunken, drabbing Bayles and his fellowes and many others of the Rouge Route' and 'the Common Cryers of Oranges, Oysters, fruits, etc.', also seemed invulnerable. Boghurst thought that this confirmed the theory of the Dutch physician Diemerbrooke, who considered, without any other evidence, that plague 'left rotten bodies alone and fastened on the sound'. Thus the idea spread that an inoculation of French Pox would give immunity against plague. Hundreds of gullible people promptly rushed to the hackney prostitutes in the hope of contracting it; most were not disappointed. Hodges reported that 'many were hereby encouraged to seek the most lascivious and filthy Prostitutions', but they were rapidly disillusioned in the results of these experiments, for plague, in their particular cases, seemed the 'more forcibly attracted' by a venereal disease.

Dr Thomson added soberly: 'To see a man eat and drink liberally, to be jocund, frolick, seemingly enjoying a Jubilee, to exercise Venery, and yet to carry about him the very Picture of Death within, is a Plague of the Plague.'

Indeed, after the initial shock and horror and fear which sobered 'the secure sinners' when the plague had first appeared, there were plenty who attempted to bury their fears in their tankards and in the company of prostitutes. Many comments were made about 'the prodigious mixture of Piety and Prophaneness' which characterized London life.

'In one house you might hear them roaring, under the pangs of Death,' wrote Dr Gumble in shocked amazement. 'In the next, tippling, whoring, and belching out blasphemies against God – One house shut up with a Red Cross and *Lord Have Mercy Upon Us!*, the next open to all uncleanness and impiety, being senseless of the Anger of God.'

The narrator in Defoe's *Journal of the Plague Year* described how he visited the Pye Tavern in Houndsditch to inquire about a man carried there after he had attempted to jump into a plague pit where his wife and children were buried. At one o'clock in the morning, the visitor found the inn overrun with 'a dreadful set of fellows, revelling and roaring extravagances'. Apparently they met there every night, terrorizing the landlord and his wife, who tried in vain to run the place quietly and respectably. They sat tippling and roistering in a room next to the street, and when the dead-cart passed they greeted it with 'impudent mocks and jeers, especially if they heard the poor people call upon God to have mercy upon them'.

The poor bereaved man at once became the subject of their taunts and jibes, and when reproved by his friend, they answered with 'hellish abominable raillery...horrible oaths, curses and vile expressions'.

A few days later, one of the drunkards who had tormented the distracted father by asking what he thought he was doing out of his grave, was stricken with plague himself and died in 'a most deplorable manner'. Within the week all had been carried to the pit themselves, victims of the disease at which they had jeered.

'The hottest judgment,' concluded Dr Gumble, 'did not teach many of us either to pray or repent.' Yet those who made merry were not altogether in conflict with the medical advice of the day. 'Chearfulness' was universally held to offer good protection against infection, but only such sober enjoyments as might be enjoyed by upright citizens in snuff-coloured suits without offence to the proprieties.

'Company, Wine and musick, and other lawfull diversions' were recommended, and a pint of sack a day was agreed by both Boghurst and Hodges to be 'an excellent Antidote for Melancholy people'. The interpretation of 'melancholy' referred back to the medieval idea of depression as one of the adverse 'humours' of the body. Boghurst personally thought music was an excellent specific, but hastened to add that he meant sober chamber performances, and not 'your wild, wanton hackney fiddlers, whose employment is altogether to bee condemned at such a tyme'.

Apart from the hugely increased congregations in London churches during June and July, another source of great crowds were the funerals of plague victims. So many relations, friends, neighbours and inquisitive hangers-on with nothing better to do would regularly follow the dead-carts, that in mid July the Lord Mayor informed the Alderman of every Ward that several people who had died in the previous week were, from the searchers' ignorance, reported to have suffered from diseases other than plague.

'Great audiences' had assembled at their burial, which was a grave cause of spreading the contagion. The City Fathers were urged to take more care to prevent all public burials during the epidemic. This made no difference, until the plague deaths reached such proportions that the corpses were merely tipped wholesale into the plague pits, usually even without any funeral rites. In the oppressively hot days of July and August, the City churchyards began to fill with over-hasty burials, 'in effect',

L'Estrange wrote, 'but half buried…to the certain destruction of as many as live within the reach of that Pestilent Vapour'.

The work of the gravediggers often lacked supervision, because the parish sextons and their superiors were too frightened to inspect the graves. Thus corpses lay in shallow troughs in the earth, not of the necessary depth. The consequent and frequently overpowering stench of putrifying bodies in the graveyards drove many away whose houses were near by. L'Estrange was one of them. 'The noyance' of the stench from a churchyard under his windows, crammed with the dead, finally persuaded him to seek sanctuary at Canterbury. It was none too soon, for on the very day of his departure his footman sickened and died, and two of his family also contracted plague, although they were fortunate enough to survive.

When the Great Plague neared its height, L'Estrange declared that the latest increases in the death rolls were 'undoubtedly promoted by the incorrigible licence of the multitudes that resort to publick Funerals, contrary to both order and reason'.

Pepys thought that the phenomenon was at least partly due to the natural inclination of the people to defy authority. 'But, Lord,' he wrote in amazement, 'to consider the madness of the people of the town, who will, because they are forbid, come in crowds along with the dead corpses to see them buried!'

This morbidity was totally inconsistent with other behaviour during the epidemic. Most people shunned the houses with plague crosses on the doors, kept indoors as much as possible, purchased every conceivable 'remedy' against infection, and hastily crossed the street whenever they encountered any whose duties were connected with plague. Doctors, inspectors, searchers and nurses were easily identifiable, for they were compelled to carry distinctive coloured staffs or 'wands' out of doors, to make sure that they could be recognized from a distance.

Pepys' diary for July gives a vivid picture of the spread of the plague and the gradual rundown of the City. Daily reminders of the Black Death were thrust upon him from all sides. On July 5th he noticed that a house in Pall Mall where 'in Cromwell's time, we young men used to keep our weekly clubs', was shut up, and the Park at St James's, built by disbanded soldiers, was locked and deserted.

The next day Pepys set off to visit Lord Brouncker, one of the Naval Commissioners, but quickly abandoned his intention when he found 'one of the two great houses within two doors of him being shut up'. Returning home by a roundabout route, he was shocked to discover the vast number of houses closed all along the way. On July 10th he drove in a coach to Brentford to dine with Mr Povy, treasurer of the Tangier Committee upon which Pepys served, but found Povy in great fright because one of his servants was sick with plague. Two days later, the diarist was himself observing the solemn fast appointed in the City for the Visitation of the Plague.

During the following week Pepys tried to pursue his normal social life, but found this far from easy. He had been asked by his distant cousin and patron, Lord Sandwich, to arrange a marriage between the nobleman's daughter, Lady Jemima, and Philip, the eldest son of Sir George Carteret, the Treasurer of the Navy. This duty involved making several journeys to the Carteret house near Deptford, and to Dagnams, the home of Lady Carteret's sister, outside Romford, in Essex.

Pleasant and flattering a task as this might be in other conditions, Pepys was not too sure about it then. 'Lord! to see, among other things, how all these great people here are afraid of London, being doubtful of anything that comes from thence, or that hath lately been there,' he noted, adding with some hurt pride that he had been 'forced to say that I lived wholly at Woolwich' (where his wife was in lodgings).

Lady Carteret gave him a 'bottle of plague-water' as a safeguard, and poor Pepys was so embarrassed that he wished himself away. Their fear, however, was not without cause, for their chaplain, who a week or two before had been full of theological argument when Pepys paid his last call, had since died of plague.

At the London Exchange, business had dwindled to a trickle by July 18th, and in the Spring Gardens at Vauxhall – usually a hive of gaiety and pleasure in summer – Pepys found 'not one guest' on July 22nd, despite the extraordinarily hot, fine weather. Abandoning his search for amusement, Pepys disconsolately took a coach for home, but in all the distance between Westminster and Seething Lane in the City he met only two other coaches and two carts, and the streets 'were mighty thin of people'. Three days later he drove to see the Duke of Albemarle at St James's and did not pass a single vehicle either on the outward journey or on the way back.

Pepys found the sickness 'scattered almost everywhere', and it was 'all over King Street, at the Axe, and next door to it, and in other place'. It reached his own parish, and for a terrible moment seemed to have found his house as well, his servant Will coming in complaining of a sick headache and lying down on his bed. The alarmed Pepys admitted that he was thrown into 'an extraordinary fear', and 'studied all I could to get him out of the house'. This was understandable, if it did him little credit, but fortunately for him and even more fortunately for the boy, the symptoms proved false; the boy was not seriously ill.

The fear of death was hard to dismiss, however, for the bell of a church near Pepys' home tolled five or six times a day for deaths or burials, and plague seemed to permeate every aspect of his life. With fascinated horror, he read Graunt's newly printed book on the Mortality Bills (given to him by Lord Brouncker) and studied each of the weekly Bills as they were issued. When forty died in his own parish in a single week, Pepys wrote: 'I began to think of setting things in order, which I pray God enable me...both as to soul and body.'

At Westminster, the parish officers were so pressed for burial space that they had begun to bury their dead in the open Tothill Fields, and no one could purchase a grave in the churchyards unless they were able to pay far more than it was worth.

On the last day of the month, Pepys travelled to Dagnams for the wedding he had helped to arrange. Waiting at the Isle of

Dogs for the ferry, he met a messenger on horseback who told him that the plague was in Islington and that 'Proctor the Vintner, of the Miter in Wood Street, and his son, are dead this morning there of the plague; he was the greatest vintner for some time in London for great entertainments'.

The ferry was late and so Pepys arrived when the wedding was all over, but, taking his duties seriously, he primed the young bridegroom – whom he privately considered to be rather innocent on such matters – upon his new responsibilities, and saw the pair to bed.

Totting up the balance of good and ill for the month, Pepys was satisfied enough about his contacts with the great and his own continuing health, but he ended by taking gloomy note of the mounting plague deaths all around him.

The disease now seemed to be everywhere, and the City was rapidly becoming more disorganized every day. In Newgate Prison, where jail fever was always raging in the indescribably filthy conditions, plague was also reported. Ironically, several corrupt watchmen and searchers of the dead, accused of murdering and robbing plague victims, were among those who awaited trial there. The Keeper, Mr Jackson, whose position was equivalent to a present-day Governor, also died. Few mourned his death, for the prison was run corruptly for the benefit of the jailers, and the smallest comfort had to be bought by the prisoners or their friends outside.

Newgate, a centre of homosexuality and depravity, and with a torture chamber still in regular use, was crowded when the plague began, for the most recent delivery of prisoners had been made in June, and since then neither trials nor executions had been held to thin their number. The reason for this was that at the last Old Bailey sessions, towards the end of June, a prisoner, looking very ill and emaciated, had been brought before the court. The judge, and the magistrates sitting with him, including the Lord Mayor, sent for Mr Upton, the master of the City Pesthouse, who stripped the unhappy man and found plague tokens on him. The trial was hastily abandoned and no further sittings took place until February 1666. Hangings were similarly suspended, but although some criminals thus received an unexpected seven-month extension to their lives, plague saved the hangman a job in many cases.

Far more tragic was the plight of the Quakers, packed forty or more to a cell, to await transportation to America. No ships could be found for them, and fifty-two died of the Black Death while they waited patiently, with prayer and hope, for ships that arrived months late. One of those who died was a fifteen-year-old girl, Hannah Trigg, yet still the magistrates sent fresh batches of the Friends into prison to replace those who were carried out dead.

Conditions were little better in the compters, or debtors' prisons, where bankrupts could languish for years if they could persuade no one to honour their debts and secure their release. The Lord Mayor was sufficiently moved by the wave of deaths in these establishments to appeal through the *Intelligencer* that all creditors willing to make 'a modest composition' should arrange the release of their debtors in Ludgate, Newgate, and the Poultry and Wood Street Compters. This was only a request and met with little response: the rich, to whom they owed the money, were not in London to heed it.

Sir John Lawrence did his best in the City, but he was fighting a losing battle with only a skeleton staff to assist him, and with little help from the citizens.

A man with an even tougher, lonelier job was the Duke of Albemarle, George Monck, who bore almost the entire responsibility for Central Government himself in the absence of the King and the Privy Council. Such a state of affairs did not depress him; his life had been one long sequence of hasty decisions and immense responsibility since the day when he thrashed the Under Sheriff of Devonshire, his home county, for some insult to his father. As a result he had to leave home precipitately, and he took to arms, a career in which he was extremely successful. He fought in Spain, in the Low Countries, on the Scottish border and in Ireland; and it was said that the secrets of his success were 'a talent for making himself indispensable, an imperturbable temper and an impenetrable secrecy'.

During Cromwell's day, Monck formed a new regiment, which later became the Coldstream Guards, taking their name from the small village of Coldstream on the River Tweed, where he had settled his headquarters because it commanded the best ford. He always lived rough with his men, and his own headquarters, according to Gumble, was simply a cottage 'with two great dung-hills at the door, the hall or entry as dark and narrow as a man could not turn in it'. His bed so small, 'like a bird's nest', that Monck used it as a pillow and rested his legs and body on benches.

In the confusion following Cromwell's death, Monck refused to support the Protector's incompetent son Richard, or even the King, before he was certain the time was right. Instead, his army – each man carrying his own seven-day rations of one pound of biscuits and half a pound of cheese a day – marched south to London; there Monck dissolved Parliament and then largely organized the Restoration.

As King Charles stepped ashore from his exile on the Continent, he knelt down and thanked God for his return, then drawing Monck to him, he kissed him and called him 'Father'. Monck, as always master of the situation, handed King Charles his sword and cried: 'God Save the King!' Everyone started to cheer and then a lone voice – that of the young Duke of Gloucester – cried with more sense: 'God Save General Monck!'

King Charles made him a Gentleman of the Bedchamber, a Knight of the Garter, Master of the Horse and Commander-in-Chief, and honoured him with the titles of Baron Monck, the Earl of Torrington, the Duke of Albemarle, and a pension of £7,000 a year. Both Monck and his wife were unusually fond of money. He amassed an enormous fortune, and when he died five years after the plague he left his eldest son property worth a half-million pounds. His name is still remembered from

Albemarle Street. All through the plague he stayed in London chewing tobacco, imperturbable as ever, and a great comfort to those who could not leave London. To many citizens Monck, heavy, solid, phlegmatic, a man who 'hated a coward as ill as a toad', became their living symbol of survival.

Also remaining in London was the great philanthropist, Lord Craven, an early Fellow of the Royal Society. He stayed in his enormous house at the bottom of Drury Lane throughout the epidemic and gave liberally of his money to build pesthouses and to help poor people. Having shared the King's exile during the days of the Commonwealth, Craven did not now shirk exile of another, more deadly kind.

And there were also several Justices of the Peace who lived in the Strand and Westminster, whom the King had personally asked to stay and who later received knighthoods when the plague had passed. Apart from these, only a handful of lesser officials remained, a pathetically small group of worried men to run the sickened City.

As high summer came, each day grew astonishingly, almost unbelievably hot. The sun shone with an Italian fierceness, roads crumbled to dust and dunghills steamed. The smell of death, of sweaty, unwashed bodies, of foul clothes and filthy streets grew stronger every day. Public and private prayers were said daily for rain to dampen down the dust and sweeten the air. Farmers living just outside London said enthusiastically that they had never known such a good summer for their early-ripening fruit and flowers. A shortage of hay was reported, but everything else prospered. Apples and pears, cherries and plums, raspberries, strawberries and mulberries; all ripened beautifully. Harvests were magnificent; root crops came on well, flowers and herbs blossomed, and all growing things were, in the words of one husbandman, 'plentiful, large, faire and wholesome'. Farm animals and wild creatures of the fields and woods were also 'as healthfull, strong to labour, wholesome to eate as ever they were in any yeare'. Cherries and grapes, usually too dear for the poor, were selling at unprecedentedly low prices. The only drawback was in the scarcity of customers in London for such a wealth of good things.

Yet, to many, this strange lush, luxuriant growth seemed to possess the seeds of something evil. It was as though Nature was running wild, and many people would not eat fruit or pick flowers for fear they should be poisoned. They felt they had grown so fast and richly through feeding on the dead that lay buried so near them in almost any open space.

'Now Roses and other sweet flowers wither in the Gardens, are disregarded in the Markets,' wrote Dr Vincent, 'and people dare not offer them to their noses, lest with their sweet savour, that which is infectious should be attracted.' The distinctive smell of the Plague was heavy and sickly sweet; the scent of hawthorn and mayflower blossom; the smell of death.

CHAPTER FIVE

No Mercy for the Stricken

By the end of July, when the official death roll from the plague was admitted to be around 2,000 a week, most of London's rich and influential citizens had already made the best use of their advantages and left the capital as early as they could. The poorer people were still in two minds about whether to go or whether to stay. If they decided to leave, they faced almost inevitable ruin through abandoning their humble jobs or shops – usually no more than a front room in their houses. Despite this, flight offered the chance of survival, and many thus gathered up what belongings they could carry and fled, reasoning that their future could take care of itself.

The Lord Mayor, Sir John Lawrence, was becoming increasingly reluctant to give his townsmen permission to leave London. Parish clerks and magistrates, who were authorized to issue documents saying that the evacuees were free from plague, shared this reluctance. Sir John, a man of energy and decision, who from the first onslaught of the epidemic declared he would remain in the City at the service of the citizens, realized the enormous hostility those in the country felt towards people from London. They hated them because they feared they would bring plague to their villages; they seized this chance of repaying real or imagined slights or insults Londoners had given them when they did not need their help and mercy.

Further, since London largely depended for milk and food on farms around its walls, the Lord Mayor did not wish to risk antagonizing the farmers. He therefore began to refuse 'free from infection' certificates to the thousands of Londoners who wanted them. The professional forgers offered counterfeit papers at high prices. To curb these activities the authorities printed warning notices in the *Intelligencer* announcing that false certificates, supposedly signed by parish officers at St Gregory's, near St Paul's, St Botolph's, Bishopsgate, and St Mary Abchurch were in existence. In future, parish officials would only sign printed certificates, and then only for people who were personally known to them.

Outside London no one wanted to have anything to do with anyone from the capital. Even the *Intelligencer*, after printing the news 'it hath pleased God to suffer this City to be visited with the Plague', later admitted that this had 'cut off all communication and correspondence' with the provinces.

Only the Lord Mayor's intelligent anticipation of this possibility saved the City from famine. Sir John ordered his City officers to organize special routes for country people bringing in food to market. They would thus not see and be frightened by sights already so familiar to Londoners: bodies black with putrefaction, naked and dead, piled in pyramids on the stinking, unsprung dead-carts; mounds of corpses waiting on the edge of mass burial grounds while enfeebled, half-witted or intoxicated diggers reluctantly dug their graves; streets awash with excreta, sour with vomit, foul with pools of urine, amid which strange flowers bloomed with a fearful beauty.

They could dispose of their goods without actually meeting their customers, and when they returned home they would have no stories of horror to pass on to their wives and friends.

The Lord Mayor also ordered that all goods sent from London to the provinces should be carefully inspected, so that nothing should be dispatched from infected premises. Even so, some bales of cloth, bound for the little village of Eyam, in Derbyshire, did carry the infection, with results remembered still, as we shall see. These measures certainly encouraged timid, superstitious country people to maintain a trickle of trade with London, but for many of them fear of plague overcame even their desire for profit.

The Mayor of Gloucester, for example, although a practising apothecary, refused to admit pipes of wine from the capital until they had first been dragged through the River Severn. This, he declared, would remove infection. After a considerable quantity of wine had thus been rendered undrinkable, His Worship agreed to allow casks into his town if water had been poured over them. 'Soe the vintner's man took a dish of water...and sprinkled each vessel a little and soe made them wholesome,' wrote Boghurst in disgust. 'Notwithstanding they had come a hundred mile in the air and it had rained on them much by the way...'

In an age and to a people to whom hygiene and even rudimentary cleanliness was alien, water was believed to hold the power of killing infection. Many farmers who brought their vegetables to London refused to accept direct payment. The coins were placed in a bucket of water for them. After an hour or so they poured away the water and pocketed the money.

Most country folk brought up their produce to fields on the City outskirts – such as Spitalfields, Bunhill Fields and open ground between Islington and the City walls. Londoners then shouted out what vegetables and fruit they needed; the farmers called back the price required, some long-distance haggling followed and a figure was finally agreed. The buyers put their silver and gold and copper coins into jars of water sharpened with vinegar, and then retreated to a distance of perhaps fifty feet, and waited. After some time, the villagers walked up to these jars, poured away the liquid and pocketed the coins.

As plague spread out to the countryside, 'plague stones', rocks with hollow places gouged out, were set up in many market places. Goods for sale were left near them with a note giving the price required; the buyers dropped their money into the hollows in the stones, which were usually filled with water or vinegar. Examples of these stones survived until recently at Grayingham, in Lincolnshire; outside the West Gate at Winchester, and at

Stretford, Manchester.

By such delusions, London was saved from complete starvation, and throughout the epidemic the penny loaf never dropped to less than nine and a half ounces; its normal weight was about eleven ounces. This was partly due to the courage of Essex shipmasters, who all through that summer delivered corn to the Port of London. By special order of the Corporation, they were allowed a commission of a farthing for every quarter of corn landed. Whether by oversight or as a continuing expression of the City's gratitude, this bounty continued for nearly 200 years after the end of the plague.

Those who could afford to buy bulk supplies of sugar, flour and oatmeal had stocked their cupboards and attics well. They had thus no need to go out into the streets and so risk infection. As always, the poor and the improvident suffered the worst hardships, and it was certainly not without reason that the epidemic became widely known as 'the Poore Men's Plague'.

Dr Vincent wrote that month that 'the Plague compasseth the walls of the City like a flood, and poureth in upon it...yea, there are not so many houses shut up by the Plague, as by the owners' forsaking of them for fear of it'. Defoe estimated that 10,000 houses were shut up and that 200,000 people had fled, while Vincent emphasized that most of these were 'the rich and middle sort', whereas 'the poor are forced to stay and abide the storm'.

Even L'Estrange, in the *Intelligencer*, appealed for charity on behalf of the suffering poor in the plague-stricken parishes. 'The weight of it,' he wrote on July 22nd, 'hath hitherto lain only upon the Poor, which are either crowded up into corners, and smothered for want of Aire, or are otherwise lost for want of Seasonable Attendance, and Remedies.' Many others, he continued, were lost 'through want of Bread; which is no wonder in several of the Out-parishes that are very populous, and whence the Rich have withdrawn themselves'.

L'Estrange appealed to readers of means to follow the example of some wealthy people who had given money to help parishes they had left, warning that 'one of the most Crying Sins' was for Christians to be 'uncompassionate one of another'. He was not always so pious and solicitous, and frequently referred irritably in his columns to the 'sluttishness' of the poor in the 'Close and filthy Allyes', as being largely responsible for the spread of the disease.

There is little doubt that L'Estrange was instructed at Court to make this appeal, for a fortnight earlier a Royal Proclamation had been published ordering general fasts throughout the country 'to the end that Prayers and Supplications may everywhere be offered up unto Almighty God for the removal of the heavy Judgment of Plague and Pestilence'. Special prayers were published in an eighty-page booklet, and by the King's command collections taken in churches for the relief of the poor in the plague areas, everyone being asked to give 'chearfully and freely'.

The instigation of such public appeals was as far as the Court or national government went towards providing plague relief. Not one farthing from the national coffers was yielded up, and although it was widely rumoured at the time (and later alleged by Defoe) that King Charles provided £1,000 a week throughout the epidemic from the Royal Purse, no evidence of this exists. If anyone was charged with the distribution of Royal largesse he apparently did not think it necessary to keep a record of how such generous funds were used. Apart from a payment of £100 for relief in Westminster, a record of which does survive, the King apparently contributed no money at all. Several rich noblemen gave larger individual sums; and lesser amounts flowed steadily in to the Bishop of London, Humphrey Henchman, and to the Lord Mayor. A typical example was an early gift of £61 collected between twenty-five Londoners, who had travelled to Bristol to escape plague, and this – and other sums like this – no doubt helped them salve their consciences.

Apart from such charity, the parishes both within and without the City were left to manage as best they could. 'Pest rates' and 'poor relief rates' of a few pence per household were levied, but with so many houses empty the actual amounts raised were small compared with the need. When the death totals began to soar towards the peak of the plague in August, these pathetic parish funds were exhausted within days. Even the temporary allocation of a few hundred pounds a week from the City exchequer had little real effect.

When a few cases of plague were reported in Brentford and other riverside villages west of London, the King thought it wise to move farther afield, and on July 27th the entire Court set off from Hampton Court for Salisbury. An interested spectator was the indefatigable Pepys, who took great delight in 'the young pretty ladies dressed like men', for the dusty journey, with velvet coats, beribboned caps and lace bands at their wrists. Pepys thought the male habit became them all, except for the Duchess of York, the plain and ungainly daughter of the Lord Chancellor, Lord Clarendon. Afterwards, the diarist went on to a friend's house at Clapham, where he enjoyed dinner, a pleasant walk in the gardens, and 'a little opportunity to kiss and spend some time with the ladies above', who included his host's daughter, 'a buxom lass', quite unlike the Duchess.

The King received a Royal welcome at Salisbury, although his Court soon became less popular. Courtiers turned local people out of their houses to make room for themselves, the City purse was lightened by 'homage' fees which had to be paid to the King's retinue by ancient custom, and residents were even compelled to build a new pesthouse, to elaborate further the precautions taken for the protection of Charles and his circle. Neither King nor Court contributed to this last project, and there was general relief when in September – after several plague deaths in and around Salisbury – the Court took horse on to Oxford.

Few Londoners who fled the capital late in July or early in August received so comfortable a welcome as King Charles and his courtiers. Although Vincent was generally right when he said that the London poor was compelled to 'stay and abide the storm', many poor people, having seen friends and relations die around them, decided that the uncertainty of flight was preferable to the seemingly certain alternatives of plague and starvation in London. With usually no more than a bundle of personal belongings, which they carried on the end of a stick over their shoulder, Dick Whittington fashion; with a few shillings capital, and their certificates of health sewn into their coats where robbers would be unlikely to find them, they trudged away along the dust-laden highways to an uncertain future, an unknown destination.

They walked because they could not afford to ride; and indeed by then most of the available horses and carts and carriages in the capital had also disappeared. Those horses still in London were impressed to draw the carts of corpses. Once out in the country, these evacuees found to their amazement that they were pariahs, social outcasts, as welcome as lepers. No work existed for them; locally established labourers and craftsmen hated them in case they took their jobs; everyone feared and dreaded them as potential sources of pestilence.

Self-preservation quickly took precedence over any feelings of common humanity. Towns and villages, which had earlier welcomed well-to-do refugees, and derived much profit from them, now paid guards with firearms to stand on their approach roads and turn away anyone even suspected to have come from London, regardless of who they were, or what papers they carried. Many towns not only refused evacuees the permission to stay a night within their boundaries; they would not even allow hungry and travel-stained Londoners to pass through their streets. Nor would anyone sell them a loaf of bread or a hunk of cheese to help them on their way. In the oppressive heat, straggling parties of runaways were forced to make long, wearisome detours across fields and rough country to avoid towns. With many areas affected by heat and drought for months, with streams and ponds dried up, they soon became delirious with weariness and thirst.

At Guildford, where the town worthies smugly reported themselves 'still happily free', the magistrates actually fixed lids and padlocks on the wells to prevent Londoners using them. Townspeople were warned not to receive lodgers or to admit coaches and wagons unless they knew beyond doubt their town of origin.

The authorities at Oxford were equally terrified of infection. Oxford had been ravaged by plague in the Middle Ages because, according to a contemporary account, 'they used to kill all manner of Cattle within the Walls and suffer their Dung and Offal to lie in the Streets'. Now, by order of the Mayor and the Vice-Chancellor of the University, a constant night watch was set at the four entrances to the city to prevent strangers coming in under cover of darkness. Scuffles between the watchers and the watched provided entertainment to undergraduates, who would walk out in the evenings to jest with the guards. Undergraduates were warned 'to prevent goods and winter clothing' being sent to them from London, for it was widely believed that plague was spread by infected clothing and material. Richard Baxter, a dissenting minister who fled to Buckinghamshire, reported that even a hundred miles from London people were fearful of buying anything from mercers and drapers.

Letters from London were no less suspect than their writers. Country folk held such notes in tongs and tried to rub away any infection by scraping them against various rough surfaces, such as a stone or the doorstep. Others put their correspondence in sieves and shook the letters about in the hope that any 'pestilential matter' on it would fall out through the holes in the bottom. Many letters were washed in water and then put before the fire to dry, becoming quite illegible in the process. Others favoured the 'airing' of their mail, and so pegged out letters on their roofs or stuck them on top of a high hedge or a pole, and waited for two or three days before they read them in the hope that by then the wind would have blown away any germs. Another practice was to press letters for a period between two cold stones; yet another, to spear the letter on a toasting fork and hold it before the fire.

John Allin, who stayed in London throughout most of the

Great Plague, living in Horsleydown in St Olave's parish, was upset to learn that some of his acquaintances in the country were reluctant to receive his letters. In correspondence with Philip Fryth, a solicitor, and Samuel Jeake, an historian, both of whom lived in Allin's former parish of Rye, Sussex, he thanked them for not sharing the fears of their more nervous friends. 'Were my penn infectious, my hand would soone let it drop,' he commented.

Others thought differently, and Boghurst provided a further example of the country's fears when he told how a messenger from a rural area came to his apothecary's shop and delivered a letter to his wife on the end of a long pole, 'because hee would not venture too near her'.

These testimonies of the terror Black Death produced go some way towards explaining, if not excusing, the shared and almost universal hostility of country people to Londoners. Always intensely superstitious and fearful of unnatural happenings, they had no compassion for the refugees who, in steadily increasing distress and numbers, were forced to wander hopelessly like nomads about the countryside during those summer weeks.

They were driven away from towns and hamlets with curses and blows; watchdogs were set on them as they approached farms; villagers pelted them with stones and manure; constables threatened them with firearms. They were forced to live like beasts, tearing up turnips and parsnips from the fields to eat raw; chewing cabbage leaves, stealing apples, sleeping in ditches and under hedges. Many, especially the older ones, sickened and died, some from plague germs carried within them from London, but more from exposure and starvation. Their bodies were left where they dropped, beside the highways, in the fields, or where they had crawled away to die alone, in barns and against hayricks.

Rarely did any of the local people care or dare to bury the bodies of the strangers. Their corpses rotted in the sunshine, torn and picked at by dogs, rats and birds of prey. A clergyman,

Richard Baxter, knew of a Welsh Nonconformist minister named Roberts who fled the capital only to find that 'none durst entertain him'. The poor man died alone on a bale of straw in the fields between Oswestry and Shrewsbury. A Londoner, who was turned away from Dorchester, crawled into a hut on a farm just outside the town, where he died, presumably of plague. The townspeople were so terrified that they dug a vast pit by the side of the hut, into which they toppled the entire building, and the corpse it contained, and covered them over with earth. No one had been prepared to risk even entering the shack to remove the body.

Numbers of refugees managed to creep into country towns despite the guards, by crossing fields and fording rivers, but they looked so thin and ragged and their accents sounded so strange that they were soon discovered. They were immediately driven out into the fields or else imprisoned. A relation of Sir Ralph Verney, writing to him from Chelmsford, where a number were incarcerated in this way, said 'thos which bee shut up would run About did not sum stand with guns redy to shoot them if they stur'.

In Northamptonshire, too, improvised pesthouses were constantly guarded by citizens with firearms. In these circumstances few refugees, denied food, water or medical aid, recovered.

People in many provincial towns, who were unfortunate enough to contract plague themselves, fared little better than the refugees. Locals commandeered hovels and pig styes and banished the sufferers to them.

A dog was blamed for spreading plague to Buckinghamshire where many died, some in the small village of Lavendon, and a crude pesthouse was set up to accommodate the sufferers near Aylesbury. Once inside it, the doors were nailed shut and the victims abandoned to their fate. Local farmers refused to let them out even to collect firewood, but some managed to escape through loose boards, and at night they stole gates and sheep hurdles which they carried back to burn for their cooking fires.

In Scotland, people took a more humane and realistic view of these unnecessary sufferings, which did nothing to stem the plague's advance, and still remained entirely free from the disease. On July 14th, after King Charles' flight from London, the Scots realized that the King would not leave his capital without good reason, and immediately prohibited all trade between Scotland and infected areas until November 1st. Strict quarantine was imposed upon shipping, and all land traffic was ordered to be held at the border until it had been fully investigated. Scotsmen returning to their homes from plague-afflicted towns were confined to their houses for one month, and it was announced at the start that any disobedience would be punished by death or confiscation of goods 'without mercy'. These regulations were extended until the summer of the following year, and proved entirely successful.

If countrymen were cruel to strangers from London, the citizens remaining in the capital proved they could be just as callous to each other. According to the Mortality Bills, 15,207 died from all causes within the City walls during that year, 9,877 of them from plague; that is less than one-seventh of the capital's total death roll.

But the ruthlessness of the City to their own people was as much responsible for this seemingly good result as the slightly better conditions there when compared with the out-parishes. Once plague had struck, the City authorities did their best to clear their ninety-seven parishes of everyone who was not a householder. Strangers, visitors, guests and relatives were at liberty to die wherever they pleased, so long as they did not die within the City boundaries.

Thousands of people usually lodged in the City, most of them impecunious craftsmen or apprentices articled for years to their masters; plus servants and tradesmen who had come to London in the hope of employment. Once their employers had fled and they faced destitution, the City Corporation hounded them out.

An order was made forbidding anyone within the City

boundary to take in lodgers; the penalty for disobedience was to have the house shut up as though it had been infected with plague. In each ward, efforts were made to persuade local residents to give notice to lodgers already in their houses; since many of the lodgers were out of work and behind with their rent, this was not difficult.

Once out on the streets, thousands of homeless, hungry people, their few belongings or sets of craftsmen's tools impounded by landlords to whom they owed money, were in an even worse plight than those wretches who had fled to the country. There were no root-crops to tear up in London; they had to beg or steal their food. They were forced to break into empty shops, houses, warehouses in a search for bread or money. No one would shelter them for they simply represented more mouths to feed, and as many more risks of catching plague. They therefore tried to seek refuge in the slums of the Liberties and out-parishes, where the plague was already taking its heaviest toll. Even there, parish constables and officers did all they could to drive out strangers who ventured in, so that they would not become a charge upon local poor relief.

The wandering wretches already sickening with plague were in the worst case of all. Weak with retching and fever, tortured with sores and buboes, half blind and delirious, often barely able to stand, they were encouraged on their way with sticks and stones. If they were too weak to walk, constables dragged or carried them over their parish boundary and dumped them at the roadside to die on someone else's territory and so at the expense of another parish.

Parish records of that summer contain records of dozens of payments of a shilling or even half a crown made to parish officers and others for 'carrying a visited woman out of ye parish'; for 'carrying a sick man out of the parish to prevent further charge'; or 'to getting a big-bellied woman out of ye parish for fear she should give birth and produce yet one more mouth to feed'. Other payments were made to the sufferers themselves – generally sixpence or a shilling – in return for their promise to quit the district and not return. Frequently a constable saw they fulfilled their part of the bargain, and then relieved them of their money. The same coins could thus be used again and again.

None suffered from the Black Death so badly as women expecting babies, whether they were respectable housewives used to substantial homes or forlorn and friendless unmarried women roaming the streets. Boghurst calculated that barely one in fifty pregnant women who contracted plague survived. If they recovered from the plague, they invariably had miscarriages which were fatal. The numbers of stillborn children quickly doubled during that summer; often the cause was more a complete lack of attention during confinement than any direct consequence of bubonic plague. Midwives could rarely be persuaded to attend women in houses stricken with plague, and as one recorded sadly, 'an incredible number of women…were delivered and spoiled by the rashness and ignorance of those who pretended to lay them'.

Expectant mothers with plague already upon them had virtually no chance of life, even if they reached the stage of being confined. No one would come near to help them in case they caught plague themselves, and so mother and half-born infant died together. Many unhappy women who had sickened during pregnancy procured unskilful and fatal abortions in a pitiful effort to escape this fate. Figures given in the Mortality Bills speak worlds in terms of this suffering. Under the headings of 'Childbed', 'Abortive' and 'Stillborn', a total of 172 deaths were listed for a nine-week period from January to early March 1665. In a similar time at the height of the plague – during August and September – this total increased to 432.

The Bills, of course, do not tell anything like the full story of these deaths, but they admit that in 1665, 652 women died in childbed compared with only 189 in the previous year, and that the number of abortions and stillbirths greatly increased.

Defoe cited the case of a young mother who sent for an apothecary because her baby seemed unwell. When the man arrived, the poor woman was suckling the child, all unaware of the meaning of the strange marks on her bared breast; they were plague tokens. He carried the child into another room, and when he opened its clothing he found the same dreaded spots and pustules on the baby's body. Mother and child were dead before morning.

Another mother, exhausted by a difficult birth, put out her child to a wet nurse, who within a few days died of the plague. No one would have anything to do with the infant, and so the mother took it back and tried to feed it herself. The baby, already infected by the nurse, passed the plague on to its mother; she died.

Another domestic tragedy recorded was that of a tradesman at Smithfield whose young wife, expecting her first baby, was stricken with plague. When her labour pains began, he ran distractedly from house to house knocking on each door, begging the people inside to help him. No one would do so, for they knew he came from a house of plague. Finally, the young man ran home and helped to deliver a dead baby; his wife died an hour later. The husband's body was found next morning when the constables visited the house to mark it with the red cross.

Dr Hodges had known and treated many of these poor people since they had been children; their sufferings saddened him as though they had been his own. 'Death was the sure Midwife to all children,' he wrote, 'and infants passed immediately from the Womb to the Grave; who would not burst with Grief, to see the stock for a future Generation hang upon the Breasts of a dead Mother, or the Marriage-Bed changed the first Night into a Sepulchre, and the unhappy Pair meet with Death in their first Embraces?'

Many expressed the earnest hope that if ever a plague epidemic should again strike London, then means should be found to evacuate all expectant mothers and children, for in the terrible agony of the City none suffered so cruelly and so needlessly as they. This was a pious and humane hope for the future; it did not help the women most concerned, nor did it benefit the older children, who faced little hope of survival in shuttered plague houses. Young people, indeed, seemed particularly susceptible to the disease and rarely possessed the resistance needed for recovery. Large families were common then, and thousands of parents were forced to watch nine or ten children die one after the other. Nearly every week throughout that summer distracted mothers murdered sick children rather than allow them to suffer any longer; suicides became a commonplace.

In the midst of this gloom and horror, Samuel Pepys told a heartening story of an infant snatched from certain death in one of these locked houses. One morning he put on his 'coloured silk suit, very fine', and his new periwigg, 'bought a good while since, but durst not wear because the plague was in Westminster when I bought it'.

Thus splendidly attired, Pepys set off for a consultation with the Justices of the Peace at Greenwich, where Alderman Hooker had a complaint to make against a man who had brought a child there from an infected house in the City.

Apparently, a saddler who lived in Gracechurch Street, and 'a very able citizen', had seen his house bolted up when his children became infected with plague. He and his wife watched them die one after the other. Eventually, only one healthy child remained, a baby in arms. While they despaired of escaping themselves, their one desire was to save the life of this last child, and they persuaded a friend to help them smuggle it from their house. The baby, naked so as to prevent it from carrying infection in any clothes, was carefully lowered from a window into the arms of this man, who wrapped it in some clothes and carried it off to Greenwich in his arms. Although information was laid against the man who succoured the child, the magistrates were so touched by the story that they took no action and agreed to allow the baby to stay within their jurisdiction, and be cared for.

Pepys thought the story 'very passionate', but soon returned to the subject of his new periwigg, wondering what would be the fashion after the epidemic, 'for nobody will dare to buy any haire, for fear of the infection, that it had been cut off the heads of people dead of the plague'.

Not all those whose compassion moved them to try to save the lives of innocent children incarcerated in plague houses were so fortunate as the man from Greenwich. Several people, just as kind-hearted, accepted the children of infected families in this way, and were committed for trial by the Justices for endangering the health of their parishes by breaking the quarantine laws.

As August began with a day of blazing sunshine, Dr Vincent wrote sadly: 'Now Death rides triumphantly on his pale Horse through our streets, and breaks into every House... Now people fall as thick as leaves from the Trees in Autumn, when they are shaken by a mighty Wind. Now there is a dismal solitude...' And indeed it seemed to many as though their only hope of survival lay in a self-imposed isolation from their fellows. They began to live hermit-like existences in their shuttered homes; others left their houses and bought, borrowed or stole a boat, and decided to live on the river until the plague should pass.

The Thames soon became crowded with vessels, ranging in size from substantial merchantmen and coasters to small open wherries and dinghies with canvas awnings. All were moored well out into mid-stream and packed with the families of their owners and crews. It was estimated that more than 10,000 people took to the river in this way, and of these a far greater proportion survived than among the families who preferred to stay on land. The richer and more prudent stocked their craft with provisions to last a number of weeks, so that they were able to remain independent of supplies from shops and farms, but fresh supplies could always be obtained fairly cheaply.

Impoverished watermen, their living gone with the decline of traffic on the river, were grateful of any chance to earn a few coppers, and they would row for miles past the infected area of the City to buy fresh food and bring it back to sell to people living on the river.

Nevertheless, plague did penetrate some of the ships; the corpses were simply thrown into the river to float away and add to the pollution. The worst-hit ship in London was the *Black Eagle*, earmarked for the transportation of Quakers and other dissenters to the West Indies, and lying below Greenwich. Fifty-five Friends were taken from Newgate – where the plague was already severe – to the ship in July, but they refused to board her. Some were forcibly embarked, and the rest marched back to jail.

A week or two later they returned to Greenwich and troops used lifting tackle to rope the struggling victims together and heave them aboard, where they were locked below decks in appalling conditions. Plague rapidly broke out among them, and half had died, many of them women, even before the voyage began.

While the ship still lay in the Thames her master, one Captain Fudge, was arrested on a charge of debt, and the crew took advantage of his absence to mutiny. Nevertheless, the vessel did set off and reached Plymouth, where she was refused permission to land. The acting master headed her out to sea, with some vague plan of his own to be a pirate. This came to nothing, for a Dutch vessel captured the *Black Eagle* and embarked the surviving Quakers for Holland, where they were released.

Previous experience of plague both in England and on the Continent should have demonstrated clearly that people stood a far better chance of survival if they could stay in the open air. Yet in London throughout that summer thousands of houses were tightly sealed and shuttered in the sweltering heat. The widespread belief that plague was carried in the air was zealously fostered, not only by charlatans with quack remedies to sell, but also by some of the most reputable medical authorities of the day. In their frantic efforts to escape a purely imaginary 'pestilential effluvium', frightened and ignorant people closed all their windows; they stuffed cushions into fireplaces, blankets into gaps beneath doors, and even plugged keyholes with twists of paper or wooden wedges.

It was widely believed that the burning of 'noxious materials' inside the houses would purify any infected air. As a result, householders lit fires containing brimstone, saltpetre, tar, frankincense, and even old boots and bits of leather harness. The heavy blue smoke thickened the atmosphere, and sent plague victims, already fighting for breath, into fatal paroxysms of coughing. Others used 'stink pots' – iron braziers or huge jars made of fire-brick – in which they burned strong herbs such as juniper berries, wormwood, tamarisk, cypress bark, aloes, rosemary and cloves, even human faeces. To strengthen the smell, they sprinkled their floors liberally with sour vinegar and urine. Then, in shuttered houses, with chimneys blocked, rooms grey with smoke and foul with the stench of this burning rubbish, families sat, grimly determined to endure the smarting smoke, convinced they were immune from plague.

In a letter to the office of the Secretary of State, James Hickes, postmaster at the Letter Office, spoke of 'airing' letters over boiling vinegar, and complained that his office was 'so fumed, morning and night', that he and his staff could barely see each other through the smoke, 'yet had the contagion been catching through the mail we had been dead long ago'.

A nineteen-page pamphlet, entitled *The Plague's Approved Physitian*, which claimed to 'shew the naturall causes of the infection of the Ayre, and of the Plague', was one of dozens produced by medical imposters. It was simply a mass of superstitions, old wives' tales and lists of traditional specifics, yet copies were sold by the hundred in booksellers' shops clustered around St Paul's. The *Approved Physitian* announced that the 'speciall cause of the Pestilence' was 'infected, corrupted and putrified air'. This 'poisonous effluvium' was not produced by 'unburied carcases' and stinking ditches and drains, which was reasonable enough, but it came mainly from 'influences, aspects, conjunctions and opposition of ill planets, the Eclipse of the Sunne and Moone, through the immoderate heate of the Aire, where the temperature of the aire is turned from his naturall state to excessive heate and moisture, which is the worst temperament of the Aire; vapours being drawn up...doe rot, putrifie, and corrupt'.

After this involved reasoning, the author prescribed a multitude of remedies to his readers. They were advised to 'goe out seldom', and light fires daily upon which a couple of dozen different substances should be heaped, 'for there is a marvelous great vertue and strength in fire, to purge, correct and amend the rottennesse and corruption of the ayre'. During the day, 'all should studiously avoid dancing, running, leaping about, lechery and baths', for such activities opened the pores and allowed 'the bad aires to enter which invenome, infect and indanger the whole body'. At night, people should sleep in 'a close Chamber, well stopp'd and the windowes and doors shut'.

Apart from the paradox of blaming heat and evaporation on the one hand, and yet recommending heat in the people's homes on the other, the author felt obliged to admit that since plague was caused by 'the breathing in of pestilent and corrupt Ayre' which everyone in London had to do, 'whether wee will or no', the only true remedy was thus to run away. Those who could not afford to flee he advised to be gay, for 'heavie thoughts and sighing doe much distemper the body'.

In the public mind, then, air was highly suspect, and people did their best to purify it, or better still, to drive it away altogether. Thus gunshots, which rang out regularly all over the capital during those three months of June, July and August, bore further witness to the ignorance of the times. Believing that the wind carried the disease from street to street, men fired guns out of their windows, convinced that the explosions would drive away deadly air, which had gathered around their houses, or that the acrid fumes from the powder would kill the 'venomous Miasmata' in the atmosphere. The College of Physicians recommended this frequent firing of guns. Even Dr Hodges, who was careful to say no more than that the air might be a vehicle for the plague 'contaminatory seeds', approved this practice on the ground that 'configurations of particules in the ether might be radically changed by such detonations'.

Boghurst, who scoffed at such ideas, reported that many people were impressed by a widely current rumour that a detachment of soldiers had saved an unidentified town from plague by firing their muskets into the sky from the streets. The apothecary also mentioned that one of the reasons why the keeping of caged birds became so popular in London during the plague, was that their owners believed the fluttering wings of the birds kept up a constant circulation of the air, and so prevented it from becoming stagnant or laden with disease.

Some fanatics were not content to discharge firearms into the air; they lit powerful squibs and shallow pans of gunpowder within their rooms. The thunder of these explosions, which deafened some and blinded others, brought down flaking plaster, blew out windows and set many of the timbered houses on fire. It is surprising, with the drought and heat of that summer, and the frequent detonations and explosions rumbling in the narrow streets, that London did not catch fire then instead of a year later.

This fear of fresh air produced a rather pathetic petition to King Charles from a prisoner in the Tower. He humbly requested that he might be allowed to take the air on the battlements with his Keeper, which he had been forbidden to do 'since the increase of the sickness'. The request was allowed.

All through the epidemic, authorities were so worried at the ineffectiveness of all known remedies that they gladly experimented with anything that seemed to offer the slightest hope of checking the plague. Thus they became involved with a French charlatan, one James Augier. In May, Augier had made an offer of 'certain Remedies and Medicaments for stopping the Contagion of the Plague, and for disinfecting houses already infected'. He backed his proposal with certificates which confirmed his claim that he had played a major role in halting the spread of plague in Lyons, Toulouse and Paris. In fact, he had printed these references himself in London. The plausible

Frenchman gained an audience with Lord Arlington, the Secretary of State, and even with the Privy Council, who decided to investigate his offer. A committee was set up of Sir John Robinson, Lieutenant of the Tower, Sir George Charnock, King's Serjeant-at-Arms in Ordinary, four Serjeant-at-Arms from the House of Commons, and a Middlesex Justice of the Peace.

On June 8th, at the committee's request, Augier sent his servant, Richard Goodale, into the house of Jonas Charles in Newton Street, St Giles-in-the-Fields, where four people had already 'dyed full of the spots'. The house was a rambling rabbit-warren, all passages and steps and floors on different levels, built of timber and plaster, with latticed windows and steep, rickety stairs. Eight people were still there, two of them suffering from plague. Goodale gave them all a draught of some medicine Augier had mixed and, more important, fumigated the house with a compound which included brimstone. After this, no one else died in that house.

Similar results were obtained when Augier's remedies were tried out in other infected premises. Jonas Charles was so impressed that he and several others, 'conceiving their lives thereby preserved', offered to take the specifics into other infected premises.

On June 29th the *Intelligencer* printed an announcement by Lord Arlington, 'to satisfie all persons of the great care of the Rt Hon the Lords of His Majestie's most honourable Privy Council, for prevention of spreading of the Infection', and ordering Justices of the Peace throughout London to deal with Augier. Six addresses were given where Augier's concoctions could be obtained, with the comment that the remedy had given 'abundant satisfaction'; and a promise was made to publish 'A Fuller Narrative of the Experiment of the said Remedies and Medicines'. The Lord Mayor was ordered to encourage and reward Augier, and indeed he was paid £20 out of the St Giles parish funds alone.

It seems that everyone was quickly disillusioned with the Frenchman, for within a few weeks all mention of him ceased.

None of the thousands of remedies tried made the slightest difference to the rising tide of plague. Either Augier's initial success was coincidental, or quite by accident and in ignorance he had discovered an amalgam of chemicals that sent the rats scurrying out of the tumbledown house in St Giles; and with them went the plague.

Many people had a private interest in promoting various fumigants or other specifics. L'Estrange, in the *Intelligencer*, made repeated references to a compound called 'Burneby's Powder', invented by Dr Tobias Whitaker, Physician-in-Ordinary to the King, on the slender basis that it had been used in half a dozen infected houses. Some people had afterwards recovered from plague, and other houses had remained free from infection. Later, L'Estrange declared that 'Dr Whitaker and other Persons of Quality' had confirmed that this was the very same remedy which had been 'so famous in the late Plague in Holland'. He did not add that no cure had been found for cases of the late plague in Holland, either.

Many people, who could not afford such specifics, kept goats tethered in their houses and hung dead toads from the ceilings in the hope and belief that these strong smells would in some way purify the atmosphere. The stench soon became so foul that householders were forced to retreat to the upper storeys of their houses in order to breath at all.

'I have not spent two farthings this yeare about correcting the aire in my house,' declared Boghurst, who was contemptuous of such practices. 'Yet I think I had as wholesome aire as my neighbours, many of which filled their houses every day with smoke.' Nobody in Boghurst's home either sickened or died throughout the epidemic; this was remarkable, for he was in contact with the plague every day throughout the epidemic.

CHAPTER SIX

Symptoms, Cures and Preventatives

The full impact of the Great Plague which engulfed London in August and September can only be understood against the background of its virulence, and the complete lack of any cure. For one thing it was sometimes difficult to diagnose because it began with different symptoms in different people. Apart from fever, headaches, and the presence of swellings, nearly half its victims went mad before they died. Some became berserk, 'running wildly about the streets', as Hodges described them, before collapsing, 'ignorant of their condition or where they were'.

Dr Vincent, walking tirelessly from house to house to comfort the afflicted, and say prayers for the dying, frequently saw denuded sufferers 'rising out of the beds and leaping about their rooms'; others stood 'crying and roaring at their windows, some coming forth almost naked and running into the streets'. Other victims developed murderous tendencies towards their own families. Friends and relatives lashed them to their beds with ropes, even chains, in case they ran amok and killed them all. Many sufferers, filled with gloom and fear for the future, took their own lives rather than linger on in this twilight world of fear and madness.

Plague took other disguises that seemed more merciful, if no less deadly. The sufferers would first be overcome with lassitude, and Hodges noted that 'many, in the middle of their Employ, with their Friends in Conversation, or in other Engagements, would suddenly, without any reluctance, fall into profound Sleeps'. They lay for several hours or days in a deep coma from which they rarely awakened. Some who contracted this variety of the plague simply did not wake up; of all the victims, theirs was probably the kindest end.

The handful of doctors who fought the plague throughout the summer searched blindly and unsuccessfully among all these complexities of the disease for some consistent cure. In the majority of cases, just when they thought 'the Conquest quite obtained, Death ran away with the Victory'. Yet sometimes patients whose lives they despaired of saving, mysteriously revived, 'much to the Disreputation of our Art'.

Doctors engaged in vehement and often bitter controversies about the relative values of different treatment; at times these disputes between medical men raged as furiously as the plague they sought to cure. On the one side were the Galenists, so-called after the Greek physician of the second century AD; doctors who prescribed natural remedies and vegetable medicines rather than those made from synthetic chemicals. On the other stood the 'chemical' doctors (sometimes loosely called Paracelsists, after the ancient alchemist, Paracelsus), who took the opposite view. But both groups shared broad agreement about the dreadful symptoms of the pestilence, and on one unquestionable fact: the plague was one of the most agonizing diseases in the world.

The cases of patients who responded to treatment and lived – either as a result, in spite of it, or because they would have recovered anyway – are recounted with justifiable pride by the courageous physicians who attended them; but they were very few. One reason for this was that doctors had not only to fight against all kinds of deceiving symptoms, but also against floods of ridiculous superstitions and 'cures' invented and sold by quacks.

Some of these charlatans made fortunes through the fear, ignorance and illiteracy which prevailed. Their activities hindered genuine physicians, and helped the plague to spread; they also killed thousands of Londoners who otherwise might have survived. The charlatans recklessly advocated sometimes perilous medieval remedies, such as bleeding, purging and inducing the patient to vomit, although such exercises were condemned by orthodox medical men.

Hodges declared that the strong emetics sold by these 'strangers to Learning as well as Physick' – containing ingredients as diverse as gunpowder and frogs' legs – frequently overtaxed the patient's strength and led to death.

Boghurst recorded that a quack named Gray, who lived in Gutter Lane, Cheapside, sold purging pills to all who came to him, irrespective of their symptoms, and whether they needed medical, surgical or gynaecological care.

The College of Physicians produced a pamphlet intended to help sufferers, but this simply contained details of treatments and medicines that had been devised nearly two centuries before, and which were of little therapeutic value. Indeed, two of their remedies, 'Matthias Plague-water, or Aqua Epidemica' and an 'Electuary of London-Treacle and Wood-Sorrel', were the subject of scorn by Dr Thomson. 'I am persuaded a Leg of Veal and Green-Sauce is far better,' he said grumpily.

Thomson, a Paracelsist, lost no chance of attacking Galenists (many of whom were members of the College), and declared that their rejection of the three traditional medical stand-bys – bleeding, purging and vomiting – was not on medical grounds, but because they were too frightened to administer the knife or the emetics. 'I plainly smell the Reason…they would fain have their fees, but are loath to fetch them,' he said sarcastically.

Boghurst despaired that 'the physitians, almost all going out of town', left the poor people prey to the 'timberheaded, upstart Empyricks' who 'made sad work both with people's bodyes and purses'. Only a few of the youngest doctors and independent apothecaries remained to care for between 30,000 and 40,000 sick, whereas 400 or 500 would not have been enough. 'Yet another tyme, when there dies 200 or 300 a week, you should have 500 or 600 hanging after them if they bee well lined with white Metall. 'Tis the rich whose persons are guarded with Angels.'[1]

The labels attached to the specifics, sold at fantastic prices by the quack doctors and pedlars, were sometimes written in pseudo-Latin, to impress the simple-minded. Always they had fanciful descriptions: 'Quintessence Animae Mundi'; 'Oil of the Heathen Gods'; 'Powdered Unicorn's Horn'. Such found ready purchasers at prices of anything up to £3 an ounce. At present day values this would be well over £50. The *Intelligencer* printed regular advertisements for such concoctions. 'Constantine Rhodocanace's Grecian – wherewith Hippocrates, the Prince of all Physicians, preserved the whole land of Greece...'

'Lady Kent's Powder, approved by all learned Physicians at home and abroad, for a most Sovereign Remedy against all Pestilential Fevers, now in the hands of a Person of Quality who had the honor to wait upon the said Countess till her death.'

Some people advertised as infallible plague cures the same medicaments they had previously recommended for other illnesses without notable success. One such was Thomas See, a physician, who decided to boost the sales of his cough mixture, 'a Sovereign Internal Balsam', by declaring that it was also 'an effectual Preservative from the Plague, and any other contagious disease, and all infectious air, as also an experienced Remedy for Coughs, Consumptions, Ptisicks, and any other Distemper of the Lungs'. In case any of his patients suffered from other complaints in addition to those listed, he added that his Balsam strengthened the stomach, helped digestion and performed 'many other wondrous functions'.

The prospect of a vast new market for their medicines even brought foreign charlatans to London. One 'Doctor Stephanus Chrysolitus, a famous Physitian, lately arrived in these parts, having travelled in several Countries which have been infected with the Plague', tried to boost the sales of imported raisins by advertising how 'by the blessing of God', he had discovered that infection could be prevented by eating 'Raisins of the Sun in the morning fasting, and Malaga Raisins either baked or boyled, and this he hath published for the publick good'. This discovery also did some good to Dr Chrysolitus; he made a small fortune out of it.

Many quacks claimed that their specific had saved thousands from death in the last plague epidemic in London – eighteen years ago. They were good enough psychologists to realise that few possessed memories sufficiently long to dispute this statement. 'The Great Cordial' of Dr Trig, that 'wrought such famous Cures in the last great Plague', secured brisk business for its manufacturer. So did the 'Sovereign Drink' of John Sly of Aldgate, and the 'Antidote or Pectoral' prepared by unnamed yet 'Eminent Physicians' who made similar claims for it.

Most of the concoctions were advertised in the *Intelligencer* or upon posters pasted up on walls, but in addition there were what one licensed physician called 'mountebanks and ignorant old women' practising in private houses or dirty little shops all over London. They hung signs depicting a Black Boy, a Green Dragon, a Blazing Star or a Scarab over their doors: their potions were often poisonous. They would charge as much as half a crown for a single pill, three-and-sixpence for a medicinal draught, and five shillings for a plaster to draw out the poison from plague swellings upon the body. The labouring man of the day was well paid at a few shillings a week, so the profits were clearly enormous.

Boghurst, recording that 'Preposterous Physicks' killed many people, said that a man in his parish named Matthews concocted and advertised a pill which would make people 'sweat out plague fever'. His ingredients included hellebore and opium. Those who bought his pills certainly sweated; then they choked and died.

Another popular 'remedy' was the arsenical amulet, which gullible folk wore around their necks to 'draw away the poison'. Doctors warned that the caustic quality of arsenic was more likely to inflame the body than afford protection. Hodges attended an elderly lawyer who wore one of these amulets on his chest. Swellings rose beneath it; in three days the man was dead.

One quack pressed some powder into Dr Hodges' hands, assuring him that it was from the horn of the unicorn. He claimed that it would not only cure plague, but had actually revived birds, cats and dogs which had been liberally dosed with poison. The doctor took leave to doubt whether such a beast as the unicorn existed at all; and even if it did, he was sure that its horn possessed no such magical properties. In any case, the price (about £5 an ounce), was beyond the reach of any but the very wealthy, although hart's horn could be bought more cheaply.

Hodges uncompromisingly declared that the quacks were 'traitors' and should be punished as such, for 'hardly a Person escaped that trusted to their Delusions', and their remedies were 'often more Fatal than the Plague'. Yet although responsible doctors begged magistrates to stop the activities of these charlatans, the Justices of the Peace held that this was none of their concern.

Dr Thomson, in his pamphlet *Loimotomia, or The Pest Anatomized*, gave a list of false remedies, and when he reached 'bezoarstone of the East' it became too much for him to continue. 'Strange that they omitted Gold,' he remarked acidly, 'but that I believe they mean to put into their own Purse.'

Charlatans who had no remedies to sell – and some who had run out of their ingredients – wrote pamphlets about preventing or treating plague. These found a ready readership. *The Plague's Approved Physitian*, which was widely distributed, gave the following instructions for dealing with plague tumours:

'*If there doe a botch appeare*: Take a Pigeon and plucke the feathers off her taile, very bare, and set her taile to the sore, and shee will draw out the venom till she die; then take another and set too likewise, continuing so till all the venome be drawne out, which you shall see by the Pigeons,

for they will die with the venome as long as there is any in
(the tumour): also a chicken or henne is very good.'

Yet this advice was hardly more incongruous than the
directions the College of Physicians gave for the same
operation:

'Take a greate onion, hollow it, put into it a fig, rue cut
small, and a dram of Venice treacle; put it close stopt in wet
paper, and roast it in the embers; apply it hot unto the
tumour; lay three or four, one after another; let one lie
three hours.'

The fearful agony caused by such experiments drove many
people mad. The cutting of plague buboes, some of them 'as big
as a penny loaf' was common, and amateur surgeons would
then pour a mixture of salt and vinegar into the wound.

'To what purpose I do not know unless they delighted to
torment people,' wrote Boghurst, 'for it put them to as much
paine as if they had been on the wrack, worse than Death
itselfe.'

In vain did conscientious doctors point out that the infinite
variations of plague called for close observation and perhaps
different treatment for each patient. Hodges noted that 'A
Person of Distinction and great Humanity' learned of a mineral
remedy used in France, and obtained samples. The authorities
ordered City doctors to try it out 'with due Caution', but to their
chagrin it simply 'threw the patients into their last Sleep'. This
demonstrated the danger of 'universal' remedies and unknown
foreign medicines.

The symptoms of plague, and the visible manifestations of
the disease were as complicated as they were agonizing. Usually,
the first sign was an icy chill, followed by a shivering fit like a
malarial ague. This, thought Hodges, was probably due to the
'Pestilential Ferment insinuating itself in to the Blood and Juices
of the Body'. Then came convulsions, after which the wretched

sufferer was seized with an overwhelming nausea. Any attempt to feed the patient would be met with expressions of loathing, and 'even the Mention of Food was irksome'.

Severe vomiting and stomach pains followed, and the patient might retch for hours on end, bringing up nothing but ropy saliva, flecked with blood. The next stage was marked by great depression and a general lack of confidence – an almost invariable plague symptom – and most sufferers then endured headaches of steadily increasing ferocity. Hodges considered that these were caused by 'the Membranes of the Brain being pricked and vellicated by the Poisonous Spicula'; others might disagree with this diagnosis, but no one disagreed about the pain.

Every patient also suffered from vertigo so severely that they had difficulty in keeping their balance, and many could barely stand upright. Hodges ascribed this to the 'caustick and narcotick Nature of the venom'.

The plague then generally took one of two paths. Some fell into deep coma, breathing heavily with eyes half open. If they recovered consciousness at all, it was only when the plague tokens appeared on their bodies, and then they lost their power of reason. 'Many persons who had continued in a Delirium throughout their Sickness, so soon as the Tokens appear'd came to Themselves, and apprehended that they were in a hopeful and recovering Condition.' Boghurst reported that a number of his patients recovered consciousness but had lost their memory and their senses, and so were 'meere Ideotts'. Those who escaped this coma were driven into a 'raving phrensy', with a high fever, 'parts both internal and external extreamly suffering'.

Except for rare cases in which the victims died quickly and without obvious signs of illness, none escaped this fever and delirium, which was usually accompanied by violent palpitations of the heart. One doctor described this symptom as 'the Heart's struggle to throw off what is offensive', and went on to describe a rare case which came his way. A youth of fourteen, who had apparently escaped infection, although his mother and several other children in his family were sick, was suddenly seized 'with such a Palpitation at Heart, that I and several others could hear it at some Considerable Distance'. The lad died quickly, no medicine proving of the slightest use to him.

Other common symptoms in plague cases included bleeding from the nose or mouth, partial paralysis of the neck and face, haemorrhoids, stomach disorders which made the sufferers complain that 'their bowels were in a presse', feelings of suffocation in the throat and chest, constant deep sighing and hiccoughing, partial deafness and blindness. A 'lisping faultering voice', the shaking of the head in 'an extraordinary hideous manner', and an insatiable thirst, were all equally ominous signs.

Dr Thomson took particular notice of the stomach disorders, and believing that the venom of the pestilence 'was channelled to that Centre and Metropolis of the body' and to 'its compeer, the Spleen', thought that much of the trouble originated from those organs. The 'stomach's ferment', he observed, sometimes engendered a black juice which appeared either in the saliva or the urine. This was a certain sign of death. But Thomson had to admit that in other cases a 'very laudable urine' was a danger signal, and that a lack of any distinctive symptoms sometimes made plague impossible to diagnose. It was easiest and safest to treat all diseases as though they were plague, unless and until they proved otherwise.

Boghurst considered the 'stopping of the stomach' to be a very serious symptom. Only one of his patients survived this, a woman who 'stammered soe you could not understand what she said'. The apothecary cured her by the eccentric method of laying 'a great Mastiff Puppy Dogge upon her breast two or three hours together, and made her drink Dill, Pennyroyall, Fenill and Aniseed Water, for she was a fat woman and could beare it'.

The plague had as many consequences and opposites as it had symptoms. While in the grip of the fever, for instance, some were unable to perspire at all, yet others sweated copiously. Experienced doctors 'could prognosticate the Event of the

Distemper from the colour of the Cloaths or Linen tinged with the Sweat'. Often the miserable victims exuded so terrible an odour that even their close relatives could not bear to stay in the sick-room; the patients thus cried out in vain for help.

One 'being sick alone, and it is like Frantick, burnt himself in his bed'. The same 'morbid ferment' often issued from the bodies of the newly-dead which overflowed the churchyards and plague pits. Over these graveyards throughout that summer, there hung a sour miasma of death, unmistakable and perpetual, thick with a fog of flies.

After the fever and delirium, outward signs of plague generally appeared upon the body of the victim in the shape of rising and swellings of various kinds, and then came the dreaded 'tokens' which usually signified the approach of death. The most innocuous of the swellings were 'pustles' or blisters, and when these alone appeared recovery was possible; more deadly were the buboes, carbuncles and parotides. Recovery after these appeared was very rare.

The buboes were either soft, white swellings, 'tumified and inflamed', or red, wedge-shaped excrescences, 'indolent and hard', that could persist for weeks. They mainly attacked the groin, armpits and neck, causing great pain. They could be as small as 'a Hen's egg', or as large as 'a half-penny loaf', but most were the size of a man's fist, and some as large as a penny loaf. In several cases treated, for which records remain, the plague settled in one large swelling under the chin 'soe that it hung down like a bag upon the brest'. Generally, a patient had only one or two buboes, but the worst cases produced as many as five or six.

Rarely did any reputable medical men try to lance these buboes, for, in the absence of anaesthetics, it was difficult to hold the patient down during the long and excruciating agony of such an operation. Sufferers complained of a sensation of extreme burning before the white buboes began to suppurate. All that could be done to help was to apply plasters in the hope that the swelling would break. Quacks, of course, lanced, cut, hacked and burned buboes for their fee of a shilling or two, without regard for the insupportable pain they caused. Their acts of butchery were, in fact, virtual acts of murder.

Plague victims who had eluded the vigilance of the authorities were frequently recognized in the streets, for buboes in the groin made them 'hop and go lame'. Dr Thomson, who three times contracted plague and survived, although each time his life was despaired of, once endured a bubo in his groin for four months.

Hodges saw that these 'Pestilential Sores' first arose with 'a very small pustle', surrounded by a circle of a 'red, flaming Colour'. They became hard and scaly, and were usually three or four fingers in diameter, although some were as big as nine inches across. Occasionally they turned gangrenous. One French quack lanced them with a sharpened needle and tried to pluck out the cores with pincers. Other 'Madd ways' were burning with hot coals or irons.

One of the doctor's patients, a young woman, complained of a small carbuncle on one finger, and after treatment he thought her cured. But, 'with her old Nurse supping plentifully upon French beans, that very Night, the Distemper returned'. A new carbuncle arose, and the girl died after only one day's delirium. This was not quite the end of the story, for 'After the Bearers came that Night to bury her, and talked of fetching the old Woman next, as a Person dead, the poor wretch, as awakened from Sleep, cried out she was not dead; but she disappointed not their Agreement, and died time enough to be carried away the same Night to the burying Place'.

The doctor's daily experience soon persuaded him that when any swellings turned black and insensitive, or the buboes collapsed and fell in suddenly, 'I always looked upon my Labours to be defeated'.

The tokens – 'those stigmata nigra' as Thomson called them – were the surest signs of death. Hodges thought them to be 'mortifications caused by the Extinction of Natural Heat upon the account of highly prevailing Malignity'. They usually appeared upon the neck, breast, back and thighs, and were round, often with hard centres 'like little Kernels under the skin'. They varied in size, but were sometimes as 'big as a silver penny'. If they could be gently pricked with a sharp needle without discomfort to the patient, they were 'Fatal…the most certain Forerunners of Death'.

The tokens varied in colour. Some were reddish, surrounded by a blue circle; others were faint blue with a black circle about them; still more were purple tinged with black. 'Sanguine or Flegmatick' people had scarlet and red tokens, and so did those with fresh complexions, while black tokens appeared mostly on those with swarthier skins and 'melancholic disposition'. Purple tokens were seen on people of all outlooks and complexions, and frequently turned violet or pale blue after death. Doctors called them 'exanthemata', for there was 'noe proper name in Latin', but it was generally felt that the popular name of 'tokens' was fitly applied, for the marks were considered to be 'tokens of disease, death and God's wrath for the sins of Man'.

The black variety gave plague its dramatic title of the 'Black Death' and with some cause; any victim spotted with black tokens rarely lived for more than three hours after their first appearance.

At times, death and the tokens arrived together, and the victims were stricken and carried off in the dead-carts with incredible rapidity. One doctor was called to visit 'a Maid whose Temper seem'd good, her Pulse equal and strong, her Senses perfect…She complain'd of no Disorder or Pain, and concluded herself secure'. He opened her bodice to examine her, and wrote later: 'I view'd her Breast and discovered very many Tokens. I left her with a Prognostick, and within 2 or 3 hours she died.'

A few days later, another physician was called to see 'an ancient Woman, and found her at Dinner with a Chicken before her, on which she fed greedily, and had eaten half before I came. After a due Enquiry into her Case, finding no Satisfaction either from her Pulse or Temper, I, searching her Breast, observ'd the Tokens, and she expired within one or two hours'.

Only a few doctors and apothecaries believed that the rate of their patients' pulses could have any significance. A butcher from Westminster told his chemist that a doctor had assured him that he had a good pulse; he was quickly disillusioned. 'I told him it was the worst signe hee had about him, and threatened him much,' said the chemist, 'wherefore he discarded mee and tooke the Doctor, but in 2 or 3 days hee dyed.'

More fortunate was a certain Mr Stafford of Acton, who contracted plague a fortnight after his wedding. His pulse was very intermittent, but although an apothecary was sure he would perish, the new husband was restored to health 'and arrived at the joyes of life'.

The psychological effects of plague were no less marked than the physical. That the sufferers should often have been seized with uncontrollable fear is understandable in view of the symptoms, and many also endured dreadful nightmares. 'Some would dream that they were among Graves and Tombs in Churchyards, others that they tumbled down from some high place and fell amongst Coffins,' wrote one apothecary, emphasizing that melancholy was the downfall of many who might otherwise have survived.

A maid who had caught the Plague in Westminster fell into this acute depression, but her apothecary 'bid her, instead of sighing, to humm it up, and ordered her friends that they should…make her as chearefull and merry as they could'. With such stimulus the girl recovered, although it was calculated that less than one in ten of people usually prone to sadness were as fortunate.

One girl escaped to a doctor from a shut-up plague house in which the rest of her family had died. She pointed to a strange mark on her leg. Was it a plague token? Was she also doomed to die within a few hours? The doctor found that it was only a wart, and reassured her and sent her off with a bottle of prophylactic. 'Had her mind not been set at rest,' he wrote afterwards, 'I really believe she would have died merely by the Force of her Imagination.'

All observers agreed that those who were fearless mostly escaped, while the nervous, who would not take 'money, goods or letters without washing or airing', or who went about 'stopping their noses and running aside upon seeing a dunghill, meeting a searcher or corpse' usually contracted the disease.

Many unqualified quacks threw nervous patients into paroxysms of fear and dread by hurrying into their sickroom and at once 'peering into their breasts or armes for tokens', a practice condemned by those who recommended more subtle methods.

Excessive drinking was very dangerous, for drunkards who became infected with plague, in the words of one physician, grew 'light-headed and dyed mad', very often within forty-eight hours. Drinkers of brandy seemed particularly prone to such an end.

Of all the plague preventatives in use, smoking – and to a lesser extent, chewing tobacco – was the one most universally accepted and believed in. Men, women and even children lit pipes night and morning, or chewed quids of strong black leaf, spitting out the bitter dark juice on to the floor. The bearers, the searchers and buriers of the dead, watchmen and the plague nurses constantly smoked evil-smelling clay pipes to protect themselves from germs. Dozens of white splinters from these pipes were found among the bones of plague victims when nineteenth-century excavations uncovered some of London's plague burial grounds.

For many years after the Great Plague the belief persisted that no tobacconist in London at that time caught the disease. The antiquary, Thomas Hearne, wrote that 'smoaking was looked upon as a most excellent preservative; in so much so that even children were obliged to smoak'. Hearne had an acquaintance, Tom Rogers, a yeoman beadle, who had been a schoolboy at Eton during that summer, and he remembered how all the Eton boys were made to smoke every morning. Rogers was 'never whipped so much in his life as he was one morning for not smoaking'.

Neither Boghurst nor Hodges, who were non-smokers, believed that tobacco had any medicinal qualities, and the doctor declared that he was 'the professed enemy' of the weed. The apothecary noted: 'I never took a pipe this yeare, nor ever doe or will doe.' As thousands of tobacco smokers also died of plague, their attitude was reasonable.

In September, as plague deaths reached their zenith, rumours grew that several doctors had died as a direct result of dissecting a plague corpse.

John Allin, writing to friends in Sussex on September 14th, declared that Dr George Starkey, 'with about six more of them chymicall practitioners', had given money for 'the most infected body' they could find, in order to dissect it. Allin was a Galenist and bitingly sarcastic about the Paracelsists' rejection of Galenical medicines, and their confidence in their own chemical remedies. He declared that when the doctors opened up the cadaver 'a stinch ascended from the body, and infected them every one, and it is said that they are all dead since, the most of them distractedly madd'.

Allin interpreted this result as God's resolve to 'stain the pride' of doctors foolish enough to hold up their own theories against the conventional Galenical theory of medicine.

Although there were many rumours of such a dissection, there is little further evidence that it ever took place. Dr Thomson, however, did anatomize a diseased corpse, and as a result he caught plague, although he survived. On a hot August day he visited 'a lusty proper man, by name William Pick, living in Petticoat Lane'. His condition was desperate (largely, thought Thomson, because he had already been nearly killed by Galenical treatment), although he recovered after Thomson's attentions. Someone in the house told the doctor that one of Pick's servants, a boy about fifteen years old, was also seriously ill. Thomson examined the lad and found that he was indeed 'labouring under the most horrid symptoms, raving as it were extimulated by som Fury'. Within an hour the boy was dead.

Thomson immediately asked permission to dissect the body, and was elated when Pick agreed, for his previous efforts to obtain a corpse had always proved unsuccessful. Within a few minutes of the death, Thomson had his instruments prepared, his knives sharpened and announced himself ready to begin.

Because the house was dark and the air close, it was agreed that the operation would best be performed outside in the backyard. Dr Thomson placed a porringer full of burning sulphur by the side of the body with the intention of killing any 'noxious stinch' that might be given off, and then, waving aside the anxious protests of those members of the Pick family who had not caught plague, and had liked the dead boy well, he set to work. He first noted that the skin was 'beset with spots black and blew' (the tokens) 'more remarkable for multitude than any I have yet seen'. When he opened the body, he found that the stomach, liver and spleen, kidneys and other organs were mostly 'exsanguine' and filled with ichorous liquid varying in colour from yellow to inky black, and 'other foul matter'. He was astonished to find 'that not one spoonfull of that ruddy liquor properly called blood could be obtained in this Pestilential body'. It seemed that plague had somehow contaminated the whole bloodstream. The boy's lungs were also badly affected, with 'severall large ill favoured marks much tumified and distended'.

After this post-mortem examination, Dr Thomson wrapped the boy's body in an old blanket to conceal the fearful incisions he had made and it was taken away on the dead-cart. As Thomson also left, in the opposite direction, carrying his instruments in a bag and musing over what he had discovered, he was not to know at what cost it had been bought. Within twelve hours, he found a strange numbness in his right hand – the hand, he quickly remembered, that he had plunged into the poisoned body to remove some organs while they were still warm.

Thomson washed his hand carefully, and when it was dry held it over a dish of burning brimstone. He continued to visit his patients, but on the following night he awoke with the same numbness in both legs, from the thighs to his toes. He lit a candle and at once called his servant, a boy of fourteen, and asked him to bring him in some of his own medicines from his surgery. Of these he took huge doses, five times as much as he had ever prescribed for patients in twenty years of practice. Afterwards, he declared that if he had slept another two hours he would have lost his life, for his next symptoms were typical of plague – 'a grievous oppression about the Midriff', lowness of spirits, a muzzy sensation in the head, and small spots on his chest and arms.

What particularly struck him was 'a very large spot of an obscure colour, of the bigness of a single half-penny', which appeared on his right arm near the shoulder. All through that morning, he sweated in 'tedious Inquietude, with much Reluctancy, and many an Agony'. By midday he sent out for 'that Excellent expert Chymist and legitimate Physician' Dr Starkey, preferring him to any 'miserable Galenist'. Starkey was also suffering from plague, but he manfully struggled round to see Thomson, who was much heartened by the visit. That same night, Starkey collapsed and had to take to his bed.

Another of Thomson's friends, Dr Joseph Dey – also a chemical physician – was taken ill at the same time, so that Thomson had to treat himself with no other doctor to help him. He drank enormous doses of his 'Tincture Polyacea' and 'Pulvis Pestifugus', and also drank as much wine as he could stand, and, for good measure, 'Strong Beer, sweetened with a little sugar, and now and then…white-wine posset'.

Dr Starkey had given Thomson a dessicated toad 'made up in the form of a Trochist' (a circular medicinal pack). Thomson also possessed another dead toad of his own, which he had sewn up in a linen cloth against such an emergency. He hung one of these tiny cadavers around his neck and held the other close to his stomach. This second toad immediately 'became so tumified, distended to that bigness, that it was an object of wonder to those that beheld it'. Thomson explained this to his own satisfaction by the theory that 'the toad's particles' were distended 'by some cirulent emanations…carrying with them a transmutative putrefactive ferment imbibed by the Cadaver'. He remained firmly convinced that the toad's body had drawn the poison of the plague from his own.

Two or three days afterwards a bubo rose on Thomson's body, and he cut it himself, sending for 'an honest industrious young man, a great lover of Chymistry' to apply leeches to suck out the poison.

This swelling continued to discharge for three weeks. Nevertheless, barely a week after the plague's first attack, Thomson was up and walking shakily about his room. His landlady, Mrs Ladyman, had fallen dangerously ill with plague which had brought on a miscarriage. Thomson treated her, and she became one of the very few pregnant women who sickened with plague and lived. At the same time, Thomson's maid and his apprentice contracted the disease, and both also recovered, a remarkable record for the household.

Dr Thomson was forty-five at the time of the plague, and his experience very nearly overtaxed his physical endurance. In about ten days he went out again to tend his patients, but the effort was too much too soon, and he suffered a severe relapse which lasted for nearly a week.

At the same time his two friends, Dr Starkey and Dr Dey, both died. Friends kept news of their deaths from Thomson in case the knowledge should delay his recovery. Thomson had visited Dey during the evening after the dissection, to tell him what he had found, and Dey was very interested. He had himself only recently recovered from a previous plague attack, but weeks of overwork had exhausted both his strength and his spirits. He died without a struggle.

Thomson went through the rest of the epidemic unscathed, and two years later, at the age of forty-seven, married for the first time. He was a Royalist and a graduate of Leyden, and somewhat dogmatic and didactic in his opinions, but undoubtedly one of the medical heroes of the Plague Year. He scoffed at Allin's suggestion that Dey, Starkey and others died because they assisted him at the dissection, because they were not even there; he performed the operation alone.

During that year of plague, the doctors of the Restoration fought a sickness of which no one knew the origin. In these circumstances, other superstitions apart, they could not hope to win. Plague was a very old disease, yet it was not until near the close of the nineteenth century that its deadly bacillus was isolated and traced to rat fleas. A Japanese doctor discovered the bacillus during a Hong Kong epidemic in 1894, and some years afterwards, research in India, which had frequently suffered plague, revealed that it was a disease originating with rats but which could readily be passed on to human beings.

In seventeenth-century England all the necessary evidence to connect plague with the rats was available, but no one drew the right conclusion. The disease flourished in insanitary conditions where rats abounded, and it was known that 'infected' bedding or clothing seemed to harbour the pestilence. Yet the nearest the doctors of the day came to isolating it was to announce that the plague must be 'a body or concretion of many little bodyes, very subtle and invisible', containing a venom 'contrary and destructive to the vitall principles of man'.

Some scientists of the time believed that plague was in the air, as we have shown; others thought its essence was lodged in the earth, which they called 'the seminary and seed plott of pestilence'. And all through that long, hot, dry summer rats ran free and multiplied alarmingly in the slums of the stinking capital, while the dogs and cats that could have thinned their numbers were ruthlessly exterminated.

It has been said that the plague was first brought to England by rats which swarmed down the mooring lines of foreign ships in English ports, especially London and Portsmouth. That may or may not be so; it is certainly possible. Plague had thrived all over the world in the same filthy conditions which typified seventeenth-century London, and England had also suffered from it for centuries.

The black rat common in the Middle and Far East was also the species most frequently found in this country at that time, and was the most domestic of all vermin. In the East it had long been remarked that when rats began to die, human plague was never far off; the Hindu scriptures even advised men to leave their houses when they saw such signs. The virulence of plague in London was due to the rapid multiplication of the bacilli passed through flea-bites into the human body. The flea was the sole carrier of bubonic pestilence leaving dead rats to continue its parasitic life upon the human body.

Outbreaks of plague, some slight, others severe, continued in many parts of the world into the twentieth century, particularly in Egypt and the East. But the Great Plague of 1665 was the last time that the pestilence visited England in epidemic proportions. In the light of the country's backward state of medical knowledge for the next two hundred years, this was more than fortunate; it was providential.

1. Ten-shilling pieces, a doctor's usual fee.

CHAPTER SEVEN

Bring Out Your Dead

Ring a-ring a-Roses
A pocketful of poesies,
'Tishoo, 'tishoo,
We all fall down!

Few people watching a group of children dancing hand-in-hand in a circle to this well-known nursery rhyme may realize that it has its origin in the plague. Roses refer to the rosy rash of plague, ringed to signify the tokens; the poesies were herbs and spices carried to sweeten the air; sneezing was a common symptom of those close to death. The words 'we all fall down' certainly referred to Londoners during that stifling August. Death rates rose so sharply that they became unable to comprehend the magnitude of the disaster. Business, pleasure, even the Dutch war was forgotten: the one obsessing topic was the plague and how to avoid it.

The Mortality Bill published for the last week in July gave a total of 3,014 deaths – ten times the normal for a summer month – and 2,020 of these were attributed to plague. L'Estrange's newspaper hopefully reported that 'the Common voice of the Town' anticipated a fall in the figures, and the editor greeted the publication of the Bill by emphasizing that the week's mortality in the City parishes had dropped by seventeen. He had to own, however, that plague was spreading in the out-parishes, that the

Royal Exchange had been closed down, and the City was thus left 'somewhat thin of people'.

From his house in the riverside parish of St Olave's near London Bridge, John Allin also wrote in his diary his hopes that the upward trend was slackening, and he thanked God he was still able to go about his business 'without any slavish feare'. But he recorded soberly that 'many whole familyes', some of them involving as many as eighteen people of several generations, had been decimated. So deadly was the disease becoming that 'it speakes it to be more a judgement than anything else'; in these circumstances Allin considered 'true repentance was the best antidote, and pardon of sin the best cordial'.

August began, like July, with solemn fasts and lengthy services in the churches, where huge congregations prayed for delivery from the pestilence. A week later, however, 1,000 more died; 800 of them from plague.

At church on August 1st, John Evelyn heard a sermon on the theme that 'the meanes to obtaine remission of punishment was not to repine at it, but humbly submitting'. Evelyn, as a Commissioner for Seamen, could do little but follow this advice, for he had to remain in Deptford on the King's business. But he decided that, for his family, at least, flight would be better than resignation. His anxiety for their welfare was understandable; his wife Mary, whom he had married eighteen years previously when she was only twelve, had borne him five sons, all but one of whom had died in infancy, and a daughter who survived. Now she was pregnant again, and her baby was due in nine weeks.

Hurriedly, Evelyn packed off his son and the boy's tutor to his brother's house, Wotton, in Surrey, and shortly afterwards sent away the rest of the family. He stayed on at his home, Sayescourt, with a couple of servants, putting his trust in 'the providence and goodnesse of God'. He was not disappointed, for he survived the plague, later refusing a knighthood offered him by the King for his devotion to duty.

127

As the days passed, more and more people inside and outside the capital became caught up in agonies of fear and trepidation about their chances of survival. Samuel Pepys, making a trip to Dagnams from the City, found all along the route 'citizens, walking to and fro, enquire how the plague is in the City...but methought it was a sad question to be so often asked me'. He could give them little reassurance, and when he reached his destination in Essex, he was regaled with a local story of the pestilence.

At a local house, owned by one John Wright, a maid caught plague and had been hastily banished to an outhouse with a nurse to look after her. The nurse locked her in and returned to the house for some food. The girl – wearing a sack-like garment, known as a 'sick dress' – took this opportunity of climbing out of the window and ran away. When the nurse returned she stood outside with the tray and called that she would be with her in a moment. To her surprise, this brought no answer, and, not bothering to open the door, the nurse rushed to Mr Wright to tell him that the girl was dead.

The Wrights were terrified; if this news became public they would all be locked in their house for weeks. They therefore decided that the girl's body must be buried immediately before anyone had heard she was even ill. Mr Wright walked to Brentwood a mile or two away to bribe a labourer to dig the grave, for he did not want to alarm his own staff, and, plague or no plague, digging was not a job for a gentleman.

To his surprise and alarm, no one would have anything to do with his idea. Later, walking home disconsolately, convinced he would have to dig the grave himself, he was astonished to meet the girl wandering about on the common, still in her sick dress and with the marks of plague on her. At first Mr Wright thought she must be a ghost, but soon he realized some mistake had arisen and he rousted out some servants, and called for a coach. One arrived, with all blinds drawn, and Wright ordered the driver to take the girl to the nearest pesthouse. She was bundled inside, and the coach rattled away over the rutted roads, dragging a plume of yellow dust behind it.

In a narrow part of the track he met another coach, going in the opposite direction, carrying a young gallant, Sir Anthony Browne, his brother and some other friends of noble birth. The knight's brother, seeing a closed coach – usually only chosen by ladies travelling alone – thought it concealed some young lady modestly hidden from the public gaze. With the directness of the time and the imperiousness of his position, he forced the coach to stop and, ripping aside the leather curtain, thrust his head in through the window.

With horror and loathing he saw, not a pretty young girl, but a rough country servant with her face covered in sores, running with sweat and 'looking very ill, in a sick dress, and stunk mightily'. Her smell, the terrible, unforgettable smell of plague, carried to Sir Anthony's coachman, and he cried out in disgust, knowing what it meant. In an instant he had whipped up his horses and carried the party away as fast as he could.

Farther along the road, someone told them who the girl was; this 'put the young gentleman into a fright that almost cost him his life'. He was ill for some days, but recovered, although no one discovered whether the girl also survived. It seems unlikely.

Meanwhile, in London, apart from a last despairing effort at optimism from L'Estrange, the Bill for the first week of August reported 4,013 deaths – 2,817 of plague. L'Estrange wrote that most of the increase was 'in the sluttish parts of those parishes where the Poor are crowded and in multitudes infect one another', while 'in the broad and Open streets, there is but little appearance of it'; but most readers found small comfort in this claim.

Allin, offered refuge in the little Cinque Port of Rye, felt it his duty to stay on in London and do what he could, but admitted he was troubled by the 'approach of the sicknesse neerer every weeke'. In his parish, 142 died (supposedly only sixty-four of plague) in that week, and a new burial ground near his house at

Horsleydown was receiving many of the bodies. But if St Olave's was suffering, other parishes were faring much worse. At St Giles, Cripplegate, for instance, 356 people died in the first August week, and several other out-parishes each admitted more than 200 deaths.

By now the plight of London was serious enough to cause anxiety to King Charles. From his safe retreat, he wrote to the magistrates of the City and Middlesex ordering them to enforce stricter measures against the plague. They were to take great care to prevent the removal of goods or passengers from London, Westminster and the out-parishes to other towns; restrict the carriage of goods up and down the Thames; enforce more rigorously the shutting up of infected families; and see to the appointment of additional searchers of the dead and plague nurses to secure speedier segregation of the sick. Anyone who disobeyed their regulations would be punished by committal to Newgate to await the holding of the next sessions. Such instructions came far too late. Plague now controlled the capital; the time for well-meant directions was long past.

Dr Vincent, despite his compassion for people, could not resist dwelling upon the guilty terrors now being experienced by some of London's less worthy inhabitants. 'The old drunkards, and swearers, and unclean persons,' he wrote, 'see many fellow-sinners fall before their faces, expecting every hour themselves to be smitten; and the very sinking fears they have of the Plague, hath brought the Plague and Death upon many; some by the sight of a Coffin in the Streets, have fallen into a shivering, and immediately the Disease hath assaulted them, and Serjeant Death hath arrested them.'

Suffering was unfortunately not only confined to the 'unclean sinners'. For the second week of the month, the total deaths rose to 5,319 with 3,880 of these being plague mortalities. 'Death, as it were,' declared Dr Gumble, 'rode triumphant through every street, as if it would have given no quarter to any of mankind, and ravaged as if it would have swallowed all mortality. It was a grievous sight to see in that great Emporie, nothing vendible or merchantable but Coffins.'[1] When Gumble went out, he saw 'no faces but such as were covered with terrors and horrors, many walking the streets with the sores running, and many dropping down dead at your very feet'.

The break-up of the last vestiges of order in the City had already begun, and as Dr Vincent observed: 'Now the shutting up of visited houses, there being so many, is at an end and most of the well are mingled among the sick.' This tragedy and its possibilities alarmed L'Estrange, who sought some scapegoat safely distant from the King, and finally decided that people who died of plague had only themselves to blame. 'Some thousands of those which have perished in this dreadfull Mortality, have hastened there own destruction by their wilfulness,' he declared ingeniously. They had allowed themselves 'to take cold, to drink too much when in a fever, to rise and expose themselves to the air before their sweats were over' and he denounced them for daring to confound his predictions and swell the death roll.

In an attempt to allay public alarm, the authorities now ruled that burials should take place only during the hours of darkness. It thus became a nightly ritual for the convoys of dead-carts to make their ghoulish rounds of the parishes, their way lighted by 'links', or men carrying burning torches, and their progress marked by the bellman, who rang his crude iron handbell to alert mourners of their approach. The drivers, leading their horses or sitting up on the cart, perched in front of their grisly load, uttered their terrible call: 'Bring out your dead! Bring out your dead!'

This call had become the only remaining London Cry, and the corpses carried out from the houses in the stinking, sweat-soaked clothes in which they had died, or wrapped in rough grey blankets, to be heaped upon the carts, were treated with as little respect as bundles of rags and bones.

As the cart rumbled past a house where plague had struck, those inside would call to the driver to stop and collect a body. Sometimes the drivers pretended not to hear those entreaties until the frantic mourners would throw down coins to them, or trinkets; anything indeed they possessed, rather than be imprisoned for another night and day with the blackened, swollen, blue-lipped corpse of someone they had loved.

These 'bearers of the dead' were rough, drunken men, hitherto regarded as virtually unemployable, and now revelling in their sudden affluence of ten shillings a week, and their quite unexpected power. Many took a perverse pleasure in their job. Singing sailors' songs, cursing, belching, looting, they staggered up the rickety wooden stairs of afflicted houses, bent, with many grunts and mutterings, over the bodies, fixed hooks to their shrouds or blankets, and then unceremoniously dragged them back down the stairs and swung them up on their carts. Their obscenities, contrasting horribly with the weeping and last endearments of the bereaved, replaced the solemn funeral rites which in more normal times would have marked their passing.

Several parishes hired carts for the entire summer to carry their dead. St Margaret's, Westminster, now one of London's most fashionable areas, bought a sedan chair fitted with a strait-jacket, in which to carry sufferers to the pesthouse. Many districts even bought carts on the rates to keep pace with the high number of burials; their parish officers felt that this would be cheaper than hiring by the day or week. They were proved right, for the carts were in use for months, every hour of every night.

During the day, the drivers and bearers drank in such taverns as would have them – for they were in such close contact with the plague that their clothes stank continually of death and vomit and decay. Thus they dozed, unshaven, filthy, stinking: heads on some tap room table through the hot, fly-brown August afternoons. And, then, at dusk, they set about their fearful tasks.

Pepys, coming home by river one night, landed at Churchyard Stairs, and nearly fell over bearers who were stumbling with a plague corpse down some steps into a narrow alley. 'I thank God I was not much disturbed at it,' he noted stoutly, but at the same time vowed never to be out on the streets so late again, for fear of who or what he might meet.

In an endeavour to spare people such harrowing encounters, the Lord Mayor ordered householders to stay in their homes after nine o'clock every evening. This was the hour when the sick were allowed to crawl or be carried out of their foul airless rooms for a few moments to breathe some fresher air; and also the bearers were going about their work. But soon the hours of darkness were not long enough for the collection and burial of more than a thousand corpses every night, and the sick were allowed out in daylight to run screaming, foaming, often naked in the unaccustomed sunshine.

Until then, London in the daytime had been a deserted, neglected City. On August 8th, journeying back from Woolwich, where he had been visiting his wife, Pepys found that the once-bustling City was almost empty. The few people he did meet and know had nothing to tell but sad stories of the death of old friends: 'Poor Will, that used to sell us ale at the Hall-door, his wife and three children died, all, I think, in a day.'

He went on to Westminster Hall, only to hear more tales of tragedy, and returning home, 'wishing I may have taken no ill in going', resolved to venture there no more.

Vincent was also disturbed and depressed by the loneliness of London at this time. 'Every day looks with the face of a Sabbath-day,' he wrote. 'Now shops are shut in, people rare and very few that walk about, insomuch that the grass begins to spring in some places, and a deep silence is almost every place, especially within the walls; no ratling Coaches, no prancing Horses, no calling in Customers, nor offering Wares, no London-Cryes sounding in the ears.'

Almost the only voices heard were the groans and screams of the dying, and the loud cries of those they left behind. One lunatic appeared in the grass-grown streets, running, with his hair long and beard matted. He ran stripped to the waist, sometimes carrying a blazing torch, once with a brazier of hot coals perched on his head. He was demented, insensible of pain, running endlessly with the urgency of the insane, shouting, 'Oh, the great and dreadful God!'

In the most heavily affected districts, barely one house in a hundred remained free of the plague. 'Never did so many Husbands and Wives dye together; never did so many Parents carry their Children with them to the Grave, and go together into the same House under Earth, who had lived together in the same House upon it,' wrote Allin to a friend in the country. 'Now the nights are too short to bury the dead, the whole day (though at so great a length) is hardly sufficient to light the dead that fall therein, into their Beds... Death approacheth neerer and neerer, not many doores off, and the pitt open dayly within view of my chamber window. The Lord fitt mee and all of us for our last end!'

The virulence of the disease can be measured by the calamity which befell the owner of Coome Farm, an isolated property on the road between Woolwich and Greenwich, which Pepys sometimes passed as he returned from a visit to his wife. The farmer, a man with a kind heart, and realistically believing that to give shelter to beggars and desperate refugees was a lesser evil than risking their violence, allowed such wanderers to spend an occasional night in his barn. On August 22nd, Pepys was horrified to see a plague corpse, rigid and black, lying in an open coffin lying in a field close by the road. The Parish had posted a watchman at the farm gate with orders to allow no one in or out.

'This disease is making us more cruel to one another than we are to dogs,' was Pepys' opinion of this act, but despite this crude attempt at quarantine, by September 4th, twenty-one people died of plague at Coome Farm.

So rapidly did the plague spread that even Boghurst wondered whether all diseases 'turned into the plague'. Not many people afflicted in August and September lasted for more than a week after the first signs appeared, and Boghurst admitted that more than half those with medical attendance died. 'They do but of a suddaine fetch their breath a little thick and short, and are presently gone, just as you squeeze wind out of a bladder.' So painful and terrifying were the symptoms and the results that many considered 'It is a greate mercy now counted to dye of another disease'.

The overwhelming evidence of the plague's virulence, and the uselessness of all supposed cures was enough to cause many to throw away their potions and pouncet-boxes. People who had loyally taken doses of 'The King's Majesty's excellent Receipt for the Plague', as advised by the College of Physicians, died just as quickly as those who placed their faith in signs of the Zodiac, and others who put dead toads under their shirts.

'Take half an Ounce of Nutmegs,' advised the Royal prescription, 'beat them all together, put it over the fire a little, and add 3 pennyworth of Treacle, and a Quart of the best Angelica-water.

'Take it always warm, both Morning and Evening, a Spoonful or two, if you be already infected, and Sweat thereupon; if not, a Spoonful in the Morning, and half a Spoonful in the Evening, all the Time the Plague continues.'

The *Approved Physitian* had informed readers that they 'need not feare the infection' at all if they took 'a Figge or a Walnut, and in the morning fasting, take a little Rew, and a corne of bay salt and eate them together', for 'this will preserve you'. The formula for a pomander was more involved; it contained fifteen ingredients.

Such was the general anxiety to find some panacea, that as fast as these prescriptions were discredited, other suggestions were tried. Amulets made from toads, frogs, snakes, scorpions, mussels and crabs became very popular; the theory that to drink one's own urine was an excellent preservative also received much attention. Boghurst thought little of this practice and advised his friends to keep their bodies 'as charily as a Venice glass', and to maintain cleanliness and temperance in all things.

By now many of the quacks and pedlars of magical remedies had left London, and few of their products were being advertised in the *Intelligencer*. Bodily prescriptions having failed, some of the clergy began to offer spiritual cures. Typical was a pamphlet by the Rev. John Featly, former chaplain to Charles I, who offered 'A Divine Antidote against the Plague'. This consisted of 'prayers for those in shut houses with buboes and tokens'. But even Mr Featly's prayers were not notably more efficacious than the walnuts filled with mercury and the mussels they replaced.

Other theorists held that 'high and windy places' were less viable to infection. Up in Hampstead, despite the name of the Vale of Health, more than 230 people died in 100 houses. 'At the West End, a little village soe called a quarter of a mile off, at the bottom of the Hill, there died none, though there were about thirty or forty houses there.' Among other villages on high ground, Acton, Highgate and Islington suffered as badly as most.

As August advanced, contemporary observers could hardly find words to describe the state of the City of London. 'All the Musick in the night was the sad sound "Bring Out Your Dead!", which like Dung, were thrown into a cart and tumbled into a Pit without numbring,' wrote Dr Gumble.

'The day was always summoning to our Grave with Knells and tolling of Bells; and if we looked abroad, there was nothing but Cries out of Houses to pray for them.

'I cannot write this without tears, much less could I see it without grief and horrour,' he added. 'Seldom did we meet friends, but it was, as it were, the last parting in this world. The dangers of this abode (in Westminster) did exceed the hazard of many Battels.'

Hodges was in tears at what he saw and felt.

'Who can express the Calamities of such Times?' he asked. 'The whole British Nation wept for the Miseries of her Metropolis. In some Houses, Carcases lay waiting for Burial, and in others, Persons in the last Agonies; in one Room might be heard dying Groans, in another the Ravings of Delirium, and not far off Relations and Friends bewailing both their Loss and the dismal Prospect of their own sudden Departure.'

By day and night now the rutted streets were filled with carts of corpses, with labourers manhandling coffins, full and empty, pushing out of their way wretched victims who crawled painfully along, driven from their homes, seeking somewhere to die. Doctors now wore masks, shaped from leather or canvas, with long noses and eye holes; the sight of these strange apparitions added to the fears and gloom.

As Vincent passed the Artillery Ground one day, a distracted sufferer rushed past him. To Vincent's horror, the man dashed his head against the wall, driven mad by pain and hoping to kill himself. But he lacked the strength to do so, and collapsed, 'hanging with his bloody face over the rails, and bleeding upon the ground'. After some minutes the wretched man dragged himself away and lay down under a tree at Moorfields, where the clergyman went up and spoke to him. 'He could make no answer but rattled in his throat', and within half an hour was dead. The madness which plague frequently induced caused similar spectacles all over the capital.

On another day, Vincent saw a woman pass the door of his house weeping bitterly and carrying a tiny white coffin under her arms, towards a burial ground near by. 'It was the mother of the Child, and that all the Family besides was dead, and she was forced to Coffin up, and bury with her own hands this her last dead child.'

As Dr Hodges made his rounds, he saw some of the infected running wildly about the streets and alleys, 'staggering like drunken men' until they fell dead, lying under a cluster of greedy black flies for the dead-cart to make its next round. Others, at the point of death, too ill to move, lay face down on the cobbles or in doorways in a coma, 'never to be waked but by the last Trumpet', or crawled about on their hands and knees 'vomiting as if they had drunk Poison'. Not a few fell dead in the markets, ironically while 'buying Necessaries for the Support of Life'.

Under the pretext of searching their bodies, the drivers of the dead-carts removed any valuables they found, often even their fouled clothes and shoes. The sight of dead-carts rumbling past with naked arms, heads and legs sticking out of a pile of suppurating corpses disturbed even the most composed.

Earlier, the majority of the dead had at least a rough box of some sort in which to be carried to the burial ground, but by the end of August there were not enough planks left in the timberyards; and not enough carpenters to fashion them into coffins had there been time. Most of the corpses were thus wrapped only in shrouds improvised from sheets, blankets or stiff sacking. These coverings, often soaked with sweat, vomit and faeces, were easily detached in the rough handling of the bodies received from the bearers.

Many timid passers-by, suddenly confronted at a street corner by the sight of fifteen or twenty half-naked corpses, eyes and mouths wide open, heaped upon a cart, and lit only by a lantern, fainted or were seized with a fit of hysterics.

Nor were these sights the worst hazard faced by those who left their homes to buy what food they could. Some of the crazed plague victims, with death close upon them, resented the fact that others should still be healthy, and roamed the streets trying to pass on the infection.

One young wife, expecting her first baby, met one such person, 'a lusty man', as she hurried along Aldersgate Street. The road was narrow and he stopped and held out his arms so that she could not pass. He was riddled with plague; his face streamed with the pus from huge buboes. As she stared at him in horror, he announced that he would kiss her and so infect her. Why should she be well when he was ill?

Terrified, the girl tried to run back the way she had come, but, realizing that her assailant was close behind her, turned after a few steps and pushed him hard in the chest. Weakened by illness, the man staggered, but in trying to save himself he caught hold of her dress and dragged her down with him. Then, on the hot cobbles, he ripped off her skirt and assaulted her. She became hysterical with fear and shame and died several days afterwards.

Others bearing plague marks begged relentlessly at the doors of the houses as yet unvisited, exposing their streaming sores and refusing to go away until they had been given money. More forced their way in and would not leave until they had been bribed to go. As the days passed, the sums they demanded grew; the sick far outnumbered the healthy, and there were no police, no watchmen to call.

A Westminster music teacher, Mr Caesar, reported that in the narrow streets there, sufferers, apparently activated from spite and envy, would hang out of their windows 'to breathe in the faces of the well people going by'. Thomas Middleton, an officer in the Royal Navy, said that at Portsmouth some depraved plague victims were even going out at night to throw filthy plasters taken from their sores through the windows of other houses. Portsmouth was badly overcrowded, and in many houses families were sleeping nine or a dozen to a room.

Several other seaports were seriously affected, and at Ipswich, the master of a collier anchored there was thrown into great consternation when he saw a Naval press gang rowing out in a long-boat towards his vessel. His quick wits kept him his crew, for he hurriedly got out some sail cloth and ordered several of his hands to wrap themselves up in it and lie down on the deck. As the boarding party scrambled aboard, these sailors either feigned death or agonizing illness, while the master cried out a warning that his vessel had been visited with plague. The Naval party fell over themselves in the rush to regain their own boat, and rowed away at a great pace.

Meanwhile, in London, the mortality rate was so high that it was not uncommon for an inheritance to pass successively to three or four heirs in as many days. Those who attended the burials of friends in the few parishes which still had space in their churchyards, were very often 'carried to their own long home' on the next day, while in other districts Hodges noted that 'the burying places would not hold the Dead, but they were thrown into large Pits dug in waste Grounds, in Heaps thirty or forty together'.

The practice of ringing bells for the dead was soon to be abandoned, for they had seemed to grow 'hoarse with continual tolling', and the constant noisy reminder of death depressed those still alive.

Everyone knew that the plague had not yet slackened its onslaught, but few were prepared for the Mortality Bill which was issued for the last week in August. This reported a rise of almost 2,000 deaths in one week – a total of 7,496 deaths from all causes, and 6,102 of them admitted to be deaths from plague. Only seventeen of the ninety-seven City parishes remained free of plague, and none outside the walls had escaped. In St Giles, Cripplegate, alone, nearly 100 corpses were being carried to the local plague pit every day. As Pepys said, this total was 'beyond all expectation', and he at once determined to retreat while he was still able and join his wife at Woolwich.

He feared that the true death figure was nearer 10,000 and Dr Gumble – who stayed with Lord Albemarle, fearlessly chewing tobacco and drinking his specially brewed strong beer – was even more pessimistic. 'The Numbers in the printed Bills of Mortality were not half the sum of those which died,' he declared. 'I heard some judicious person affirm that the week there were put into the Bills six thousand, there died above fourteen thousand.' This was not published 'lest it should discourage the whole Nation', but in East Smithfield and some of the poorer out-parishes, the people died 'until whole streets were isolated, and death had no more spoil or prey to ravin in'.

The deaths of sextons and parish clerks, the refusal of Quakers and others to have anything to do with records, and the large numbers of poor who were tipped into mass graves without even being counted, support these suggestions. Whenever a record was kept of mortality among a limited class or in a specific area, it was found that plague rarely took less than three out of ten, and very often more than half. This point is underlined by the experience of troops left in London under Albemarle's command. He segregated them by putting their tents in Hyde Park. Although they had the best care available in

London, with special physicians appointed to look after them and ample medical supplies, a third of their number still caught plague and died.

On September 4th, Pepys wrote to Lady Carteret from the comparative safety of Woolwich, and gave his reasons for his retreat there.

He had remained in London 'till above 7,400 died in one week; and of them above 6,000 of the plague, and little noise heard day or night but tolling of bells; till I could walk Lumber (Lombard) Street, and not meet 20 persons from one end to the other, and not 50 upon the Exchange; till whole families, 10 and 12 together, have been swept away; till my very physician, Dr Burnet, who undertook to secure me against the infection, having survived the month of his own house being shut up, died himself of the plague; till the nights, though much lengthened, are grown too short to conceal the burials of those that died the day before, people being thereby constrained to borrow daylight for that service: lastly, till I could find neither meat nor drink safe, the butcheries being everywhere visited, and my brewer's house shut up, and my baker, with his whole family, dead of the plague. Yet, Madam, through God's blessing… your poor servant is in a perfect state of health'.

Pepys was one of the prosperous middle-class, who could afford to leave London, but most of the poor had nowhere else to go. Caught between starvation and plague, they were at the mercy of circumstances, and the City authorities could always enlist them for the sickening and perilous jobs of watchmen, bearers of the dead, grave diggers, nurses and the like. The miserliness of the public services can be gauged by the fact that only about £1 of public money was spent for every three plague victims who died. This sum covered everything from relief to burials.

Some labourers who dug plague pits went on strike for more money. They had been paid from 7s 6d to 10s a week for this work, according to the means of the parish where they worked, but at a time when most preferred to go hungry rather than work in the evil-smelling burial grounds, encircled by corpses, some parishes grudgingly raised the pay to 2s. a day; others had to offer a free meal as well. By such means the mass of bodies were at least assured of burial, and were not picked to the bones by birds.

1. This was no exaggeration; a London merchant, writing to a rich client on August 17th, remarked that not one merchant in a hundred was left in London.

CHAPTER EIGHT

The Plague at Eyam

The story of London under the shadow of plague, not notably heroic or charitable, is relieved by events that occurred in a remote hamlet, 160 miles away; the village of Eyam, north of Bakewell in Derbyshire, high in the bleak cloudy peaks of the Pennines.

Eyam had a population of barely 350 people living in homely little stone cottages, that stood sheltered in a valley unusually rich with trees. The cottages were clustered on each side of a short village street, which at its western end crossed a stream over Fiddler's Bridge. Most of the men and some of the women worked on farms and smallholdings.

The fact that Londoners were being carried to mass graves in their thousands throughout that terrible August meant nothing to the people of Eyam. London was only a name to them, a city that by no means all had even heard of, and which probably none had ever seen. Yet by a strange irony this remote, unlikely hamlet was to suffer a far greater loss in proportion to its size than London; and to give an example of heroism that is still remembered.

Early in September a box of old clothes and tailors' patterns was delivered by coach to the home of Edward Cooper, the local tailor, near the church. He told his servant, George Vicars, to break the cord and open it. They then discovered that the contents felt damp and fusty after their long, slow journey

143

north. Vicars shook out the clothes and hung them round the kitchen fire to dry.

This box brought more than old clothes to Eyam; it brought the plague. Vicars was taken ill within forty-eight hours of unpacking it; four days later he was dead. Cooper died two weeks afterwards. By the end of the month, seven more households had become infected, and twenty-six more people died. Only then did Eyam begin to understand that this strange sudden illness, for which there seemed no cure, must be the plague, the dreaded disease of which they had heard rumours from coaches and carriers' carts driving up from the South.

The lateness of the year and the hardness of the Derbyshire winter saved the village from immediate extinction. But even in the cold of November, with icy winds sweeping across the snow-covered Pennines, seven more died. December brought heavy frost – and nine further deaths. The local churchyard, which usually had barely half a dozen burials in one year – and those only of old people – was already overcrowded, with forty-four deaths in less than four months. By Christmas the whole village lay in the grip of a fear as hard and relentless as the frost.

In the following spring – long after plague had left London – Eyam met its full ferocity. Those who had relatives and friends in other parts of the country went to stay with them. Those who had nowhere else to go built crude huts under rocks in the dale leading to the neighbouring hamlet of Foundley. There they lived like beasts, eating roots and snaring animals until the cold of autumn drove them back to their cottages.

By the end of the month all available space in the churchyard was full, and the church closed. Its bell no longer tolled for the dead; there were too many.

William Mompesson, the rector, a man not yet thirty, who had only been in Eyam for a few months, realized that rising panic had put the whole village on the verge of flight. He called all his parishioners together and told them bluntly that many were probably already infected. It was thus their duty as Christians to stay where they were and not hazard others by visiting them. He pledged himself to stay with them in Eyam and also to do all he could to enlist aid for them.

The villagers agreed with what he said. These country people were illiterate and simple, but in the courage of this decision they showed a fortitude and unswerving sense of honour that few Londoners could approach. After the meeting, Mompesson hurried back to his rectory and wrote to the great landowner, the Duke of Devonshire, at Chatsworth, near by, declaring his intention of isolating the village if the Earl could assure him of supplies of food and other essentials. Then he decided upon a boundary line around the village, and the men of Eyam marked it out with stakes. Beyond that line no one was to go.

By the end of July fifty-seven had died.

Weeds now sprouted unchecked in gardens, and cattle and crops were left neglected in the fields beyond the boundary. Cows mooed in agony to be milked; pigs rooted like wild beasts, sheep died of thirst and exposure, for no one could reach them.

The village recluse, a man named Merril, moved out to a hut on high ground above Eyam, where he lived for months with only a cockerel for company. As he looked down upon Eyam, barely half a mile away, the village seemed already in decay. Houses were deserted, doors and window shutters banged in the wind. The only people in the overgrown main street were carrying coffins or corpses wrapped in blankets; outside in the fields beyond the cottages, the graves spread out farther every day.

The home of Talbot, the village blacksmith, was soon infected. He buried his three daughters, his wife and then one of his sons. He and his last remaining son also died of plague. In the space of a few days the whole family had been obliterated. Their burial place was a small stone enclosure on a hillock about a quarter of a mile east of the village; it still remains as a memorial of the time.

All through these months of loneliness and pain, Mompesson held two services every week in the open air in a small coombe called The Delf. He preached from a natural arch in an ivy-mantled rock, his congregation sitting or kneeling on the grass, widely spaced out as some insurance against infection.

Coffins, shrouds, even funeral services, were finally abandoned, for it became impossible to keep pace with the numbers required. The dead were swiftly carted off to burial grounds, or tumbled into pits hastily dug in cottage gardens.

By this time, plague had decimated almost every family, and many households had no one left capable of digging a grave. Earlier on, Marshall Howe, the strongest man in Eyam, a rough-tongued giant, had agreed to act as parish burier in these conditions but insisted on taking as his right all money and possessions left by the dead who had no heirs. He soon became quite well off, and would announce with satisfaction that he would never want for a pipe of tobacco while he lived. Yet his wife, Jean, who constantly begged her husband to stop this terrible work, suddenly sickened and died, and so did his young son William. Howe survived the plague, and lived for another thirty years with a strange reputation; a mixture of respect for his strength and contempt for his coarseness. For several generations afterwards, Eyam parents would frighten naughty children by threatening to send for Marshall Howe.

In the last week in August, Mompesson and his wife Catherine walked out together in a meadow behind the Rectory, a daily custom they had observed throughout the summer. As they turned back towards the house, Catherine, talking of their two children, suddenly cried out: 'The air – how sweet it smells!'

The young rector knew then that his wife was doomed; one of the early signs of the Black Death was a familiar sickly-sweet odour sometimes only felt by the victim. Later that afternoon, Catherine collapsed and was soon delirious. She was consumptive; the plague claimed her within three days. Mompesson's servants had to lead him away from her body. When he was finally persuaded to quit the room, he sobbed, 'Farewell, farewell all happy days.'

The loss of the rector's wife deeply affected the remaining villagers, even in the midst of their own sufferings, for Mompesson and Catherine had won their love and respect.

During that August month, seventy-eight people died of plague. The houses worst hit were those on the east side of Fiddler's Bridge; people living to the west shut themselves up and refused to cross the stream. One who did risk the journey, to visit his sister in Lydgate at the eastern end of Eyam, crept out early one morning only to find that she was already dead. Howe had buried her in a deserted garden.

Only one villager attempted to go beyond the boundary which isolated them; a woman driven almost frantic by the loss of her family. She made for the little market town of Tideswell, about five miles distant. But there the townspeople, knowing of Eyam's plight, maintained a watch on the road to prevent anyone entering from Eyam. Thus when the woman approached the town she was stopped and asked for her address.

'Orchard Bank,' she replied truthfully, for this was a local Eyam name for a small group of cottages.

'And where is that?' asked the watchman.

'Verily, it is the land of the living,' the woman hedged, scuttling past him. She did not get far, for he raised the alarm and she was later identified in the market place. The cry of 'The plague, the plague!' went up from all sides, and the unfortunate woman from Eyam was chased out of the town, and pelted with clods and stones to help her on her way.

All through these terrible months when plague had long since left London, there had been little contact between Eyam and the outside world. Food and supplies provided by the Duke of Devonshire were brought in by carriers from nearby villages to agreed points on the boundary. They arrived at dawn, and all they carried back were reports of the plague's progress, written by Mompesson, with money from the villagers to pay for the goods they had brought. They left coins in a hole dug in a shallow stream, afterwards known as 'Mompesson's Brook', in the hope that the water would wash away any infection. The supplies were collected daily by bearers appointed by Mompesson and the Rev. Thomas Stanley, the former Rector of Eyam until he had been ejected four years earlier as a dissenter. Stanley stayed on in the village until his death five years later; ecclesiastical politics were forgotten as he worked alongside Mompesson throughout the plague.

One of the carriers, who brought a load of fuel close to the village, afterwards caught cold. When his neighbours in his home village of Bubnell, near Chatsworth, heard that he was ill, they put a watch round his house and threatened to kill him if he tried to emerge. The Duke of Devonshire arranged for his own physician to examine the carrier. Doctor and patient met at a prearranged spot, one on each side of the Derwent River, shouting their questions and answers across the water. The doctor was soon satisfied that the carrier had nothing worse than a chill; his neighbours then agreed to let him out.

On October 11th, with only thirty-three people left alive in Eyam, the plague suddenly and unexpectedly died; its terror and shadow left the ruined village. Of the original population of 350, fifty had fled before the village was cut off. Of those 300 left behind, 259 had died. It had been a Derbyshire custom for many years to make funeral cakes, one for each villager, when anyone died, and for a long time after the plague there remained a local saying that 'two dozen funeral cakes were sufficient for the whole village'.

A day or two after the last plague death, Merril, still living his hermit-like existence in the hut high above Eyam, stood looking down at the ravaged village. He had no means of knowing that the plague was over. Then, to his surprise, his cockerel strutted past him and took wing towards the village and his old cottage down in the valley. Merril took this as a sign of hope, like Noah's dove flying from the Ark, and ventured cautiously down the street himself. When he entered his cottage, the cockerel was pecking for food.

In the following months, as the survivors were systematically burning all the bedding, clothes and furniture they could find in abandoned houses, Mompesson dictated a letter to his uncle, John Bielby, in Yorkshire; he did not want to frighten him by writing with his own hand.

'The condition of this place has been so sad, that I persuade myself it did exceed all history and example,' he said. 'Our town has become a Golgotha, the place of a skull. My ears never heard such doleful lamentations, my nose never smelled such horrid smells, and my eyes never beheld such ghastly spectacles.

'There have been seventy-six families visited within my parish, out of which 259 persons died (eight deaths were from causes other than Plague). Now, blessed be to God, all our fears are over, for none have died of Plague since the eleventh of October, and the pesthouses have been long empty.

'I intend (God willing) to spend this week in seeing all woollen clothes fumed and purified...here have been such a burning of goods that the like, I think, was never known.

'I know I have had your prayers; and I conclude that the prayers of good people have rescued me from the jaws of death.'

Mompesson stayed on at Eyam for three more years, and then accepted the living of Eakring in Nottinghamshire. When local people there heard of his experiences they feared that he would bring the plague to them. For months, Mompesson was forced to live in a hut they built for him on the parish boundary, waiting patiently for his parishioners to accept him. Eventually they did so, and he became widely revered. In later life he was offered the Deanery of Lincoln, but refused the post, afterwards becoming Prebend of York and Southwell.

Fear of the plague died slowly in Eyam. For nearly 200 years, 'The plague take thee!' was the most common local expletive, and 100 years after the Black Death, a centenary sermon in the village church 'drew forth abundant tears from the sobbing auditors'.

In 1779 Eyam was attacked by a fever epidemic in which some people complained of swellings in the neck and groin; and many thought that the ghost of the plague was returning.

Well on into the nineteenth century, skeletons were still being unearthed from underneath floorboards and in gardens. All over the village lay scattered tombstones which had been erected to honour those who had died deliberately because they did not wish to live and risk being the cause of death to others.

CHAPTER NINE

Plague Pits and Bonfires

In London during those days and weeks when plague had been gaining control in Eyam, the burial pits had become huge hummocks of the dead; even Tamberlaine's pyramids, built with the soldiers his armies slew, could not compare with these barrows.

'Now the Grave doth open its mouth without measure,' wrote Dr Vincent. 'Multitudes, Multitudes, in the valley of the shadow of death thronging daily into Eternity; the Churchyards now are stuft so full with dead corpses, that they are in many places swell'd two or three foot higher than they were before, and new ground is broken up to bury the dead.'

Despite this, the plague had still not reached its peak, although the dead-carts were in use night and day with shifts of drivers and searchers in a desperate attempt to clear the streets of corpses. So great was the carnage that the fear grew that too few would survive to bury their dead, and London would become virtually depopulated, a city of the past, empty, desolate and decayed.

The City authorities, anxious for any means to diminish the slaughter, decided to kindle giant fires in the streets to drive away the 'poisoned air', a custom of no medical value that dated back to early Elizabethan times.

The streets were already so foul with putrefying corpses and the bodies of horses, cats and dogs that the doctors protested strongly but in vain against this absurd scheme. Before the

151

College of Physicians had retreated from London, some of their number had apparently recommended such fires. This was good enough for Sir John Lawrence and the Duke of Albemarle, who were naturally prepared to try any remedy that might conceivably slow down the gigantic death rate. Thus, on September 2nd – exactly a year to the day before the start of the Great Fire which destroyed the City – the Lord Mayor issued a Proclamation which bore Albemarle's endorsement.

It stated that during plague epidemics 'in former ages' and 'in other countries', fire had been found successful in purifying the air. Accordingly, all the inhabitants of the City and Liberties were 'to furnish themselves with sufficient Quantities of Firing, to wit, of Sea Coal, or any other combustible matter, to maintain and continue fire burning constantly for three whole days, and three whole nights'.

All traffic in the streets was forbidden while these fires burned, and people were urged not to allow sparks from the fires to ignite the timber houses in the narrow alleyways and lanes.

Although many were sceptical of this latest move to check the rapid spread of death, some believed that it might work the miracle which would save the City. There was talk that Hippocrates had saved a plague-stricken town by firing a nearby forest although no one knew exactly when or where, but special prayers were said in churches in every London parish for the success of this scheme.

At eight o'clock on the evening of Tuesday, September 5th, tar torches were put to piles of wood and rubbish at scores of different sites all over the capital; at once the flames roared up, impressively hot and dangerously close to the houses. Huge coal fires were also lit at the Custom House, at Queenhithe, Billingsgate, Blackfriars, the Bridewell, at the corner of Leadenhall Street and Gracechurch Street; by the north and south gates of the Royal Exchange, at the Guildhall, by Blackwell Hall Gate, outside the Lord Mayor's house in Great St Helen's; near the west gate of St Paul's, in front of Bow Church, and at the entrance to London Bridge near St Magnus' Church.

These were official 'City bonfires' maintained at the expense of the City purse. In addition, householders in 'all streets, courts, lanes and alleys of the City and Suburbs' were compelled to club together to light, maintain and pay for their own street fires. Coal was scarce, so that anything combustible – tar barrels, old furniture, faggots, were fed into the flames as the sparks soared upwards towards the stars.

Allin wrote to his friends in the country of 'sea cole fires made in the streetes about every 12th doore', and added gloomily: 'But that will not do ye worke of stopping God's hand.'

The day after the fires were lit, Pepys – in London just long enough to pack up some belongings to take back to Woolwich – noted that they were blazing vigorously 'through the whole city'. Later in the day, journeying down the Thames to see Albemarle at the Cockpit, he was able to see them burning on both sides of the river all the way.

Householders stoked their fires in shifts, and the watchmen – with the responsibility of keeping the giant City fires going on top of their other plague duties – had little rest. For three nights and two days Londoners sweated in the heat and coughed in the smoke throughout the daylight hours, while in the cooler nights the capital became a strange and sinister sight, with deserted streets, shuttered houses, and the spectral spires of its dark skyline wavering and flickering in the eerie orange glow of the flames. On the last of the appointed days 'a smart and hasty rain' extinguished the general conflagration, making in the process a thick blanket of choking smoke which engulfed the City. Immediately afterwards, wrote Dr Hodges, 'the most fatal Night ensued, wherein more than 4,000 died'.

Whether this was a result of 'the Wet Constitution of the Air that immediately followed' or 'the suffocating Qualities of the Fuel', the doctor was not prepared to debate, but he was full of scorn for the theories of the Hippocrateans, and believed that the fires had been useless, 'a showy and expensive Project'.

In this he was undoubtedly right, for the interception of colliers by Dutch privateers, and the understandable reluctance of coal ships to put in at any plague port, had raised the price of coal to £4 a chaldron (thirty-six bushels). Defoe calculated that the City's official fires alone burned 100 chaldrons, or £400 worth of fuel, and the Lord Mayor estimated that each householder would have to contribute between 1s 6d and 2s for their fires – three or four times the amount levied as a rate for pest and poor relief.

Many wealthy people who had left the capital in the spring were not greatly concerned at the suffering and liabilities they had left behind them. Eventually the Lord Mayor gave notice that unless they paid up immediately their houses would be forcibly opened by the constables and their household goods sold to meet the liability.

The rain, which stopped the City's costly fires, also damped official enthusiasm for continuing with this scheme. No attempt was made to rekindle the great black mounds of steaming ashes, and for once the air was clear of the acrid blue smoke. Most people were grateful for this. 'May Posterity be warned,' wrote one, 'and not, like Empyricks, apply a Remedy where they are ignorant of the Cause.'

The Mortality Bill for that week was printed the day before the fires went out. Pepys, who had to visit the Tower on business of his own, sent out a lackey for a copy immediately he arrived. He read with horror of 8,252 deaths, of which 6,988 were due to plague. Pepys thought the Bill 'a most dreadful number', and his despair was reflected all over London. Evelyn, who was in Westminster to seek Lord Albemarle's permission to commandeer a ship for plague-ridden seamen, noted: 'I went all along the City and Suburbs from Kent Streete to St James's, a dismal passage and dangerous, to see so many Confines exposed in the streetes, and the streete thin of people, the shops shut up, and all in mournful silence, as not knowing whose turne might be next.'

The Intelligencer put into words the thoughts of all London: 'God in His Mercy remove this heavy Judgment.'

While the King's loyal subjects were dying in such great numbers in the capital, King Charles and his court were disturbed in their round of pleasure-making at Salisbury by two or three deaths in and near that city, which were suspected to have been caused by plague. It was thus decided that the King should spend a week or two hunting in Wiltshire, and then move on to Oxford, where the Queen could join him.

At the end of August, Parliament had again been prorogued, and it was due to meet in Oxford, 'on weighty and urgent affairs'. But since most MPs were in their country houses, a large assembly was not expected.[1] In fact, it was smaller than had been anticipated; barely half the Members arrived. The main business engaging their attention was the voting of further large sums of money for the pursuance of the Dutch war. The House also passed the Five Mile Act against dissenters, and then most of the Members returned to their country homes. There had been little debate in the House, and it was recorded that 'The Expedition that was used in all Business out of Fear of the Sickness, and out of an impatient Desire to be separated, was very notorious.'

The Commons did appoint a committee to draw up a Bill for more effective measures to prevent the spread of plague, but this was later defeated in the Lords; they refused to sanction any Act which did not expressly exempt the houses of noblemen from plague regulations. Their Lordships also insisted that their London homes should not be liable to search or to be shut up, and also that no pesthouse should be built anywhere near the property of a peer. Efforts were made at a compromise, but the noble lords were adamant, and that Parliamentary session ended.

The weather in London during the second week of September, while these deliberations were going on elsewhere in more pleasant surroundings, was cooler than it had been all summer. This fact may have helped to bring about the first decrease in the

Bills since the plague began, for the Bill for that same week showed 562 fewer deaths than the week before. The *Intelligencer* sounded a note of restrained optimism in reporting the drop in mortality. 'The weather has been very sharp of late for this time of the year, and has undoubtedly made a quick riddance of such bodies as were before tainted,' their editorial writer noted, and went on to suggest that the figures for the following week would show a further decrease.

Others were less sanguine. Pepys took a walk through the City, talking to as few people as possible, and thought that plague cases had actually increased. In Fenchurch Street, he met bearers with a load of plague corpses at noon, and, hastily moving out of their way, he came face to face with 'a person sick of the sores, close by me in Gracechurch in a hackney-coach'. The Angel Tavern, at the bottom of Tower Hill, was shut and deserted; he was disturbed to learn that the last time he had called in there for a glass of ale, one of the household had actually been dying of the plague.

All the news he heard was of death; past, present and to come.

'Poor Payne, my waiter, hath buried a child and is dying himself… A labourer I sent but the other day to Dagnams, to know how they did there, is dead of the plague… One of my own watermen, that carried me daily, fell sick as soon as he had landed me on Friday morning last, when I had been all night upon the water, and I believe he did get his infection that day at Banford, and is now dead of the plague…

'And lastly, both my servants, W. Hewer and Tom Edwards, have lost their fathers, both in St Sepulchre's parish, of the plague this week.'

These sad reports put the diarist into 'great apprehensions of melancholy, and with good reason. But I put off my thoughts of sadness as much as I can, the rather to keep my wife in good heart and family also'.

Only four days previously, Pepys' wife had heard that her father was very sick and his house shut up. Pepys promised to help his in-laws, but he had worries with his job as well. Plague was on the increase in most of the main ports, and the Navy Office had no plans for the Fleet at the end of their summer campaign against the Dutch.

The sailors, who had spent months at sea, in cramped, foul, unventilated quarters deep in the hulls of the creaking wooden ships, were restless for shore leave. It was suggested to Pepys that since Chatham, Woolwich and Deptford – all on the Thames – were probably too near London for safety, they might be allowed ashore on the Isle of Wight. Plague, however, had already been reported there; one man had died and two women who had changed the sheets of his bed died soon afterwards. The Navy replied that they had no wish to come anywhere near London; Pepys heard that the crews would rather lose three months' pay and be paid off in Portsmouth than collect all their back pay in the capital.

Even in the throes of the worst weeks of the plague, religious controversy continued as vehemently as ever. From the north of England alarming reports went to the Secretary of State's office in London about the activities of dissenters. It was said that fanatics were 'openly rejoicing' in any Dutch successes in the war, hoping that the Hollanders would soon be able to attack the English coast and so create ideal conditions for an uprising against the Monarchy. Some were even grateful for the violence of the plague, which had occupied all the attention of the administration and so prevented the stern measures normally taken to suppress their activities.

Meanwhile, England's foreign trade was suffering badly. The main Continental ports were closed to all ships from Britain, and goods lay rotting in warehouses in London and all around the coast.

Worse was yet to come; the peak of plague casualties came in the third week of September – the 12th to the 19th – when 8,297 deaths were recorded, 7,165 of them from plague. Hodges reckoned that at least 12,000 people died that week. The French Ambassador, Count Cominges, reported to Paris that, in his opinion, the true figure was 14,000.

Pepys, up to see the Duke of Albemarle on September 20th, the day before the publication of this fearful Bill, was told this news in advance.

'Lord!' he wrote, 'what a sad time it is to see no boats upon the river, and grass grows all up and down White Hall Court, and nobody but poor wretches in the streets! And, which is worst of all, the Duke showed us the number of the Plague this week, brought in last night from the Lord Mayor; that it is encreased about 600 more than the last, which is quite contrary to our hopes and expectations, from the coldness of the late season.'

Now London lay at the extremity of her agony. The plague pits which had been dug on vacant spaces all over the City and suburbs were hopelessly inadequate for this harvest of death. They overflowed with spotted, mutilated corpses, eyes ripped out by birds and rats and prowling ravenous dogs.

The sun unexpectedly returned to the capital after the short spell of cooler weather and rain, and the grave-diggers, fuming with cheap spirits, with their clothes stiff and stinking with putrefaction, dug like madmen in an attempt to keep pace with the seemingly endless succession of dead-carts that moved to and fro between the streets and the pits. At night, these grisly scenes were lit by flickering torches as the men worked on in shifts through the dark hours; to many it resembled a scene from Hell, with which the Puritan preachers had threatened their flocks so short a time before.

It was no longer possible to bury the victims within twenty-four hours of their death, and for as long as two or three days bodies were piled in the streets, stacked against the walls of houses like wax figures, until graves could be prepared. The numbers of the dead far exceeded the living left in London, who toiled to bury them.

Near Aldgate churchyard the parish authorities sunk a pit fifty feet long, twenty feet across and about ten feet deep. The first body was tipped into this on September 6th, and soon it was full of corpses, either naked or at best wrapped in old shirts or strips of blanket. Day after day, as more cadavers were shovelled in from the dead-carts at one end, labourers hacked away earth and stones at the other to enlarge the pit. Finally they could extend it no more; a wall was in the way. So they began to dig down. They reached a depth of twenty feet before they came to water, which bubbled in among the rotting corpses.

Within a fortnight this mass grave, now big enough to swallow up a couple of ships of the line, had received 1,114 bodies; the topmost lay at ground level. A mound of earth was thrown on top so that the last corpses would be covered by enough earth to preserve them from scavenging dogs.

The plague was also producing more painful and ugly sights than at any other time; never before had the swellings grown so huge and distended, like great shining bladders, nor had they been so agonizing and difficult to treat. Demented with pain, the sick ran screaming about the streets, foaming at their mouths. At Cripplegate plague pit, delirious sufferers plunged in among the corpses, shouting that they could not recover and so would bury themselves. Some were levered out of that sink of decay with long shepherds' crooks or hooks. Others lay in a coma and could not be roused. They died when more bodies were piled in upon them. Many victims, all reason gone, ran or danced, laughing and shouting about the streets with the hideous strength of the insane. One man skipped through the weed-grown streets for nearly six hours quite naked, until he suddenly dropped dead.

In the midst of these sights, sounds and the smell of death that had lingered over the City for months, those who still were healthy had become fatalistic. They believed that they had no hope of survival and so all precautions seemed futile. They did not expect to live long so they determined to enjoy what time they had left; they drank heavily, visited friends, even held parties, seemingly indifferent to the disease that had so far spared them.

Dr Vincent, still preaching from the City pulpits, lived in a household of eight – three men, three youths, an elderly woman and a maid. Towards the end of September, with plague raging all around them, and neighbours dying on either side, the plague touched his own home.

'The Cup was put into our hand to drink, after a Neighbour-family had tasted it, with whom we had much sweet society in this time of sorrow,' he wrote. 'And first our Maid was smitten; it began with a shivering and trembling in her flesh and quickly seized on her spirits.'

On the Monday of that week, Vincent went out to visit a friend in the City, whose husband had recently died of plague, and discovered that the widow had also become infected; her own death was only hours way. He went on to another house to pray with a man widowed a few days previously, and found that he was also infected and resigned to death.

When Dr Vincent returned home his maid was dying and another member of his household was delirious and in a high fever. On Thursday the maid died 'full of tokens'. On Friday one of his male servants had a swelling in his groin, and by Sunday he too was dead.

On the same day another servant fell ill, and was dead on the following Wednesday. On the Thursday, the master of the house fell sick. Within forty-eight hours the rashes and rings of spots appeared. Vincent went up to the sick room to pray with him, for all hope was abandoned. The man actually told him where he wished to be buried, and the text he wanted to be recited over his body. Then, to everyone's surprise, he suddenly recovered.

The Mortality Bill for the third week in September showed the beginning of the plague's decline in London, although in some places, and in the village of Eyam, it had still not yet reached its peak. Six thousand four hundred and sixty died in London that week, 5,553 of them from plague, but despite this drop of 1,800 in the death roll, there appeared little reason for optimism, for the London scene was becoming more horrifying than ever.

The rate of survival among the bearers and buriers had been surprisingly high in the early stages of the epidemic, but now scores of them were dying, others were refusing to drive the dead-carts. In several parishes, including Shoreditch and Aldgate, drivers had actually died while making their rounds. In one instance the horses panicked, and the cart, loaded with dead, raced through the streets at a wild pace, swaying crazily over the cobbles, until it finally overturned and tipped the corpses out on to the ground. Other drivers fell dead in the street and then their carts moved aimlessly about at the whim of the horses. One cart, which regularly delivered bodies to the plague pit in Finsbury Fields, was found upside down at the bottom of a newly-dug plague pit, the horses still in the shafts and kicking feebly. The driver, his whip still in his hand, was dead.

Anyone sick or even sleeping was in danger of being flung into a cart and carried away to the plague pit. Sometimes their cries of fear and terror led others to light torches and search for them amid the bodies, but in many cases it seemed impossible to tell the living from the dead, and no search was made. The deep coma into which many sufferers fell deceived their relatives into thinking they were dead; no death certificates existed; probably not one corpse in fifty was even seen by anyone with proper medical qualifications.

One who narrowly escaped such a fate was a Scotsman from the Highlands, who had come to London to work as a street musician a few months before the plague began. He walked up and down Holborn, near St Andrew's Church, every day, blowing a set of miniature bagpipes, followed by his pet dog. After each tune he would take off his cap and hold it out as an invitation to passers-by to drop in a coin. Since few people left in London at this time could afford to give him any money, he was soon nearly starving, but still went on with his routine, hoping that somehow things would improve. To those who asked how he was faring, he would reply that the dead-cart had not collected him yet, but the bearers had promised to call for him next week.

One day in September, someone unexpectedly invited him to celebrate his survival with a drink. The piper was hungry and cold and the grog fumed inside his empty stomach like fire. It was months since he had tasted strong drink, and when he came out into the rainy afternoon he immediately collapsed in the street dead drunk, near Cripplegate. He lay there until dusk, when some people who lived near by thought he was another plague corpse, and brought a body out of their house and laid it beside him to be collected by the dead-cart.

In the early evening John Hayward, the under-sexton of the parish of St Stephen's, Coleman Street, and a bearer throughout the plague, came by with the parish dead-cart. He noticed these two bodies, and hooked them up by their belts and added them to his load. Then he went on and collected several more bodies before finally turning back towards the nearest plague pit.

By this time, the drunken piper was half-buried under corpses. His dog ran faithfully behind the cart, whining and whimpering. As they neared the pit it jumped up on to the vehicle and began to bark loudly. This familiar sound aroused the piper, who slowly crawled out from under the stinking pile of bodies, still befuddled with drink, and with no idea where he was.

Some association of ideas between the barking of his dog and his calling made him raise his pipes to his lips. He began to play a Highland lament, wild and shrill and off-key. Hayward and his bellman, who was walking up in front with the two horses, looked around in amazement at this eerie sound. In the flickering light from their resin torches they could see an unsteady figure on top of the corpses trying to play some half-seen instrument. They at once dropped the reins and fled, believing that Satan was riding on their cart. The horses went on for a few yards and then stopped, heads down.

The piper shook the body next to him, thinking it asleep. The head rolled over and the Scotsman peered into a dead, bloated face. At the sight, soberness returned. He vaulted out of the cart and ran away in the opposite direction, to his lodgings. Miraculously, he did not catch the plague and the story of his experience spread around London. A rich man with nothing better to do with his money even gave him a pension, and commissioned a statue of him by Caius Gabriel Cibber, a well-known sculptor of the day, which showed him with his dog, his pipes and a cask of liquor. This survives; it was bought by the Victoria and Albert Museum, where it was put on view.

Hayward, who had been so alarmed by the sound of pipe music, worked tirelessly throughout the plague to keep the streets and houses of his large parish clear of the festering bodies which lay about for weeks in many other districts. His wife was a plague nurse, and her honesty earned her the commendation of the parish officers.

But by being kind and sincere they were certainly in the minority. Most bearers and plague nurses had notorious reputations. One bearer, named Buckingham, would follow his dead-cart, shouting: 'Faggots, faggots! Five for sixpence!' Sometimes he would hold up a dead child by an arm or leg, and wave the tiny, rigid cadaver above his head like a butcher displaying a carcase of meat. When his cart was full and he reached the plague pit, he would lash his torch to a wheel and then go down among the dead and undress the bodies of young women. He was one of several bearers who practised necrophily.

Dr Gumble, Albemarle's chaplain, could not bring himself to be specific about these horrors, and would only admit that 'in the very Pesthouses such wickednesses were committed as is not to be named'. The miserable and helpless sick incarcerated in these barracks were entirely at the whim and mercy of anyone set to watch over them. There was a complete lack of any responsible supervision, which might have afforded them protection from robbery, rape and depravity.

Although Buckingham escaped the plague he did not altogether escape punishment. Angry citizens reported him to the magistrates, and as a result of their testimony he was publicly whipped outside the City pesthouse, and then flogged through the streets. In addition he was jailed for a year and debarred forever from being employed in any similar way; it was by no means an extreme penalty in those days.

The Mortality Bill for the last week of September showed a further drop in the City death roll. Of the 5,720 whose deaths were recorded in the parish registers that week, 4,929 died of the plague. In Stepney, 631 died in that week, and Allin's parish of St Olave's buried 281, with the plague still spreading insidiously from street to street.

'It is very hot near me,' he wrote to a friend, but he was trying to live up to his responsibility as a clergyman by going out to preach, for there was no shortage of 'imployment...in this scarcity of ministers'.

Allin still held to an almost childlike faith in alchemical remedies. 'Freind,' he wrote to a correspondent of September 22nd, 'get a piece of angell gold, if you can of Elizabethan coins (it is ye best), which is phylosophicall gold, and keepe it allways in your mouth when you walke out or any sicke persons come to you; you will find strange effects of it for good in freedom of breathing, etc, as I have done, if you lye with it in your mouth without your teeth, as I doe, viz, in one side between your cheke and gumme, and so turning it sometimes on one side, sometimes on ye other.'

The first week of October brought a further decrease in the Bill; 5,068 deaths, 4,327 from plague, but two City parishes were stricken.[2] Nearly 64,000 had died altogether in less than eleven weeks. Evelyn, returning from a visit to his wife, who had given birth to her baby, rode by coach through the City on October 10th.

'Having occasion to light out of the coach in several places about businesse of money...I was invironed with multitudes of poore, pestiferous creatures, begging almes.' The shops were still closely shuttered, and the capital presented 'a dreadfull prospect'.

The worst ravages of the plague had been among the poor, and for months yet they were still to suffer cruelly. Even in the following January, Pepys, riding through the City in Lord Brouncker's coach, noted: 'Lord! What staring to see a nobleman's coach come to town. And porters everywhere to bow to us; and such begging of beggars!'

Gradually, with the colder weather, the virulence of the plague declined and dwindled, but its mark remained, and for the rest of the year there was little life in the streets of London.

In the second week of October, only 3,219 died (2,665 from plague), and the *Intelligencer* reported that hope was reviving in the town, for 'the distemper itself is observed not to be so mortal as it was, the greater part of the Infected now escaping'.

On October 14th, Allin announced that the death rate was falling in his parish, but that plague 'doth yet creepe into fresh houses still'. Like many of those who had stuck it out, he was utterly exhausted. 'My head aketh,' he wrote despairingly, and his worries were not lightened by what he thought to be adverse portents in his horoscope.

Pepys also found little to cheer him. His landlady at Woolwich determined to make capital of the disaster, and raised her charges to £5 10s a month for three rooms, including breakfast and dinner.

On October 16th the diarist was in London, but he could not accustom himself to the grim scene. 'Upon the Exchange, which is very empty, God knows!' he wrote, 'I walked to the Tower; but Lord! how empty the streets are, and melancholy, so many poor, sick people in the streets full of sores; and so many sad stories overheard as I walk, everybody talking of this one dead, and that man sick, and so many in this place, and so many in that.

'And they tell me that in Westminster, there is never a physician, and but one apothecary left, all being dead; but that there are great hopes of a great decrease this week; God send it!'

The hopes were justified, for the death roll dropped abruptly to 1,806 (1,421 of plague) in the third week of October, and twenty-eight of the City parishes were able to report themselves entirely free of plague deaths. Yet the City was still a place of death; the only people Pepys met were searchers of the dead, with their white rods of office; burial parties still were the main traffic in the streets. On October 29th he saw in Woolwich 'two women crying and carrying a man's coffin between them; I suppose the husband of one of them, which, methinks, is a sad thing'.

November began with reports of a new attack of plague at Lambeth, St Martin's and in Westminster, and when the Bill for the first week came out on November 9th, the numbers had risen again to 1,787 deaths, more than 1,400 of them plague. The relapse was general, for only twenty parishes were now free. The following week, however, saw the beginning of the final decline; 1,359 died (1,050 from plague), but this was the last time that deaths exceeded a thousand in any one week.

The weather was turning very cold, and this added to the dwindling numbers of the dead, and gave some people confidence to return to London. Those who risked a return to their homes were fearful, said Vincent, 'lest some of the after drops of the storm should fall upon them'. Their fears were justified for, writing in mid-November, Allin recorded: 'It is yet dying time with us…truly God seems now in divers places to visit the second time, after they have beene all well six to eight weekes; and fresh houses in divers places, besides some whole familyes swept away that have returned to ye City already.'

The evacuees were shocked by the sad appearance of the capital. Beggars squatted amid the muck and withered weeds at every street corner, displaying their sores and suppurations in plasters, begging for coppers to buy food. Windows gaped emptily without glass; whole houses, streets, squares had been looted and stripped of everything that could be carried away.

In the third week of November, more than 900 died, with at least 600 plague deaths, and there was still no general move to revive the life of London. As autumn merged into winter, the Bills dwindled to 400 or 500 a week, but the hardships of the poor continued. The weather was freezing (Allin commenting that 'it pincheth soarly here') and coal became dreadfully expensive. Lord Albemarle, the Earl of Craven and the Lord Lieutenant of the Tower did their best to persuade shipping to bring in fuel, but it was a slow business; a letter to Newcastle, where most of the coal came from, took several days to deliver, for the roads were impassable in places.

Cold winds cut through the rags the slum dwellers wore; they had little to eat and nothing left to burn. Plague still killed two or three hundred people a week, and those who had come back from the country seemed particularly prone to the disease.

'Divers persons and familyes at their returne home have mett with what they fled from,' noted Allin gloomily, and he was further depressed by seeing another strange comet in the sky, which he thought might presage a new outbreak. Coincidentally, the totals in Bills for the next two weeks rose by thirty or forty.

The Court remained at Oxford, occupying themselves with the arts of leisure and of love. 'There's no other plague here but the infection of love; no other discourse but of ballets, danse and fine clouse...none other fight than for "I am yours",' wrote one indignant observer. It was even suggested there that the King should proclaim that anyone showing signs of melancholy in the town should be stuck in the pillory and whipped until he had learned to become 'Merry à la mode'.

There were exceptions to this attitude. Sir William Coventry wrote to Pepys in November: 'I could heartily wish the Court were nearer London, to bee ready both to advise and execute better than at this distance wee can doe. I hope a little more decrease of the plague will make somebody valiant enough to advise it.'

An implicit indictment of Charles and his circle can be read between the lines of many such letters, but the writers were careful not to name names; critics could have short lives, even if they escaped the plague.

---

1. In the words of Clarendon, the Lord Chancellor, it was considered 'a very inconvenient Season for all Persons of Quality to travel from their own Habitations'.
2. Pepys, who stopped to talk to a constable on his way home one evening, was brushed by bearers carrying a plague corpse. But even he was becoming resigned, noting that such experiences were becoming so common that 'I am come almost to think nothing of it'.

CHAPTER TEN

The End of the Pestilence

Towards the end of November it became clear that the strength of the plague had genuinely and permanently diminished, and the painfully slow revival of London began. Cases of plague were still reported, mostly in the slums on the fringe of the City, but its malignity had largely disappeared, and Dr Hodges was able to report what he called 'a new Dawn of Health' in the City.

All through December, the numbers of dead in Mortality Bills fluctuated – now causing fears that the plague was returning, now hopes that it was receding.

Encouraged by the Mortality Bill for the last week in November, which listed only 544 deaths, of which 333 were admitted to be from plague, Pepys and his wife paid a fleeting visit to their little house by the Navy Office. Coming home from work on December 4th, the diarist wrote: 'It was a joyful thing for us to meet here, for which God be praised!' Pepys was anxious to return permanently, for he was reluctant to continue the expense of temporary lodgings elsewhere, but only a week later he was questioning whether it would be advisable. In the Bill for the first week in December, the number of deaths declined to 428, of which 210 were due to plague.

The next week's Bill listed fifty-seven deaths within the City out of the total of 442 in all London – 243 from plague – and what Pepys called his 'poor little parish' of St Olave's had six deaths – the highest for any City parish. This alarming development was probably the temporary result of a short spell of unexpectedly warm weather which for a few days broke the incessant hard frost.

In the third week of December 525 died, 281 from plague, and sixty-six of these in the City. This increase caused some alarm, for it was feared that the spring would certainly bring another fierce epidemic. Christmas week brought more cheering news, with the lowest Bill since the onset of the plague; of the 350 who died, only 152 were plague cases. This Bill was not published until December 27th, and so Christmas came and went with little attempt to make it a festive occasion. Church bells were silent, and only a few Christmas services were held in the City's 109 churches, for many clergymen had still not returned to London. In the fashionable areas, such as Covent Garden and Westminster, the great houses stood shuttered and completely empty, except for a few servants in their rooms high up under the eaves.

Funerals were still the most common sight in the streets, with beggars running them a close second. Forges and manufactories were empty and boarded up; their workers had no means of making any money apart from begging at street corners, or stealing from deserted houses, but most of their fittings and furniture had been stolen long ago.

So great had been the emphasis on death and funerals for so long that Pepys, attending church on Christmas morning, was amazed to see a wedding in progress. He made a special note of this in his diary, for it was something 'I have not seen for many a day'.

A few shops opened briefly for Christmas, and the removal of their dusty shutters for the resumption of business was one of the first signs that life was beginning to return to the capital. Passing by an oyster shop in Gracechurch Street, which he had patronized before the plague, Pepys was delighted to find it open and apparently well stocked. He bought two barrels of oysters, but his appetite was not increased when he heard that they came from Colchester, famous even then for its 'natives', where the plague was said to be depopulating the town. Despite this, he found the oysters 'very good'.

By the end of the year, many of the houses in the poorer districts began to be opened up, as more and more of London's refugee citizens returned. They made little attempt to air or disinfect their homes. Hodges was disgusted that so many would enter 'Houses and Rooms where infected Persons had but a little before breathed their last'. In their tiredness they even slept in 'Beds where Persons had died', and which had not yet been 'Cleaned from the Stench of the Diseased'.

The talk in the streets and the few open shops was anxious inquiry as to whether friends and relatives survived. Possibly only one in fifty Londoners could read or write, and so the poor relied almost exclusively on word of mouth.

Had this cousin been seen in Chelmsford? Did that man, who *might* be Uncle Samuel, really have a deformed hand by which he could be recognized?

It was a slow, unsatisfactory business, trying to trace people who were probably dead, and if not could either have left London or even been press-ganged into the Navy to fight the Dutch.

All through the cold weather the stench of death and decomposition lingered on, rising in foul, seeping waves from burial mounds which contained hundreds of corpses. All further burials in City churchyards were expressly forbidden, for fear that disturbances of plague graves might bring about a new onslaught of the disease. Even so, the rank smell of such giant putrefaction soured the air and made it impossible for people to move back into houses that stood near churchyards. Hundreds of people appealed to the City Corporation and to Justices of the Peace for something to be done about this constant smell.

Pepys, who attended St Olave's Church in January for a service in commemoration of the execution of King Charles I, was horrified at it as he walked through the churchyard.

'This is the first time I have been in the church since I left London for the Plague,' he wrote afterwards, 'and it frighted me more than I thought it could have done, to see so many graves lie so high upon the churchyard, where people have been buried of the plague. I was much troubled…and do not think to go through it again a good while.'

All over the City people were 'solicitous to have their churchyards covered with lime', as a possible means of cleansing them. Albemarle and Craven proposed that every burial place should be covered by a twelve-inch layer of unslaked lime, and then a similar covering of fresh earth. But to do this would have required thousands of tons of lime, taking weeks to dig it out of the chalk pits in Kent and transport it to London by barge or cart; the plan was sound but impossible to execute. The graves remained as they were until gradually the corpses rotted away and the mounds fell in and then the smell disappeared.

Returning to his home at Acton at this time, Richard Baxter, the Puritan divine, found his church's yard 'like a plow'd field with Graves, and many of my Neighbours dead'.

Craven suggested to the magistrates at Westminster that they should order all bedding to be taken out of the infected houses and aired, and then all such rooms should be given at least one coat of whitewash to purify them.

To encourage people to keep their homes clean, daily collections of refuse were instituted. The dead-carts were now transformed into dust-carts, and the handbells which had rung for bodies were now sounded to warn the people to sweep their garbage out into the streets. The bearers of the dead were still in work; they became 'rakers', who piled refuse into the carts and dumped it in new laystalls sited outside the City walls, some distance from the houses.

Those who still caught plague were kept under guard in their homes for forty days' quarantine, and parish constables were given strict orders to clear all verminous beggars from the streets.

These measures, which could well have been instituted earlier, had there been people capable of implementing them, helped to reduce the death rate in the New Year. During January, 253 people died in London, and of these only seventy were from plague. It was the first time that less than a hundred people had died from plague in any single week, and with only thirty-one parishes infected, the danger had almost gone.

Pepys returned to his house in Seething Lane, but caution continued to be his watchword. 'Home to my wife,' he wrote, 'and angry about her desiring a maid yet, before the plague is quite over…I will not venture my family by encreasing it, before it is safe.'

All through that year Albemarle in the Cockpit had struggled through a mass of complicated paperwork while politicians and public officials were miles away on their country estates. Dr Gumble, whose faithful friendship did much to sustain him, declared that Albemarle was always 'loaded with business'. In the absence of the King, he was in constant correspondence with Clarendon, the Lord Chancellor, with Secretaries of State and others. In addition to his own duties as C-in-C of the Army, he took over much of the responsibility of the Fleet, acting as a liaison between its Commanders, the Officers of Ordnance and the Navy Commissioners.

As well as all this, Albemarle directed the administration of the capital which lay outside the City walls, giving advice to the magistrates and Deputy Lieutenants of Middlesex and Southwark, arranging for essential supplies to be brought in, and endeavouring to organize some relief for the poor. Although the City itself was largely administered by the Lord Mayor, he invariably consulted Albemarle before instituting anything of importance.

The Navy Office had been moved out to Greenwich, in view of the Dutch war, for it was imperative that it should continue to operate on as nearly normal a scale as possible. The Exchequer had evacuated to Nonsuch, not far from Epsom in Surrey; the Michaelmas Law Term had been held at Oxford; the Exchange had either been closed or virtually deserted. Thus, apart from the Customs, no Government department remained in London.

Similarly, nearly all of the merchanting and manufacturing centres in the City had been empty and forsaken except for a few clerks and servants left behind to guard their masters' property; the imposing premises of the financial houses had presented forlorn and shuttered frontages to a deserted Lombard Street overgrown with weeds and dandelions.

Thus national and local administration had fallen gravely into neglect, and in an economy where the men were divided into three groups – those who worked, those who prayed and those who fought – the breakdown of commerce, finance and trade had been reflected in widespread poverty all over London.

The attitude of the King and the Court provided a yardstick by which the wealthy noblemen and rich bankers and merchants measured their own behaviour. Until King Charles considered it safe to return to Westminster, they were unlikely to come back themselves, and without them the crippling after-effects of the plague would become steadily worse.

On January 5th the King, still in Oxford, ordered the Exchequer to return to Westminster and reopen there on the 20th of the month. A week later, on the advice of the Privy Council, he ordered that the next legal term should be held at Windsor Castle, so as to avoid too precipitate a return to London. Nevertheless, Windsor was on the way to town; this was an encouraging sign.

The lawyers were especially pleased; they had endured a miserable time away from the Inns of Court. At the Michaelmas Law term in Oxford, most of the jury cases were postponed (except those in which the King had some interest), and no Chancery business was taken.

The lawyers, who were not admitted to the University City unless they could produce certificates of health, had been, according to a Frenchman, Denis de Repas, 'the jest of the Court and the hate of all the people'. In a letter to a friend, he declared that Oxford was full of lawyers whose clothes were as much out-of-date as their speech, 'which none can understand but when they ask for their fees'. He added: 'They generally curse this towne by reason that they cannot gett any lodgin. They did lay sixty last night in a barne full of haye, not far from my lodgin.'

The *Oxford Gazette*, edited by Henry Muddiman, which had replaced the *Intelligencer*, which had ceased publication in November, reported on January 15th that the King hoped 'with some impatience' that further decline of the pestilence would permit his return to London, which he had 'a very longing desire to do'. King Charles II was a prudent, cautious man, however, and his desire to be back in his Palace at Whitehall did not exceed his desire to remain alive and healthy. He was no doubt troubled by reports that plague deaths had suddenly and inexplicably increased to 158 in the second week in January.

Pepys, who had helped to reopen the Navy Office six days before, shared this alarm. On January 13th, when he went out to dinner at Covent Garden with Lord Brouncker and his mistress, Mrs Williams, he recorded that the occasion was 'pretty merry, though not perfectly so, because of the fear that there is of a great encrease again of the plague this week'. When he heard the totals of the next Bill, he was 'mightily troubled at the news…much the saddest news that the plague hath brought me from the beginning of it; because of the lateness of the year, and the fear we may with reason have of its continuing with us next summer'.

It was remarkable, he wrote three days later, how 'infinitely naked' Covent Garden and the fashionable districts to the west of the City were in comparison with the City itself, which was 'almost as full again of people as ever it was'.

The next Bill was more reassuring; plague deaths were only seventy-nine and the King, who had received an urgent appeal from Albemarle to meet him, decided to risk a journey to Hampton Court. He arrived with the Duke of York and some of his chief ministers on January 27th. Thereafter Albemarle would visit Charles daily, driving out each morning in his huge carriage, returning each night to London when the day's business was complete.

In the last week of the month, when snow lay thickly over London and the surrounding countryside, only fifty-six people died from plague. Of these, only two were in Westminster. The *Gazette* thus reported that the King had determined, 'for the encouragement of his City of London, as for the better convenience of his great and weighty Affairs of State', to return to Westminster. After making this historic announcement, the *Oxford Gazette* became the *London Gazette*, which has continued as the organ of Royal and official news ever since.

On February 1st, King Charles travelled back by coach to St James's Palace. Despite the snow and icy weather, thousands lined the route to cheer his progress. The bells of the churches sounded peal after peal, and bonfires, identical to those which had burned in an attempt to drive away the pestilence in September, blazed in the London streets that evening. The mass reaction was one of relief tinged with hope – relief that the plague was now officially over, hope for a new return to prosperity.

Both hopes were borne out. As the flight of the King and Court had precipitated the mass evacuation of London by its wealthy citizens, so the King's return encouraged thousands to return after him. Clarendon said that for a few days after his return to Westminster, the only coaches on the streets belonged to the Royal Household, 'so much were all men terrified from returning to a place of so much mortality'. But directly the news was known throughout the countryside that the King was back in Whitehall, the streets were soon crowded with the returning coaches of great families, and carts piled high with their belongings.

The Queen drove to Syon House, where Charles collected her, and together they sailed majestically down the Thames to Westminster in the Royal Barge. The Judges adjourned their courts at Windsor, and within days were again sitting at Westminster Hall. Despite this, Parliament was twice more prorogued, finally until September 1666, and there is no indication that the MPs were anything but grateful for being thus excused attendance in London.

But if they were timid, others were less so. 'Before the end of March,' wrote Clarendon, 'the streets were as full, the Exchange as much crowded, the people in all places as numerous, as they had ever been seen, few persons missing any of their acquaintance…'

The persons to whom the Chancellor referred, of course, had not been in London during the plague, but on their country estates miles away.

The frequent deaths of clerks and sextons of parishes hindered the accuracy of the weekly returns. 'Of the Anabaptists and other sectaries, who abounded in the City, very few left their habitations, and multitudes of them died, whereof no churchwarden or other officers had notice; but they found burials according to their own fancies in small gardens, or the next fields.'

More women and children, according to the Chancellor, died than men, and the greatest proportion were obviously among 'the lowest and poorest part of the people'.

Some of the rich prodigals did not escape the scorn of those who stayed behind. Pepys, although he had retreated as far away as Woolwich, certainly had little sympathy for them. At the first assembly of Gresham College, in Bishopsgate, since the plague, Dr Jonathan Goddard, the Professor of Physics, 'did fill us with talk, in defence of his and his fellow physicians going out of town in the plague-time; saying that their particular patients were most gone out of town, and they left at liberty, and a great deal more…'

'My wife and I the first time together at church since the plague,' he wrote later, 'and now only because of Mr Mills, his coming home to preach his first sermon; expecting a great excuse for leaving the parish before anybody went, and now staying until all are come home; but he made but a very poor and short excuse, and a bad sermon.'

With frost and snow now covering the graves in St Olave's churchyard, Pepys was not so afraid of venturing through it as he had been a few days before. And a week later, when Sir Thomas Harvey attended a meeting at the Navy Office, having been out of London throughout the plague, Pepys noted with satisfaction 'he was coldly received by us, and went away before we rose also, to make himself appear a man less necessary'.

Despite the outward appearance of normality, even a small variation in the number of plague deaths published in the Bills caused a wave of gloom to sweep through London. In April and May these figures rose again to between forty and sixty, largely because of outbreaks in Lambeth, Deptford and other out-parishes which suffered most as the tide of plague receded from the centre of the City.

The spring was again very hot, and the Black Death continued to harass many towns outside the capital. Colchester, with about 5,000 deaths, lost most of its inhabitants; the rest fled and the town became virtually empty, with only beggars walking the deserted streets. More than £1,000 was collected by the London Diocese for its relief. Along the Thames, too, the riverside towns of Deptford, Greenwich, Erith and Chatham were all seriously affected, and the Privy Council issued special plague instructions to their administrators.

Allin, who had also survived, left Southwark for Woolwich; he was still refused a physician's licence, but went on practising without one. Not long after his arrival, he was again plunged into the thick of plague, and once more he did wonderful work and lived to remember these days.

After a sharp rise of fifty-eight deaths in the second week of May, the Bills for the City of London dropped to between twenty and thirty plague cases a week, and all but one or two of these were in the out-parishes. The summer came without the epidemic which many people had secretly expected and dreaded, and news of a single infected house became a topic of interest and surprise.

Many new plague regulations came into force in May 1666, after the need for them had passed, but they were in any case of little value. The Privy Council ordered pesthouses to be built in every major city and town, but few were actually constructed, for the civic authorities concerned had other plans for their money. All householders in time of future plague would 'Keep shut all windows opening towards Infected Houses'; 'Fires in movable Pans, or otherwise', were to be made in all 'necessary publique Meetings in Churches, etc, and the convenient Fumes to correct the Air to be burnt thereon'; and local authorities were ordered to ensure that 'no Swine, Dogs, Cats or tame Pigeons be permitted to pass up and down in Street, or from house to house, in places Infected'.

The toll of the Great Plague in London had made 1665 the most disastrous year in the history of the capital. In the Bills alone, 97,306 deaths were recorded, 68,596 of them from plague; of these, 15,207 (9,877 plague) took place within the 446 acres covered by the City. These figures are only fractions of the real totals. Clarendon thought that 'many who could compute very well, concluded that there were in truth double that number that were mentioned in the Bills who died, and that in one week, when the Bill mentioned 6,000, there had in truth 14,000 died'.

Despite the number of deaths and the gloom of the City, this terrible summer was soon forgotten. The remarkable resilience of the human mind was shown by the fact that people 'had the courage to marry again, and betake to the Means of repairing the past Mortality; and even Women before deemed barren, were said to prove Prolifick'. According to one estimate, the loss of nearly 100,000 people was hardly noticeable after a few months.

John Graunt, in his *Observations on the Bills of Mortality*, was also sanguine on the subject, calculating that all those who died would be replaced in two years. He explained away the smaller birth rate in London than elsewhere by the fact that many of its courtiers and wealthy classes kept their families in the country, while others sent their wives to the country for confinements. Scarcely half the people, he believed, saw any need to have their children christened; only 9,967 were christened in London during the plague year, and since no other registration of births existed, this was clearly a most conservative estimate of births.

London remained the goal of people who wanted to grow rich and successful; there was no shortage of replacements for those who had perished. Their jobs were eagerly taken by new immigrants, and the City soon recovered its usual bustle.

Dr Gumble saw all official reports that had flowed in to Albemarle throughout the plague year, and hazarded a guess at the total plague mortality in England.

'This Judgment,' he wrote, 'the next year took its circuit, and visited many great Cities and Towns in the Nation, so that in 1665 and 1666 there died about two hundred thousand persons of men, women and children of the pestilence, which was a visitation beyond any formerly in this Nation; and I hope and pray that God will never send the like, and that we nor our Posterity after us may never feel such another Judgment.'

London was indeed spared further horrors of the plague, but the Great Fire, which began within weeks, was as damaging in terms of property as the plague had been in terms of human life.

Many people considered that both disasters must be the work of God's hand, as a punishment for their sins. In his pamphlet, *God's Terrible Voice in the City*, Dr Vincent was convinced that if only citizens had truly mourned their dead and repented, then they would have been spared the Fire. Ironically, the rich largely escaped harm from the plague, which was thus called 'the poore men's plague', but in the fire the poor had little to lose. Many of the rich and prosperous merchants and property owners, however, were ruined. They had saved their lives in the country only to lose their fortunes on their return to London.

CHAPTER ELEVEN

A Fire in Pudding Lane

Shortly before midnight on Saturday, September 1st, 1666, Thomas Farynor, King Charles' baker, and his daughter Hannah, climbed the rickety stairs from the bakery to their bedroom in their wood-framed house in Pudding Lane, near London Bridge.

Two hours later they were awake, gasping and choking in thick clouds of acrid smoke that billowed up these stairs. A pile of faggots and dry brushwood for the oven had somehow caught alight; the whole ground floor was an inferno.

Farynor quickly realized that escape down the stairs was impossible, so, seizing his daughter's arm, he pulled her to a garret window and helped her out on to the roof. Then, calling to his two servants to follow him, he climbed out himself. His manservant obeyed; the other, a maid, stayed behind screaming in terror, as afraid of the height as of the fire.

Hunched up, on hands and feet, the three frightened people crept over the tiles to the roof of the house next door. They reached this and then realized that the maid was not with them. By then it was too late to go back for her. Their house and bakery was aroar with flames; the maid's screams of terror were soon drowned by the crash of falling beams.

Thus, in that hour, as the capital slept, the Great Fire of London began, and claimed its first life.

The baker's house in Pudding Lane, 'not ten doores from Thames Street', as one contemporary described it, was one of a double row of tumbledown Tudor buildings that stretched down the hill almost to the Thames-side at Fresh Wharf. It was a narrow, rather dark street, held to be 'fitter for a wheelbarrow' than for a cart or carriage, paved with rough cobbles, and typical of many in this congested part of the City. The houses leaned drunkenly towards each other, their overhanging gables almost meeting above the centre of the roadway. For the most part they were built of timber, with walls weatherproofed with a thick coating of pitch; this was peeling off in hard black flakes after a long spell of dry, hot weather.

As well as the perpetual sour smell of the river, which was a sewer and depository for all other refuse, a state of affairs very much apparent at low tide when the exposed banks of stinking grey mud laying steaming in the sunshine, Pudding Lane was also strong with certain indigenous smells. Thames Street was the centre of the City's wharves and warehouses. On to each of the many lanes and alleys that branched away from it opened storage sheds and cellars, packed with casks of oil, brandy, pitch and tar; boxes of sugar, butter, and leather for the Cordwainers' Company. On the wharves near by stood stacks of timber and pyramids of coal. All these stocks were easy to ignite and the store houses were crammed, for after the plague the merchants lived in hopes of early prosperity with the return of the rich to the capital. Many also believed that the end of the war against the Dutch was in sight, and this would increase future trade. But instead of bringing work and wealth to London, these expensive and highly combustible materials essential to prosperity were to provide the fuel for ruin.

At first, the fire which gutted Farynor's house confined itself to a few buildings round about; indeed, a merchant who lived next door had time to remove all his goods before his property was burned down. Others followed his example, and soon Pudding Lane was strewn with heaps of furniture: chairs, beds, boxes, plus masses of trading stock; all this effectively blocked its narrow way to anyone who came to help fight the fire. There was no proper fire brigade in all the kingdom but certain City

Companies owned pumps and engines and sets of leather and metal buckets which could be used should their own premises catch fire. But on that September midnight no one thought of seeking any outside aid; a fire was no new thing in the City anyway and they all seemed to burn out quite quickly; so the flames marched from house to house, unchecked and unhindered.

Until two o'clock in the morning, the blaze was still localized, but then a keen wind, sweeping in from the north-east, began to fan the flames. Showers of sparks were carried across to the next street west, Fish Street Hill. They quickly set fire to piles of hay and straw in the yard of the Star Inn, a coaching house, and soon the wooden galleried building was burning like a torch.

At three o'clock, someone awoke the Lord Mayor, Sir Thomas Bludworth, at his home in Gracechurch Street (above Fish Street Hill). He arrived with some of his City Officers, annoyed at being roused from bed in the early hours for such an unimportant reason as a fire; he had been drinking heavily on the previous evening, and an early call was not to his liking.

After taking a cursory look at damage so far, he gave his opinion on the whole matter. 'Pish,' he said irritably, 'A woman might pisse it out.'

As an anonymous lawyer of the Middle Temple wrote later, Sir Thomas, also known as 'Bludder', was 'not long ere undeceived of his foolish confidence'.

In fairness to Bludworth, however, fires were frequent in the narrow streets, so thick with houses; often several buildings closely clustered together, and sometimes a whole row would burn to the ground before anyone except those immediately concerned did anything about it. Although a more serious outbreak sometimes occurred, such fires usually burned themselves out before widespread damage compelled the authorities to take notice. The fuel which the fire fed in Pudding Lane, and the breeze that fanned it, changed its character entirely. Indeed, by the time the Lord Mayor arrived, the fire had a firm grip on the Lane, and was also spreading rapidly down

Fish Street Hill, which led directly to the entrance to London Bridge.

Samuel Pepys and his family had long been in bed, but some of his maids had stayed up late to prepare for a dinner which the diarist was to give next day.

'Jane [one of these maids] called us up about three in the morning, to tell us of a great fire they saw in the City,' he wrote later. 'So I rose, and slipped on my night gown, and went to her window; and thought it to be on the back-side of Marke-lane at the farthest; but being unused to such fires as followed, I thought it far enough off; and so went to bed again, and to sleep.'

While he slept the wind rose even more strongly, and the situation worsened hourly. This finally became clear to Bludworth, and so with some other City magistrates he organized a chain of leather buckets with which citizens, awakened by hammering on their front doors and throwing stones up against their windows, attempted to douse the blaze by throwing water on it. But the fire was already too hot and too strong for them; it reached out two long arms of flame down Pudding Lane and Fish Street Hill; these met in Thames Street, and thereafter burned with redoubled vigour as the packed storehouses took light.

Attempts were then made to bring in some of the rudimentary fire-engines owned by the City companies and parishes, but it proved impossible to make much use of them owing to the exceptional narrowness of the alleys and lanes, the piles of furniture and effects dragged out into the street, and the crowds of people who came to see what was happening. According to a contemporary report, 'the engines had no liberty to play...but some of them were tumbled down in the river, and among the rest, that of Clerkenwell, esteemed one of the best'.

The first fire-engine, a German invention, had appeared in London thirty-three years earlier, and had been used against the fire which destroyed a large number of houses on London Bridge in 1633. It simply consisted of a crude pump, mounted on a carriage, that could project a stream of water for some distance; but it was very heavy, unwieldy and badly suited to steep, cobbled streets. Smaller appliances were 'three-man fire squirts', which ejected thin streams of water. No fire brigade existed in London for another hundred years, and it took hours to raise the parish officers and officials of the Liveried Companies and from them extract the necessary permission to use any privately owned and run machines.

By seven o'clock in the morning, any chance of checking the blaze with buckets or engines had gone. A long stretch of Thames Street was well alight, and periodic explosions marked the firing of stores of pitch, brimstone, oil and spirits. The heat became so great that no one could stand nearer than 100 paces from the edge of the conflagration. One spectator wrote afterwards that the deadly 'sulphureous' nature of the fire at this stage was evidenced by 'the melting of bells, iron, pots, glasses and other metallick things and in the calcining of stones and bricks'. From the molten metal to which the church bell of All-Hallows-the-Great was reduced, a new bell was cast and hung in the rebuilt church a few years after the Great Fire.

Fed by the blazing wares of the Thames Street merchants, the fire engulfed the church of St Magnus the Martyr, which stood at the entrance to London Bridge. The flames completely gutted the building within minutes; then a sheet of fire burst out through the roof with a mighty roar, rising far above the surrounding rooftops. The flames rushed on towards the bridge with its narrow roadway and packed masses of timber houses on each side, supported above the water by nineteen thick stone arches. About fifty houses had been destroyed at the northern end of the bridge in the fire thirty-three years earlier. All had since been rebuilt, but now the Great Fire swept through the gate-house and out on to the bridge. By eight o'clock in the morning, a third of its length was burning.

Gables and roofs crashed down in showers of sparks across the narrow thoroughfare, making it impassable, while other houses, burning fiercely, toppled backwards into the river.

Clouds of hissing steam billowed up as the smoking and flaming debris hit the water. The whole bridge seemed certain to be destroyed; it would have been had the fire not been checked when it reached an empty space too wide to jump between the buildings.

Those who lived on the bridge had received ample warning of the danger, and so not one life was lost; but the survival of the southern half of the ancient structure was surprising. Sparks from the blaze were carried right across the river to the City of Southwark on the south bank, where a stable in Horse Shoe Alley, near Winchester Stairs, caught fire; two houses burned away within half an hour, before labourers with sledge hammers and iron bars broke down a third and so checked the blaze.

At the entrance to London Bridge, the fire again split into two directions. One wall of flame was blown westwards along Thames Street by the fierce prevailing wind, and threatened the main body of the City. So greedily did the flames leap from property to property that Vincent called the sight 'the astonishment of the beholders'. Indeed its speed and ferocity stupefied everyone; they could do nothing but watch its progress with a kind of mesmerized terror.

'All Men stood amazed, as Spectators only, no Man knowing what Remedy to apply, nor the Magistrates what Orders to give,' Lord Clarendon, the Lord Chancellor, wrote later.

By this time none but desperate measures could have helped to prevent the fire from consuming the capital. Without exception, contemporary reporters of the early stages of the disaster indicted Bludworth and his subordinates for their lack of effort at a time when all could still be saved. Pepys, commenting on September 7th, when the City was no more than a smouldering ruin, wrote that 'People do all the world over cry out at the simplicity of my Lord Mayor in generall; and more particularly in this business of the fire, laying it all upon him'.

According to Vincent, the confusion into which the Lord Mayor and some of his brother magistrates were thrown had meant that 'councel is taken away: and London, so famous for wisdom and dexterity, can now find neither brains nor hands to prevent its ruine'.

Far more deadly were the charges that Clarendon later made. He stated unequivocally that although Bludworth hastened to Pudding Lane, 'his Consternation equal to that of other men', he completely failed either to assert his authority as chief City magistrate or to take any decisive action. When he arrived, the wind had not yet spread the flames to the warehouses, and prompt action could probably have isolated and localized the blaze. But all that was academic as the fire roared on, and before daybreak St Margaret's Church in Fish Street Hill began to burn.

Citizens beseeched the Lord Mayor to pull down houses in the path of the fire to create gaps which the flames could not leap; the fire would thus die because of lack of fuel. Bludworth could not bring himself to authorize this imperative step. 'Who will pay for the damage?' he asked cautiously, fearing that the householders concerned might have a case against the City. As the fire crackled past with the black soot and dust of burning buildings settling on everyone and everything like some strange feathery rain, he was again implored to give this permission. Again he refused, adding that he 'durst not do it without the consent of the owners'.

The warehouses were all burning and in the words of Archdeacon Laurence Echard, the 'raging East Wind fomented it to an incredible Degree, which in a moment rais'd the Fire from the Bottom to the Tops of Houses, and scatter'd prodigious Flakes in all Places, which were mounted so vastly high into the Air, as if Heaven and Earth were threatened with the same Conflagration'. The fury of the flames, he added, 'soon became insuperable against all the Arts of Men, and Power of Engines'.

By midday, the Lord Mayor at last realized that the only hope was to authorize the demolition of properties in the path of the fire, as he had been advised hours previously. 'Firehooks' – huge iron hooks attached to long poles and ropes – were kept in churches and official buildings for such a purpose. Men would swarm up the walls and bury the hooks in the roof trees of the houses. Then teams of men and horses would pull the ropes until the timber frame of the property fell apart and the whole shoddy structure collapsed. Now Bludworth gave orders for this to begin, but once more his judgement was wrong. He began the demolitions too close to the fire, misjudging the speed of its progress. In some streets, the fire took hold on the empty, abandoned houses as the sweating teams were still desperately trying to pull them apart. In others, there was no time to clear the huge piles of wooden debris from the streets after a house had been torn down before the fire lit them; they only served to feed the flames until they reached the next line of houses.

The east wind was possibly the supreme factor in the destruction of London. Throughout the four days in which most of the damage was done, it blew so strongly that it had the same effect as a gigantic bellows, magnified by the narrow streets along the Thames. Whichever way people ran they seemed to be in its teeth, for the twisting lanes and alleys were like tunnels that increased its pressure. This produced strange results; in some places the flames seemed to fly in spirals around certain houses persuading the superstitious that 'this fire was miraculous'.

In the Inner Temple, some barristers decided that it would not be fitting for them to save the furnishings and law books of their learned friends who were out of London for the summer vacation 'because it was against the Law to break up any man's Chambers'. One observer noted that 'the unusual negligence at first, and a confidence of easily quenching the fire, on a sudden changed into a general consternation and despondency, all people choosing rather by flight to save their Goods than by a vigorous opposition to save their Houses and the City'.

This pattern was repeated all over the capital. People feverishly dragged their belongings from their homes and shops to what they imagined was safety, leaving the fire to creep up on them unchecked. The flames moved so swiftly that in many cases before they had time to remove their possessions farther than the street outside their front doors the houses were alight behind them.

Pepys was awake about seven that morning, and at once looked out of the window to see whether the fire had grown during the night; he thought that it did not look 'so much as it was, and further off'. A few minutes later he realized his mistake.

'By and by Jane comes and tells me that she hears that above 300 houses have been burned down tonight by the fire we saw, and that it is now burning down all Fish Street, by London Bridge. So I made myself ready presently, and walked to the Tower; and there got up upon one of the high places, Sir J. Robinson's [1] little son going up with me; and there I did see the houses at that end of the bridge all on fire, and an infinite great fire on this and the other side the end of the bridge; which, among other people, did trouble me for poor little Michell and Sarah on the bridge.

'So down, with my heart full of trouble, to the Lieutenant of the Tower, who tells me that it begun this morning in the King's baker's house in Pudding Lane, and that it hath burned down St Magnus' Church and most part of Fish Street already.'

Pepys rushed down to the waterside where boats plied for hire, like river taxis: one carried him downstream to London Bridge, where he saw 'a lamentable fire. Poor Michell's house, as far as the Old Swann, already burned that way, and the fire running further, that in a very little time, it got as far as the Steele Yard, while I was there'.

The Steele Yard, headquarters of the prosperous Hanse merchants from Germany, stood at least a quarter of a mile west of the outbreak, near where Cannon Street Station is now. Between these points the whole Thames bank was blazing fiercely. The Fishmonger's Hall, between Thames Street and the river, was gutted; so were the maze of narrow little alleys which gave access to the wharves: Churchyard Alley, Red Cross Alley,

Black Raven Alley, Catherine Wheele Alley, Old Swan Alley, Red Bull Alley.

Thames Street also continued to blaze, and, as the day wore on, the flames began to creep farther and farther back from the river, attacking St Michael's Lane, Crooked Lane and St Martin's Lane. Soon the fire had devastated an area the shape of a bow; its string was the straight line of the river bank and its crescent steadily widened to encroach farther and farther upon the City.

While Pepys was there that morning, he saw the panic begin, 'every body endeavouring to remove their goods, and flinging into the river, or bringing them into lighters that lay off; poor people staying in their houses as long as till the very fire touched them, and then running into boats, or clambering from one pair of stairs, by the waterside, to another'.

And then, out of all that tableau of devastation, Pepys' sharp eye caught one tiny detail: 'The poor pigeons were loth to leave their houses, but hovered about the windows and balconys, till they burned their wings and fell down.'

After remaining for an hour, he became highly alarmed. He had 'seen the fire rage every way; and nobody, to my sight, endeavouring to quench it, but to remove their goods, and leave all to the fire…and the wind mighty high, and driving it into the City; and everything, after so long a drought, proving combustible, even the very stones of churches'.

The fire burned on for 200 yards east of London Bridge against the wind, far enough to burn down another church, St Botolph's, Billingsgate, between Thames Street and the river.

More serious was its spread to the north. By noon, the flames had reached the church of St Laurence Poultney, not fifty yards from Cannon Street. The horrified spectators saw flying sparks ignite its lofty spire, one of the highest of the forest of steeples which rose clear of the City skyline. In a short while the steeple was enveloped in flames, which melted its leaden skin, while the main body of the church underneath was left untouched. Then the spire collapsed in a mass of flaming debris which then ignited the main fabric of the building. Quickly it burned to the ground.

At lunch with his family at Sayes Court, Deptford, John Evelyn received intelligence of the fire and at once 'took Coach and went to the bank side in Southwark, where we beheld that dismal spectacle, the whole Citty in dreadful flames neere the Water side, and [it] had now consumed all the houses from the bridge, all Thames Streete and upwards towards Cheape side, downe to Three Cranes' – a wharf just west of the Steele Yard.

By early afternoon the fire had already wrought terrible havoc. The Dyers Hall and Watermens Hall, two more City Companies, lay in ruins; so did Coldharbour, a warren of tenements below Thames Street which had long been notorious as a hiding place for criminals and debtors on the run. At one side of the lane which led down from Thames Street to Coldharbour stood the little church of All Hallows-the-Less, which had been gutted in a few minutes. Next to this building was a more imposing church. All Hallows-the-Great, with a very fine tower. The blaze swept through its choir and side chapels, and left only a blackened skeleton of beams and walls. Afterwards, only the tower remained to mark the spot where the church had once stood.

London's churches were three times as numerous as those of any other city in the world, but within four days eighty-seven of the City's ninety-seven parish churches lay smouldering in ruins. Although Sir Christopher Wren used some of their debris for rebuilding, thirty-six of these devastated churches were never replaced.

A lawyer from the Middle Temple went up the Thames by boat to see the fire early in the afternoon, landed at Paul's Wharf and began to walk towards the fire. 'We were stopped in Cannon Street by the abundance of goods and carts with which it was filled,' he wrote afterwards. 'Here we met my Lord Mayor on horseback, with a few attendants, looking like one affrighted out of his wits.'

Early that day, the City had been thrown into a panic by rumours that the fire was the fiendish work of foreign incendiaries, or Papists intent upon the destruction of what they considered a heathen city. The lawyer found the streets full of people, certain that the French and Dutch were on the way. 'It was already imagined the design of the French and Dutch in revenge of what our forces had lately done at Brandaris upon the island Schelling.' (The British Fleet had burnt that town five or six weeks before.) 'The riding of a hot-headed fellow through the streets (with more speed and fear than wit) crying "Arm, Arm!" had frightened most of the people out of the churches.'

Later, he passed a party of forty horses of the Lifeguard in Cornhill, some companies of the King's regiments, and detachments of the Train-bands (London's citizen-soldiery) marching into the City.

Vincent was another who saw these train-bands plodding through the streets to look for 'Outlandishmen' following reports that foreigners had been seen throwing fireballs into houses. The rumours became more and more lurid as the day wore on, ending in the widespread conviction that at least 4,000 Frenchmen and other adherents of the Church of Rome were roaming the capital, armed with swords and daggers and intent on firing as many parishes as they could. As a stern opponent of the Roman Church, Dr Vincent was convinced that the Great Fire was 'a Papish design'.

All through that fatal Sunday, lack of water hindered the efforts of the fire-fighters. The area of the City the fire had attacked on the first day was supplied from the Thames by several 'water machines' underneath some of the London Bridge arches, at the northern end. The fast-flowing river water was collected by scoops in great wheels which forced it through wooden and leaden pipes that then carried it for nearly half a mile into the City.

This complicated and leaky installation had been set up seventy years earlier; it was the custom when fire broke out in any neighbourhood for those concerned to punch holes in these pipes and draw off what water they needed to put it out. By the time of the Great Fire, a few crude hydrants had been placed in the pipes, but again they had to be smashed in many places to fill the buckets.

Early that Sunday morning the pipes ran dry, for the flames that damaged London Bridge also put the water wheels out of action. Men standing helplessly with empty buckets watched the flames double their intensity, until sheets of fire hundreds of feet long were blowing across the tops of neighbouring houses, now and then igniting properties up to a hundred yards away from the main conflagration.

Samuel Pepys took a coach to the Palace at Whitehall and asked for an early audience with the King. It was granted immediately. Pepys told Charles bluntly that unless he would order houses to be pulled down, 'nothing could stop the fire'.

The King commanded Pepys to return, and find the Lord Mayor and instruct him 'to spare no houses whatever, but to pull down any building in the path of the fire'. The King's brother, the Duke of York, added that Bludworth could have as many soldiers as he needed.

Pepys hurried away and borrowed a coach to take him back to St Paul's, where the crowds were so dense that his coach could make no progress, so he left it and continued on foot through Watling Street. His way was constantly impeded, 'every creature coming away loaden with goods to save, and here and there, sick people carried away in beds'. The street was jammed with carts overloaded with furniture and household fittings, while the poorer people struggled along with fantastic loads upon their backs.

Already carts were in such great demand that their owners were asking £5 a load; within days their price would climb to £30 – in normal times more than enough to buy several carts and horses outright. The Thames watermen were also grateful to the fire, for every available boat was hired to carry persons and property from the blazing riverside. When the final tally of losses from the catastrophe was reckoned up, an estimated two million pounds had been spent on removing goods from the City.

At last Pepys found the Lord Mayor in Cannon Street; the fire was so close that they could both feel its heat although the street itself was still free of flame. It was at once obvious that Bludworth was completely unhinged by the disaster. He was 'like a man spent, with a handkercher about his neck'. When he heard the orders from King Charles, he cried, 'like a fainting woman', 'Lord! What can I do? I am spent: people will not obey me. I have been pulling down houses; but the fire overtakes us faster than we can do it.'

Bludworth added that he needed no more soldiers, 'and that, for himself, he must go and refresh himself, having been up all night. So he left me...'

This was the man in whom the City had placed its trust; a fellow citizen described him as 'a person delighting more in drinking and dancing than is necessary for such a magistrate'. His authority was little regarded, yet a Lord Mayor of different calibre could have changed the face of history with his deeds.

With no leaders, no instructions, people wandered aimlessly about, telling each other how dreadful the fire was, and yet doing nothing to stop its march. One man, Isaac Houblon, a rich merchant with his fine clothing streaked by dirt and his face running with sweat, stood at the door of his house in Dowgate, receiving some of his brother's goods, which had been carried out from houses already blazing. The furniture and stores had twice been shifted already; soon they had to be moved a third time when Houblon's house was also swept away by the advancing line of fire. This case was typical of hundreds; and yet a determined attempt to confine the fire in its early stage could have saved both houses and their contents.

Instead of attending Sunday services in the churches, people carried their possessions to church and dumped their carpets and clothes into the pews and aisles, in the hope that the thick stone walls would afford some protection from the flames.

Pepys returned home to dinner, but soon afterwards was out again watching the fire. He and a friend, Mr Moone, walked back through the City streets, where now all was pandemonium.

Men and women ran aimlessly about in the roadways, some crying in terror, others cursing, others searching desperately for friends or relatives or people to whom they had entrusted their belongings. Horses and carts were now so numerous they were 'ready to run over one another'. Owners were whipping their huge Shire horses as they stumbled over the cobbles, pulling wagons of goods out of Cannon Street and up to Lombard Street, although Cannon Street had itself received tons of evacuated property only a few hours previously.

By late afternoon it was apparent that no act of man was likely to stop the fire; only a change in the weather could prevent its farther spread. That change did not come. The drought which had already lasted for weeks showed no sign of breaking, and the easterly wind continued to blow as strongly as ever, fanning the flames to a white-hot fury.

From Westminster, King Charles and his brother sailed downstream in the Royal Barge to see for themselves what was happening in the City; and Pepys, who had also taken again to the water, met them and accompanied them to Queenhithe. The King ordered that more houses must be demolished with all speed, but the men had not time to clear a substantial channel before the flames overtook them and they had to begin again farther up the street.

That afternoon the Thames was as thick with lighters, barges and smaller craft as it had been during the latter weeks of plague. Only this time, instead of containing families and friends with as much food as the vessels could carry, they were loaded to the gunwales with the contents of entire households. In the water, wooden chairs, beds, chests of drawers and tables, thrown into the river by desperate people who could neither hire nor afford a boat, bobbed along haphazardly. Some were roped together, but even so their owners held little hope of recovering them. Yet this slight possibility was preferable to certain loss in the fire.

One possession seemed prized above all else by many families. 'I observed,' wrote Pepys, 'that hardly one lighter or boat in three that had the goods of a house in, but there was a pair of virginalls in it.' The virginal – similar to the spinet or small harpsichord – was the most favoured musical instrument of the time. It took the name from the virtuous young ladies who would sing prettily to their own accompaniment.

Before nightfall the wind increased, and great clouds of billowing smoke and showers of sparks lifted high above the riverside and over the water, finally to be blown back across the City. The boats scurried like busy water-beetles to and fro over the river to dump goods and refugees at landing stages at Southwark and other points on the south bank that were still free of fire.

These craft frequently collided with other boats hired by sightseers, some of whom treated the outing as an excursion; many were drunk, and in the dense smoke clouds which often lay low upon the water, neither crew could see the other. The rude shouts and jokes of the revellers in the smoke mingled with the anguished cries of people who saw their entire worldly possessions disappearing into the darkness. Small pieces of still-burning fabric and paper – even slivers of wood – floated by on the breeze. Some settled on the boats, others on houses not yet reached by fire. Within seconds they were blazing furiously.

Bad as the sight of black smoke and yellow flames had been by day, the scene became infinitely more terrible by night. The glow from the flames turned orange and rose high into the darkness. By its brilliance the dismal, badly lit streets of London were illuminated as never before. The night burned far brighter than the day; the fire was many times stronger than it had been only a few hours earlier, yet still nothing drastic was attempted to quench it; and still those not immediately affected did not realize that it could possibly affect them. There have been worse cases of official inertia and private folly, but not many and not much.

People still crowded the riverside in boats, on foot, riding in coaches and carts, to watch the flames crackle and roar unchecked northwards into Cannon Street and Eastcheap, as though this were a display of pyrotechnics put on for their benefit.

Families whose houses had already been burned had nowhere to go and frequently no work – for often their workshops were also destroyed. They also had no food, and worse, no hope, for no provision was made for them and they knew that none would be.

Archdeacon Echard considered that 'the distracted Looks of so many Citizens, the Wailings of miserable Women, and the Cries of poor Children and decrepid old People' were 'the most killing Sight of all'. Those fortunate enough to have friends outside the immediate arc of fire sought shelter for the night with them, but other families, their homes reduced to ashes, wandered wretchedly about the streets until dawn.

In a wide strip immediately around the fire, all but an optimistic few packed up their households in feverish haste. Throughout that night the narrow streets were heaped with piles of furniture and goods, and choked with handcarts, horse carts and wheelbarrows hired to carry away whatever could be saved. Already the evacuation was turning into a rout; before it had finished, thousands were sleeping rough in the fields outside the City walls.

Among the sightseers during the evening were Mr and Mrs Pepys and three friends, who, after their long sojourn upon the water, were in a little alehouse on the Thames bank some distance from the western fringe of the fire. As the darkness deepened, they 'saw the fire grow; and, as it grew darker, appeared more and more; and in corners and upon steeples, and between churches and houses, as far as we could see up the hill of the City, in a most horrid, malicious, bloody flame'.

As Clarendon remarked on that first night of the Great Fire of London, it seemed like 'a foretaste of the Last Judgment'. Pepys wisely decided that he should prepare his own belongings for flight while he still had time. His servants carried out most of the furnishings into the garden, 'it being brave, dry, and moonshine and warm weather', while a friend, Mr Hater, helped Pepys pile his iron chests into the cellars. 'We did put Mr Hater, poor man! to bed a little,' noted Pepys, 'but he got very little rest, so much noise being in my house, taking down of goods.'

Thousands were in the same predicament, for by now 'no Distance was thought secure', and many who went to bed thankful to be at a great distance from the fire awoke before morning with 'their own Houses being in a Flame'. For most, however, whether for worry or wonderment, it was a sleepless night.

One who had stayed upon the river well into the evening, to see the fire outlined against the blackness 'with all the horror and dreadfulness imaginable', was haunted by the spectacle. 'I kept my bed but few hours,' he wrote sadly to a friend, 'and slept less.'

Before King Charles went to bed he ordered the Earl of Craven to give what assistance he could to Bludworth and his fellow magistrates, and agreed that troops should patrol the city to guard against deliberate incendiaries. During the night, a large crowd collected outside the Palace, shouting and chanting, beseeching the King to save the City. The hubbub awoke him and, as he looked eastwards towards the burning City, where the tongues of flame leapt from a devastated area of more than forty acres, he saw the spires and steeples shimmering in the heat and haze.

King Charles, in the days to come, was to lead the struggle to preserve as much as possible of the capital; and later do much to ensure that a new City of London arose from the ashes of the old.

The same cannot be said for all his Court. One of them, a Mr Hugh May, went so far as to assure the King that the fire was His

Majesty's greatest blessing since the Restoration. His theory was that it had effectively destroyed a rebellious City, always a potential danger to the Crown. Charles angrily rejected this suggestion, and refused to pay heed to the expectations of the courtiers that he would not allow Londoners 'to repair and build…up again to be a Bit in his Mouth and a Bridle upon His Neck; but would keep all open, that his Troops might enter upon them whenever he thought necessary for his Service, there being no other way to govern that rude Multitude but by Force'.

Despite the tireless efforts of the King to halt the destruction from Monday onwards, such remarks were maliciously repeated all over London, and they did him great disservice. Some of the powerful merchant citizens even suspected he had deliberately instigated the fire, in order to destroy their power. Others, so Bishop Burnet noted, thought that the King's brother, the Duke of York, seemed 'a little too gay and negligent' as he rode about the fire-stricken city, and that 'his look and air discovered the pleasure he took in that dreadful spectacle'. There was, of course, not the slightest scrap of evidence against the Royal brothers, but everyone looked for scapegoats to excuse their own inertia; and if the scapegoat was Royal, then so much the better.

1. He was the Governor of the Tower.

CHAPTER TWELVE

The City Devoured

Monday was another dry and sunny day, and the east wind blew the fire farther into the heart of the City. Now no one had any doubt that all would be destroyed; there had never been a fire like this before in London. It seemed supreme, subduing all attempts to fight it. By the afternoon, smoke clouds from burning London were drifting over towns and villages more than fifty miles away, and even in Oxford, sixty miles to the west, Anthony à Wood remarked that 'the sunshine was much darkened'.

On the Monday, more than thirty hours after the fire began, King Charles and his Council acted: but although their plans were good, they came at least a day too late. Nothing could redeem the fatal neglect of Sunday, and by Monday evening the flames had devoured an area almost three times as large as it had done on the previous day. By midnight most of the City's main streets and buildings were in ruins, including the Royal Exchange, then London's most fashionable shopping centre.

Like most Londoners, Pepys was out early on that Monday morning, determined to save what he could of his own from the fire. In the event, the fire missed Seething Lane and he did not lose his home.

'About four o'clock in the morning,' he wrote, 'my Lady Batten sent me a cart to carry away all my money and plate, and best things, to Sir W Rider's at Bednall Greene, which I did, riding myself in my night gown, in the cart; and, Lord! to see how the streets and the highways are crowded with people running and riding, and getting of carts at any rate to fetch away things.

'I find Sir W Rider tired with being called up all night, and receiving things from several friends. His house full of goods, and much of Sir W Batten's and Sir W Pen's. I am eased at my heart to have my treasure so well secured.'

As Pepys returned home, he had to fight a way through the throngs of people and vehicles trying to escape from London. Neither he nor his wife slept at all that night but, tired as they were, they and the servants spent the whole of the following day 'labouring to get away the rest of our things, and did get Mr Tooker to get me a lighter to take them in, and we did carry them, myself some, over Tower Hill, which was by this time full of people's goods...and down to the lighter, which lay at the next quay, above Tower Dock.

'And here was my neighbour, Mrs —, with her pretty child, and some few of her things, which I did willingly give way to be saved with mine; but there was no passing anything through the postern, the crowd was so great.'

The scene at the postern was typical of many all over the City on that second day. Suddenly aware of the growing danger, people literally put their households on their backs and flocked to the City gates and riverside quays not yet touched by the flames. 'Now there is a general remove in the City,' recorded Vincent, 'and that in a greater hurry than before the Plague; their goods being in greater danger by the fire than their persons were by the sickness.'

Within hours the narrow lanes and streets were jammed firm with struggling men staggering under gigantic bundles wrapped in blankets; with carts, their horses rearing up, nostrils wide, terrified of the smell of burning. Gangs of men trying to drag in the fire engines could make no headway. The authorities attempted to impose some order upon the chaos by banning all further carts from the fire area. This only brought out a horde of labourers from the Liberties and out-parishes who, sensing the opportunity of making money, flocked into the City to offer their services as carriers.

John Dryden, in his poem, 'Annus Mirabilis', part of which is an heroic description of the Great Fire, wrote:

> The rich grow suppliant, and the poor grow proud.
> Those offer mighty gain, and these ask more.
> So void of pity is th' ignoble crowd,
> When others' ruine may increase their store.

Instead of making some concerted stand against the fire, time 'was all in this lost labour spent', and householders bribed, cajoled, threatened and blustered with only one end in view: to salvage as much as they could of their own property. Fantastic prices were asked and received for porters and vehicles. 'Now Carts, and Drays, and Coaches and Horses,' wrote Vincent, 'as many as could have entrance into the City were loaden, and any money is given for help, £5, £10, £20, £30 for a cart.'

Some country folk, who brought in their vehicles hoping for a quick profit, 'had the conscience to accept of the highest price, which the Citizens did then offer in their extremity; I am mistaken if such money do not burn worse than the Fire out of which it was raked'.

Merchants and their labourers trundled barrels of oil, casks of spirits and wines along the streets. The day was almost unbelievably hot, with the blazing sun and the warmth of the fire. Others dragged trolleys piled with portable belongings towards the City gates. 'Every one now becomes a porter to himself and scarcely a back either of a man or woman that hath strength, but had a burden on it,' observed Vincent.

Many awakened from sleep by the heat of the flames or the warning cries of their friends, escaped with little more than the clothes they wore. Others had to abandon their carts and wheelbarrows when streets became impassable. Some were blocked by debris from houses pulled down in the path of the flames; in others, the roadway had been torn up in the rush to uncover and breach water pipes; and at street junctions, soldiers were already posted in an endeavour to seal off the fire area. To avoid the hold-ups, many refugees took to the side streets and back alleys, which within hours were as badly blocked.

Three men who walked into the City from the Temple at about three o'clock that afternoon, and toured the western fringe of the blaze as far as Cornhill, had the greatest difficulty in making their way even on foot. One wrote afterwards that the streets were 'barricaded with goods, carts, coaches, and distracted crowds'.

The King, like most of his subjects, had also been up early that Monday morning. Soon after ten o'clock he was being rowed up and down the river in the Royal Barge, trying to gauge the extent of the fire by the riverside. He had already relieved Bludworth from further responsibility, and appointed his brother, the Duke of York, to take supreme control in the City. He also ordered that 'fire posts' should be set up at strategic points in the path of the fire, at Temple Bar in Fleet Street, Clifford's Inn Gardens, Fetter Lane, Shoe Lane and Cow Lane. The constables of the parishes concerned had to muster a hundred men for this duty. Each station was further strengthened by thirty soldiers, under an officer; and members of the Privy Council, 'noblemen and other gentlemen', under the overall authority of the Duke of York, were empowered to hire any additional labour required and to pay a shilling a head to those who were 'diligent all night'. Five pounds' worth of bread, cheese and beer were allotted to each fire post as their rations.

As this force took up its positions, the wholesale pulling down of houses around the perimeter of the fire began, but the only methods they could use – hooks and ropes – were far too slow. Hourly, the arc of fire widened as it spread north and west, and gave no time to pull down houses and drag away the debris from the approaching flames. As the official account published in the *London Gazette* expressed it, 'many attempts were made to prevent the spreading of it by pulling down houses, and making great intervals, but all in vain, the fire seising upon the timber and rubbish and so continuing itself, even through those spaces and raging in a bright flame all Monday and Tuesday'.

One effective means remained of demolishing enough property to create a substantial ditch around the fire: to blow up entire streets with barrels of gunpowder. They used this drastic remedy on the following day, but by then the Great Fire had already done its worst, and most of the City was a mass of smoking rubble, from which rose the blackened and empty shells of brick and stone buildings.

'Some stout seamen', from the Deptford and Woolwich dockyards, suggested using gunpowder very early on, so John Evelyn declared, 'early enough to have saved the whole Citty, but some tenacious and avaricious men, Aldermen &c, would not permitt, because their houses must have been of the first'.

The hopeless task facing demolition gangs in pulling down houses with the wind blowing the fire towards them, was twice emphasized during that Monday. As King Charles passed Queenhithe early in the morning, one of the teams was feverishly tearing down timber houses around the harbour and the market place just behind it, for only four houses to the east of the harbour had up to that moment survived the fire. As the King's barge sailed by, a spectator on the south bank of the river at Southwark saw flames engulf these four houses. A sheet of fire flew up from their roofs and the wind blew it across the gap the labourers had just made, and twenty houses beyond. It then ignited the turret of a large house in Thames Street and took hold within seconds. Within hours another three-quarters of a mile of the riverside, as far as the Temple, had been razed to the ground.

In the late afternoon, as the fire roared northwards into Cornhill, it again encountered a substantial gap which 200 men had worked with hooks and hammers and axes to make. As they stood back, shielding their eyes against the heat, piles of rafters and doors they had dragged into the streets to be carted away suddenly caught fire. Within seconds the flames leapt the gap they had just made; their work was all in vain. Had gunpowder been used then, or better still, on Sunday, the fire could have been contained within a much smaller area.

After the abortive attempt to check the flames at Queenhithe, they burned on westwards along the bank, and northwards towards St Paul's Cathedral. The shore installations at Queenhithe Harbour were reduced to a heap of smouldering ashes, and the flames ran right along the wharves to Baynards Castle at Blackfriars. The castle, which for 240 years had stood sentinel over the City at its west end – as had the Tower in the east – was soon burning fiercely. Its towers and battlements of flint-coloured stone, abutting directly upon the water, were blackened with smoke.

Eastwards along the river bank from London Bridge the spread was slower, for the fire had to burn in the teeth of the blustering wind. But even here the blaze fired Billingsgate at about six o'clock in the evening, causing great alarm that it might reach the Tower and the arsenal there.

To the north the flames made their most terrible inroads. In a 300-yard strip stretching from where the Mansion House now stands right down to Blackfriars, seventeen churches and dozens of streets and alleys were devastated. Among the churches was that of St Michael Paternoster Royal in College Hill, north of Thames Street, which housed the tomb of Dick Whittington, four times Lord Mayor of London. Although the church was rebuilt by Sir Christopher Wren, the tomb and the mortal remains of the most famous Lord Mayor of London were entirely destroyed.

Cannon Street was soon devastated from end to end, Eastcheap was well alight, and the bow of fire swept northwards into the City centre. 'A dreadful bow it was,' said Vincent, 'such as mine eyes had never before seen; a bow which had God's arrow in it, with a flaming point.'

By midday Gracechurch Street (which Pepys always called Gracious Street) was alight. The fire seemed inexorable; no one and nothing could halt the flames.

Lombard Street, the centre of London's banking houses, was ablaze by early afternoon, and the flames quickly swept right along, reaching Poultry by the evening. Fenchurch Street also began to burn at its western end. As the blaze found fresh fuel in Lombard Street, the flames raced farther north up the side streets to Cornhill, a wide road lined on both sides with the premises of the most prosperous merchants, and one of the City's finest shopping centres. This street was also the home of many leading mercers; so strong was the wind, that scraps of charred silk were picked up at Windsor, Beaconsfield and even Henley, thirty-three miles away.

From the south side of Cornhill, it was only a short step to Threadneedle Street and the Royal Exchange, and the fire took this in its stride. The Exchange was one of the most handsome buildings in London. Its centrepiece was a high and slender tower of stone, with a large clock and two ornate balconies near its summit, topped by a striking grasshopper windvane. Beside the tower, a pillared and vaulted gateway gave entry to the huge courtyard surrounded by cloistered walks where the merchants did business. Set in the walls above were statues of every English monarch for the last 600 years. The Exchange had a long and imposing frontage to the north of Cornhill, which contained many shops specializing in rare and exotic goods: spices, ivories, amber.

One by one the statues of the kings reeled and fell into the flames; soon only a shell of stone remained, half filled with ash while the blackened faces stared sightlessly up at the charred galleries. Only the statue of its builder, Sir Thomas Gresham, remained unharmed. A rich store of spices, owned by the East India Company, next caught fire in cellars under the Exchange, and a strong smell like burning incense wafted across the stricken streets; later this was thought to be evidence that the Great Fire had been a Papish plot. The flames ran on to engulf half Threadneedle Street and moved to within forty yards of Throgmorton Street before the day ended.

Throughout the afternoon the King and his brother rode about the streets to exhort the fire-fighters, carrying a bag containing £100 in coin, which he distributed among the most zealous, to encourage them to even greater efforts. Bishop Burnet remarked later: 'The King was never observed to be so much struck with anything in his whole life' as he was by the fire, and at times he dismounted to help labourers pull the firehooks.

On the next day, near the Temple and at Cripplegate, the two Royal brothers handed out water buckets in the chain, 'when they stood up to their ankles in water', and played a fire squirt into the burning houses for many hours, 'which people seeing, fell to work with effect, having so good fellow labourers'.

The King's actions and appearance with only a few attendants was not without risk. Many people who had lost property or position through his restoration to the throne would have liked to see him dead. But as the *London Gazette* pointed out later, 'a greater instance of the affections of this City (for Charles) could never have been given than hath now been given in this sad and deplorable accident, when, if at any time, disorder might have been expected from the losses, distraction and almost desperation of some persons in their private fortunes, thousands of people not having had habitations to cover them.

'And yet in all this time it hath been so far from any appearance of designs or attempts against His Majesties Government, that His Majesty and his Royal Brother, out of their care to stop and prevent the fire, frequently exposing their persons with very small attendants, in all parts of the town, sometimes even to be intermixed with those who laboured in the business, yet nevertheless there hath not been observed so much as a murmuring word to fall from any…beholding those frequent instances of His Majesties care of his people, forgot their own misery, and filled the streets with their prayers for His Majesty, whose trouble they seemed to compassionate before their own.'

Afterwards, the House of Commons presented him with a resolution of 'humble thanks' for his help in preventing the complete ruin of London.

Riots against the monarchy were lacking during the Great Fire, but riots against foreigners were not. Inflamed by wild rumours that the French and Dutch were spreading the blaze by hurling fireballs into premises well away from the main conflagration, crowds soon demanded vengeance. They picked up swords, knives, iron bars and axe heads that had survived the blaze and began to hunt foreigners through the streets.

It did not matter who they were or that they had lived all their lives in London, or even been born there: their names doomed them. Frenchmen and Dutchmen, who had lived and carried on business in London for generations, were seized and manhandled and their houses entered and ruined on the vague suspicion that they intended to fire them later as part of a plot to destroy the entire capital.

One of these poor wretches was a Dutch baker, Cornelius Rietveldt. When he lit his oven at his bakery in Westminster, the mob saw smoke coming out of the chimney and immediately rushed in, crying that 'the Dutch rogue' was setting the place on fire. They dragged him out into the street and beat him nearly to death. Others set about smashing his house and bakery, but only after they had first looted it of everything they could carry away.

The Duke of York, riding back to the Palace after his own efforts at fighting the fire, probably saved the man's life by ordering him to be committed to the Westminster Gatehouse. Rietveldt later petitioned successfully for his release, but financially he was ruined.

The belief that the fire was the design of England's enemies 'kindled such rage in the multitude that they killed one poor woman who had something in her apron they imagined fireballs, and sadly maimed or wounded divers others, especially Dutch and French, whose very birth was enough to condemn them'. The woman was first seen walking in Moorfields holding some young chicks in her apron. She 'was seized by the mob, who declared that she carried fireballs, and not only did they violently abuse her, but they beat her with sticks and cut off her breasts'.

Soon a foreign accent was alone sufficient to invoke violence, and only prompt action by the King, who sent his officers about the City to quiet the mob, prevented a massacre of all foreign nationals. Nevertheless, Lord Clarendon recorded that many were seized and 'after all the ill Usage that can consist in words, and some Blows and Kicks, were thrown into Prison'.

Later, Catholics also attracted the vengeance of the mass, and they were dragged struggling from their houses for no other reason than someone had heard them utter 'ambiguous words' about fire. Feelings ran so high that eventually anyone who dared to say he thought that the fire was probably accidental was suspected of being implicated in a conspiracy to destroy London. Reports of fresh outbursts of fire in distant parishes, neither confirmed nor denied, added to the general fear that the fire was the work of enemies.

One man who lived in Bread Street – destroyed by fire on Monday night – carried all his belongings to a friend's house in Holborn, then far from danger. But as he approached his destination he saw 'that very house, and none else near it, in a sudden flame'. He was sure that some enemy had set light to it with 'fireballs'. In fact, the driving wind was to blame; the 'fireballs' were simply smouldering flakes carried for miles by the wind.

Lord Clarendon described one example of the way in which fear banished reason. Lord Hollis and Lord Ashley, in charge of the Newgate Street area, saw a large, disorderly crowd, surrounding a dishevelled and frightened figure. His hat and cloak had been torn from him, and he was bruised and bleeding. Both men recognized him as a servant of the Portuguese Ambassador. Someone swore he had seen this man pull a fireball from his pocket and hurl it into a shop, which immediately burst into flames. He had fallen upon him, seizing his sword before he could draw; and at once a crowd had gathered. When they discovered that he did not even speak English, they began to beat him to death.

When Lord Hollis repeated their accusation in Portuguese to the servant, the man replied that he did not think he had even put his hand in his pocket. He had seen a piece of bread upon the ground, and had picked this up and laid it on a ledge inside a front door farther along the street. A superstition about bread was so common in Portugal that Clarendon declared that if the king of that country had seen a piece of bread upon the ground he would have picked it up and kept it until he saw a suitable place to put it down. Lord Hollis and Lord Ashley, with some of the angry citizens, went into the building and found the bread upon the ledge just as the man had said. The fire was still two doors away.

Despite this vindication, the noblemen put the prisoner under guard on the pretext that they wished to examine him later. Such excuses were frequently given to help protect the innocent, for a number of less fortunate aliens than the ambassador's man were murdered or lynched in the streets before their alleged 'crimes' could be submitted to any impartial inquiry. As one Dutchman said, 'It will be a long time before the people of London forget their rage against the foreigners.'

When the flames had died down, the jails were full of suspects, and although the King was convinced that the cause of the fire had been accidental, he did not dare to say too much in the teeth of popular opinion. Instead, he charged Sir John Keeling, the Lord Chief Justice, and others to examine the allegations against all prisoners charged with having any part in lighting it.

This panic found parallels all over the country, until it was wildly believed that the Papists intended to burn all England, town by town. At Oxford, so Anthony à Wood noted, the people were so suspicious that 'noe sorry fellow or woman could pass but they examined him, no gun or squib could go off but they thought it the fatall blow'.

On the last day of the London Fire, 'a butcher driving certaine oxen over Carfax cried to his beasts when he was under the window – "Hiup! Hiup!" – which, some taking for "Fire" run out of the church, and all the rest run after, with the semblance of death in their faces, some saying they smelled smoke, others pitch…and could not be reconciled to their error a great while'.

Foreigners were arrested and kept in custody without any charge being preferred against them in many towns, particularly along the East Anglian coast. One petty criminal, caught killing sheep, was accused of wanting their tallow for fireballs. His protest that he merely wanted to sell the carcases was waved aside.

News of the fire was slow to circulate in the provinces, as the Letter Office in London had been burned down on Sunday night. The Clerk, James Hickes, had stayed until surrounded by flames at one in the morning, and narrowly escaping injury. Later, a temporary office was set up in Covent Garden, and when the letters did start going out again, their contents reflected the wild rumours currently circulating.

'Poor London is almost burnt out,' wrote Lady Hobart from Chancery Lane to Sir Ralph Verney on the Monday.

'It began on Saturday night and has burnt ever since, and is at this time more fierce than ever, it did begin in Pudding Lane at a bakers, where a Dutch rogue lay… 'Tis thought Fleet Street will be burnt by tomorrow, there is nothing left in any house there, nor in the Temple… 'Tis the Dutch who fire, there was one taken in Westminster setting his outhouse on fire and they have attempted to fire many places and there is an abundance taken with grenades and powder!'

Although, as Lady Hobart said, all the carts and drays for ten miles around were being used night and day to move what belongings had been saved, 'I am almost out of my wits, we have packed up all our goods and cannot get a cart for money, they give five and ten pound for carts, I cannot get one for twenty pound to go out of town…and I fear I shall lose all I have and must run away.'

Dr Denton, physician to the King, wrote a letter to a friend about the fire. 'It is generally believed, but not at Court,' he wrote, 'that the Papists have designed this and more.' There were strong presumptions for this, he added, 'as gunpowder, and balls and wildfire' had been found on many of them. The people felt that if they destroyed these evildoers none were left behind to do the work, whereas if they sent them in custody to Whitehall, they were 'all dismissed'.

Dr Denton's letter mentioned another hardship brought by the fire; food was becoming very scarce. 'Nothing almost is to be gott that we have not in possession, bread, beer, meat, all in scarcity and many want it.'

As darkness fell on Monday night, London certainly presented a fearful sight. The fire still raged with unparalleled intensity, and the entire capital was brightly lit in the harsh glare of sheets of flame that rose like giant burning torches high into the sky above the devastated area, now stretching for a mile along the river bank and at least half a mile deep. The silver-grey of the moonlight was changed to red by the shroud of smoke which hung thickly over the City, reflecting the glow from the conflagration.

'All the Skie,' wrote the astonished Evelyn, 'were of a fiery aspect, like the top of a burning Oven, and the light seene about 40 miles round about.'

A schoolboy, William Taswell, standing on Westminster Pier and gazing fascinated upriver towards the heat of the flames, found that he was able to read his *Terence* as easily as if it had been daytime.

The shape of Tuesday's fire, which burned a vast area, and crossed the boundary of the City walls, was determined that evening. Four terrible lines of flame converged at the eastern end of Cheapside. One mounted from the Thames-side through Dowgate and Old Fish Street into Watling Street; a second blazed from Cornhill into Poultry and along by the Old Stocks Market (the site of the present Mansion House); a third ran down Threadneedle Street; the last burned up through

Bucklersbury. 'All these four joyning together, break into one great flame at the corner of Cheapside with such a dazzling light, and burning heat, and roaring noise by the fall of so many houses together, that was very amazing,' said Vincent.

The Poultry Compter, a debtors' prison, was totally destroyed; the prisoners were released an hour or so before the flames reached them. In Bucklersbury, the home of apothecaries and the chemical trade, tongues of fire licked into storerooms filled with highly combustible compounds and emerged with redoubled ferocity: the wind carried away the choking stench of burning sulphur.

The noise of the Great Fire had grown as deafening as its lurid light was dazzling. 'The noise and crackling and thunder of the impetuous flames, the shrieking of women and children, the hurry of people, the fall of towers, houses and churches was like a hideous storme,' was how Evelyn described it. The air became so hot that the fire-fighters could barely breathe; reluctantly they were forced to abandon their efforts.

To Vincent, the sound of the flames raging was 'as if there had been a thousand Iron Chariots beating upon the stones'. And still the wind rushed along the streets and gusted among the rooftops, ever fanning the flames to greater fury. 'If you opened your eye to the opening of the streets, where the Fire was come,' he wrote, 'you might see in some places whole streets at once in flames, that issued forth as if they had been so many great Forges from the opposite windows, which folding together, were united into one great flame throughout the whole street; and then you might see the Houses tumble, tumble, tumble, from one end of the street to the other with a great crash, leaving the foundations open to the view of the heavens.'

The people were filled with terror and 'there was nothing to be heard but crying out and lamentation, and running about like distracted creatures'.

An Italian wrote afterwards: 'One would need to have been a Nero to have watched such a spectacle without pity... Men, women and children of all ages and of all ranks, ran through the streets, their backs loaded with their most precious goods; and among them were carried many sick and disabled persons, who had been driven from their houses by the fire… As they ran they made a heartrending murmur…the miseries of this people were appalling.'

That night, the exhausted refugees, their faces blackened, backs aching and clothing covered with grime, began to camp out in the fields beyond the City wall with whatever pitiful heaps of household effects they had managed to salvage. Here the tattered belongings of the poor, and the sumptuous possessions of the rich, found a common resting place beneath the stars. Moorfields, and the open ground between the City, Finsbury and Islington, was crowded with sleeping figures wrapped like corpses in blankets or sacks.

The fields and meadows for miles around, which a year before had received bodies of plague victims the churchyards could not contain, were strewn with furniture, bundles and families; here and there a white tent gave shelter to women and children. Those whose despair had robbed them of sleep saw a constant reminder of their ruined homes in the giant, ragged tongues of flame which hourly crept nearer to the City wall, and the dull, monotonous rumble of destruction.

In four lines of his poem, Dryden caught something of the pathos of the scene:

> The most, in fields, like herded beasts lie down;
> To dews obnoxious on the grassie floor:
> And while their Babes in sleep their sorrows drown,
> Sad Parents watch the remnants of their store.

Watching the long string of people go through the City gates, Vincent was moved by the 'rueful looks, the pale cheeks, the tears trickling down, the smiting of the breast and the wringing of the hands; to hear the sighs and groans, the doleful and weeping speeches of the distressed citizens, when they were bringing forth their wives (some from their child-bed) and their little ones (some from their sick bed) out of their houses, and sending them into the Countries or somewhere into the Fields'.

Even in the fields, a mile away from the blaze, the refugees could feel 'intolerable heat and drought, as if they had been in the middle of the fire'. Many walked farther away still, until all the villages around London were crowded by refugees without homes or hope.

CHAPTER THIRTEEN

The Fire Spreads Westwards

By midnight on Tuesday, the old City of London had been almost entirely burned away. As gales swept East Coast ports, the wind blew the flames across London at incredible speed until they burst out beyond the City wall, leapt the Fleet Ditch, and roared on into Fleet Street, razing all buildings on either side to the ground within hours.

Afterwards, a foreign observer wrote that 'in an hour's walk, from the Temple to the Tower, there is, within the walls, hardly anything left standing, and without the walls, in Fleet Street and from Holborn to Fleet Bridge, all is in ruins'.

St Paul's Cathedral burned until the lead on its roof ran down the streets like lava; the Guildhall blazed like a torch throughout the night 'as if it had been a Palace of Gold, or a great building of burnished Brass'. Newgate Prison, set in the City wall, and the gateway, were also destroyed, and the Sessions House at the Old Bailey was levelled. Of all the famous buildings of London, only the Tower was saved; even there the flames, burning back in the teeth of the easterly wind, reached the moat.

The fire raged with such ferocity throughout that Tuesday that in the morning Lord Arlington reported to Sir William Clifford, Comptroller of the Royal Household, that 'no art or pains can meddle with it'. The vast pall of thick yellow smoke which rose over the capital had brought night at noon. When the sun, shining in the cloudless skies above, made its brief appearances, the people saw it burning red, in Vincent's words, 'with a colour like blood'; as the long lines of refugees trudged away from the stricken City, they walked for miles beneath the deep, choking shadow of London's funeral shroud of smoke.

The bands of troops and labourers the King had organized made tremendous efforts to stem the fire, but they received little or no help from ordinary people.

'The City, for the first rank, they minded only for their own preservation; the middle sort were so distracted and amazed that they did not know what they did; the poorer, they minded nothing but pilfering,' wrote one man who worked alongside the Duke of York. 'So the City was abandoned to the Fire, and thousands believing in Mother Shipton's prophecy "That London, in sixty-six, should be burnt to ashes".'

Mother Shipton's predictions, contained in a printed tract, had been read by everyone; Pepys recorded that when news of the burning of the capital was carried to Prince Rupert, at sea with the Fleet, his only comment was that 'now Shipton's prophecy was out'.

Altogether, that Tuesday had been a terrible day; as the sun rose the fire was already, in Vincent's phrase, 'in the very bowels of the City'. The flames spread up from the Thames-side through Soper Lane, Bow Lane, Bread Street, Friday Street and The Old Change on parallel courses, and broke out in a mass of fire into Cheapside. Here stood the shops of goldsmiths and jewellers, their windows glittering with intricately worked gold ornaments and silver plate. The houses of the goldsmiths were as expensive as the goods they sold, and Cheapside, wide and well-kept, contained the finest buildings in the whole of the City, as well as the Mermaid Tavern.

Cheapside did not stand long against the fury of the fire's onslaught. 'The fire,' wrote Vincent, 'breaks furiously into the broad street, and most of that (the south) side of the way was together in flames, a dreadful spectacle! And then partly by the Fire which came down by Mercers Chapple, partly by the fall of Houses cross the way, the other side is quickly kindled, and doth not stand long after it.'

Within a few hours, Cheapside was alight from end to end, but the goldsmiths had prudently removed their treasure – said to be worth £1,200,000 – to the Tower some hours before. Their Hall, in Foster Lane, was destroyed, however, as was Goldsmiths' Row, a group of Tudor shops and houses on the south side of Cheapside. These properties, lavishly decorated and bearing a gilt facsimile of the Goldsmiths' crest, had been an architectural sight of London for many years.

As Cheapside burned, the threat to St Paul's Cathedral grew hourly. Early in the day it was decided that the only hope of saving what was left of the capital lay in making a stand upon the line of the Fleet Ditch between Holborn Bridge and the Bridewell; and to pull down every building on both sides of this. Surely the fire could not leap so large a gap.

The Duke of York took charge of the operation between the Thames and the Fleet Ditch, and Lord Craven directed works between Fleet Bridge and Holborn Bridge. All morning their teams worked, gasping for breath and soaking with sweat, for the wind fanned the heat from the approaching flames towards them although the fire was still a quarter of a mile away. So swiftly did it travel that by noon it had reached the gap in the Duke of York's sector.

As the last properties standing on the east side of the Ditch went up in flames, the wind blew across a shower of blazing flakes of debris. Exhausted, grimed, coughing in the smoke and stifling in the heat, the Duke and his men watched helplessly as they flew high above their heads, and came down like burning rain on the Bridewell and Salisbury Court, to the west of the Ditch. Within minutes a chain of smaller fires began which soon set Fleet Street alight. Their labours had all been in vain.

Meanwhile the flames burned on towards the Tower, and caused alarm for the safety of the magazines of gunpowder stored there. The previous night Lord Berkeley, the Ordnance Commissioner, had applied for a warrant 'for the delivery of all water engines remaining in store at Deptford and Woolwich'.

But the roads were jammed with carts and barrows and refugees: whether the fire engines would arrive was debatable.

Meanwhile, in Lothbury, north of the smouldering Royal Exchange, the fire received one of its first checks. A City Alderman, whose house was one of a number of large buildings, constructed partly of brick, to the north of the street, was horrified by the way people refused to make any attempt to stop the flames spreading. He ran up and down the street shouting to everyone he saw, trying to organize a team of fire-fighters. He was greeted with a mixture of contempt and insult.

He returned to his bank, unlocked his safe and brought out £100 in gold coins, which he began to distribute among the bystanders, promising them more when they started work. The sight of so much money spurred them on; the houses were isolated and saved. Another man paid £50 to a gang who saved his house at Pie Corner, Smithfield. This led to the saying that the Great Fire 'began at Pudding Lane and ended at Pie Corner'.

Not all were so generous. Pepys, in a diary entry for September 8th, testified to the meanness of some of London's wealthy citizens. He and his friends had talked 'of the low spirits of some rich men in the City, in sparing any encouragement to the poor people that wrought for the saving their houses.

'Among others, Alderman Starling, a very rich man, without children, the fire next door to him in our lane, after our men had saved his house, did give 2s 6d among thirty of them, and did quarrel with some that would remove the rubbish out of the way of the fire, saying that they come to steal.

'Sir W Coventry told me of another this morning, in Holborn, which he showed the King: that when it was offered to stop the fire near his house for such a reward that come but to 2s 6d a man, among the neighbours, he would give but 18d.'

By one o'clock on Tuesday afternoon, St Paul's Cathedral, afforded some protection by the space of the churchyard around it, was still unharmed, although surrounded by burning streets.

By two o'clock the fire had attacked the Temple. A resident, John Barker, sent an urgent message to Lord Arlington notifying him that he had escaped to take refuge with Lord Lyonberg, the Swedish Resident, in Covent Garden, but could not get transport for his books and other effects. 'At the Temple,' he wrote, 'neither boat, barge, cart nor coach is to be had, all the streets full of goods, and the fire flaming on into the very Temple.' The Swedish Resident joined Barker, asking that four waggons should be 'pressed' to carry away their possessions.

There seemed small hope now of checking the fire before it swept right through to Whitehall and the Palace. A Royal Warrant was issued agreeing to the Exchequer's removal from the Temple to Nonsuch, and to commandeer carriages and lighters for the job, 'all Mayors, Bailiffs, &c, to assist at their peril'. The King commanded the Lord-Lieutenants of Middlesex, Surrey and Hertfordshire to muster the local militia in case of need, 'the hand of God being laid upon the City by a raging fire'.

After being driven back from the line of the Fleet Ditch, the Duke of York and his men determined to make another stand at Somerset House. The blaze in Fleet Street burned so fiercely that an observer standing on the hill in Highgate eight miles away saw 'with what rage and greediness it marched...and by five o'clock was advanced as high as the Fleet conduit', just west of Shoe Lane.

As such alarming reports of its spread to the west reached the Palace, the King's possessions were hastily packed in preparation for a flight to Hampton Court by the river, scheduled for six o'clock next morning. Fire-fighters meanwhile began to pull down more houses between Somerset House and Charing Cross in a last effort to save Whitehall and Westminster.

One of them wrote afterwards: 'Night coming on, the flames increased by the wind rising, which appeared to us so terrible to see, from the very ditch the shore quite up to the Temple all in a flame, and a very great breadth. At ten o'clock at night we left Somerset House, where they began to pull down some houses in hopes to save Whitehall... Nothing can be like unto the distraction we were in, but the Day of Judgment.'

St Paul's was now beset by the flames from each quarter of the compass. On the south bank of the Thames, and from the high ground north of the City, crowds could see its giant roof, with the huge, squat tower, denuded of its spire by an earlier fire in 1561, rising dominant upon its knoll to dwarf everything else in the City. For hours the preservation of the City's chief church, in the heart of that fire, seemed to those who watched like a miracle. The cathedral was so large (222 yards long) that however fierce the flames and dense the smoke, they could never completely obscure it. But shortly before dusk some flaming sparks found a piece of wooden boarding which had been laid across the roof where the lead had broken away. By the time darkness fell, the whole roof was a mass of fire, and St Paul's was finally ablaze.

'The church,' wrote Vincent, 'though all of stone outward, though naked of houses about it, and though so high above all buildings in the City, yet within a while doth yield to the violent assaults of the conquering flames, and strangely takes Fire at the top; now the Lead melts and runs down, as if it had been snow before the Sun; and the great-beams and massy stones, with a great noise, fall upon the Pavement, and break through into Faith Church underneath; now great flakes of stone scale, and peel off strangely from the side of the Walls.'

St Faith's was a church within a church, a small parish church which occupied part of the vaults of St Paul's, and which had been adopted by London's booksellers and stationers as their own; many of them had their shops in the adjacent Paternoster Row.

On Monday night and Tuesday morning, with the fire sweeping down towards their premises, they worked desperately to carry their stocks into St Faith's, until countless thousands of valuable books – afterwards reported to Pepys to be worth 'above £150,000' – were stacked in the pews and aisles. Inside the cathedral stood piles of other assorted goods, while in the churchyard outside, enormous heaps of trading stock were stacked, notably the cloths and clothing of the mercers and drapers. Possibly a quarter of a million pounds' worth of stock was taken to St Paul's for sanctuary; not £250 worth survived the fire.

A bookseller named Martin, whose house was just inside the churchyard, saw the flames take root at the edge of that one wooden board on the cathedral roof. No hose was long enough to reach it – even if there had been water to use. Also, demolitions, and the destructions wrought by the fire in the streets round about had blocked all the surrounding streets, so that no fire-fighting force could come close enough to try and save the cathedral.

Once the fire took hold, it spread with astonishing rapidity. Above the vaulting inside the building, the roof was all timber, protected on the outside by the enormous skin of lead, no less than four or five acres in area. Through the long weeks of drought before the Great Fire, the blazing sun, day after day, had heated the lead; the wood underneath was warm and dry. This giant roof, blazing from end to end, fell down into the church below, carrying with it a thousand tons of stonework; the mighty roar of the crumbling cathedral was heard right across the City, above all the din and confusion of the fire and the thunder of gunpowder explosions bringing down the houses.

The flames, recharging themselves upon the woodwork of the inner fabric and the goods stored below, shot back out through the gaping roof and rose two or three hundred feet into the air. Inside the cathedral, the heat was so great that the outside stonework split under it, and giant pieces of stone shrapnel, weighing twenty, forty and even a hundred pounds hurtled out into the streets. 'The stones of Paules flew like granados,' declared Evelyn, 'the Lead melting downe the streetes in a streame, and the very pavements of them glowing with fiery rednesse, so as nor horse nor man was able to tread on them.'

The booksellers, who lost practically their entire stock, suffered the worst of all London traders. Their books in St Faith's burned for a week. The wind took the burning pages and scattered them for miles. Richard Baxter, out at Acton, five miles away, said that he 'saw the half-burnt leaves of Books near my Dwelling', and Pepys was told by Lady Carteret how an abundance of pieces of burnt papers were deposited at Cranborne in Windsor Forest.

'Among others, she took up one...which was a little bit of paper that had been printed, whereon there remained no more or less than these words: "Time is, it is done".'

One bookseller, a Mr Kirton, lost £5,000 worth of books – a fortune; he never recovered from the shock and died of grief in the following year. 'All the great booksellers almost undone...a great want there will be of books, especially Latin books and foreign books,' wrote Pepys. He was soon proved correct, for the prices of many books rose by four or five times, while others were virtually unobtainable.

While St Paul's blazed, the Great Fire still spread in every direction, destroying all buildings as far as London Wall and Cripplegate, on the northernmost City boundary, and attacking the busy shops and stalls of Newgate Market. The Butchers Hall, in Stinking Lane (now King Edward Street), was razed, and the flames sped on to Newgate Prison. Many quaintly named streets perished that day, among them Milk Street, Gutter Lane and Cat-eaten Street.

Newgate Jail was completely gutted; the prisoners were marched out some hours earlier to Southwark Jail. The warders or turnkeys had a difficult time on the journey, for several breaks were made and a number of notorious criminals escaped in the smoke and confusion. From the prison, the fire broke out through the City wall to engulf St Sepulchre's Church, where a knell was tolled whenever the execution cart, containing a prisoner condemned to die, with his coffin and the hangman, set out from the prison for Tyburn Tree, now the site of the Marble Arch. It was the custom to stop this cart at the church steps so that he could receive the last rites before he began his last journey through London.

All day, as the fire raged, the evacuation of the capital continued, accelerated by more rumours that the French were on their way to complete the destruction. 'The Inhabitants of a whole Street,' wrote Clarendon, 'have run in a great Tumult One Way, upon the Rumour that the French were marching at the other End of it.'

Now £40 and £50 was willingly paid for the hire of a single cart, and as one Londoner said, 'they that were most active, and befriended by their Wealth, got Carts, and saved much…the rest lost almost all'.

By Tuesday night, about 150,000 people were homeless, and most of these camped in the fields to the north of the City, squatting disconsolately among their pitiful salvage, watching St Paul's burn. The wall of flame, more than a quarter of a mile wide, swept along Fleet Street, and grew closer and closer to Whitehall.

The burning of Guildhall that evening was a sight second only to that of the death of St Paul's. 'All through the night Guild Hall was a fearful spectacle,' wrote Vincent, 'which stood the whole body of it together in view, for several hours together, after the fire had taken it, without the flames (I suppose because the timber was such solid Oake) in a bright shining coal, as if it had been a Palace of Gold, or a Great Building of burnished Brass.'

Then, suddenly, and quite unexpectedly, with the whole City ablaze and the sky for miles around almost as light as day from the livid glow of the flames, the Great Fire began to die.

The first real sign of the fire's decline came at about eleven o'clock on Tuesday night, when messengers hurried to the Duke of York at the Palace with the news that the wind had veered south and dropped in strength. The heavy walls of St Dunstan's in Fleet Street and the Temple Church were helping to contain the flames; there was a chance that they could be held and would not spread farther west. More equipment and men were rushed at once, and they worked all through the night with great success.

'We had not this mercy shown to us alone, but likewise hearts and hands from the people; the soldiers being almost all tired out with continual labour,' wrote one of them afterwards. Only in the dying hours of the Great Fire did Londoners overcome their panic and self interest sufficiently to help put out the blaze.

While the flames were being contained near the Temple, the fight to save the Tower of London continued; it was imperative that the Tower should not catch fire, for it contained enough gunpowder to destroy shipping in the river, to blow up London Bridge, and give the fire a new lease of life beyond the City wall.

After supper that evening, Pepys, whose house and office were hourly more seriously threatened, saw 'how horribly the sky looks, all on a fire in the night, enough to put us out of our wits... It looks just as if it was at us, and the whole heaven on fire.

'Now begins the practice of blowing up houses in Tower Street, those next the Tower, which at first did frighten people more than anything,' he wrote. 'But it stopped the fire where it was done, it bringing down the houses to the ground in the same places they stood, and then it was easy to quench what little fire was in it, though it kindled nothing almost.'

People who lived near the Tower were terrified by a rumour that the cannons in the fortress were being turned on their houses in order to demolish them more quickly. As the explosions shook their decrepit wooden properties, they ran out into the streets, terrified and shouting that the soldiers were murdering them. It took hours to reassure them that no guns were being used. That night, the flames burned on to the eastern end of Tower Street until nothing remained between them and the fortress but the Tower ditch, an evil-smelling stagnant pool.

Earlier, the Goldsmiths Company had taken their treasures into the Tower for safety; now these were carried out again in case the heat should melt them. By the light of the flames, a detachment of soldiers formed a chain, and handed out the gold and silver plate and heavy bags of golden coins into the hold of a vessel. This cast off immediately and sailed down river to Whitehall, where the treasures were unloaded into the Palace vaults.

The move was needless; the Tower did not burn. Instead, the wind died, and the flames died with it. All over the City the Fire of London began to go out as suddenly as it had begun.

CHAPTER FOURTEEN

The End of the Fire

By Wednesday morning it seemed that the Fire of London was virtually over. Parts of the City still burned for another forty-eight hours, and isolated pockets of fire in vaults and cellars continued to smoulder for days, and even weeks afterwards: but three days had been long enough for the world's greatest city to be reduced to charred rubble and ashes.

On Wednesday afternoon the wind died away, and the flames were out all around the perimeter, except at Cripplegate. Within the 436 acres that had been involved, some sporadic fires still burned, but they were gradually subsiding.

Then, at four o'clock, 'a lurking spark' began a new blaze in Paper-buildings, Temple, which as darkness fell lit up the devastated Thames-side for the fourth successive night. This at once began rumours that 'fifty thousand French and Dutch in arms, coming to cut our throats and spoil us of what we have saved from the flames'.

'Many Citizens, having lost their houses, and almost all that they had, are fired with rage and fury,' wrote Vincent. 'Now "Arm, Arm, Arm" doth resound the Fields and Suburbs with a dreadful voice.'

The report caused a tremendous uproar and tumult. 'Taking what weapons they could come at,' Evelyn recalled afterwards, 'they could not be stop'd from falling on some of those nations [i.e. foreigners] whom they casually met, without sense or reason, the clamor and peril growing so excessive, as made the whole Court amaz'd at it, and they did with infinite paines, and great difficulty reduce and appease the people, sending guards and troopes of souldiers, to cause them to retire into the fields againe, where they were watched all this night.'

The King was afraid that the troops would lose control, so on Thursday morning he rode out to Moorfields to address the people. A huge crowd of homeless Londoners gathered to meet him. He sat on his horse, against a background of the still smoking city, and told them frankly that the disaster was 'the hand of God' upon them all, and no plot, for he had personally examined suspected incendiaries and found nothing to support charges that the City had been deliberately fired. He begged his people 'to take no further alarm', and promised to defend them from any enemy and, more usefully, to provide food and help for them all.

As a first step to fulfil this promise, he opened the Navy stores and sent £500 worth of sea-biscuit to the hungry refugees. But even in their extremity, they found that they could not stomach this hard tack which was daily fare for those unfortunate enough to be press-ganged to serve with the Fleet. The *London Gazette* noted diplomatically that 'the people, being unaccustomed to that kind of bread, declined it, and so it was returned in great part to His Majesties stores again, without any use made of it'.

When the Duke of York, at Whitehall, received news that the Temple fire had broken out again, he immediately rode there to find that the gatemen, afraid of pilferers and looters, were refusing to allow fire-fighters in to quench the flames, which were rapidly taking hold. The Duke ordered these men to open the gates and, after a rapid survey, decided that the only hope of saving the Temple Church and Hall was to blow up property near by.

When kegs of gunpowder were brought in a barrister appeared and ordered the Duke to stop; it was against both the rules and charter of the Temple that any buildings should be exploded. 'Upon which,' wrote one of the Duke's lieutenants, 'Mr Germaine,

227

the Duke's Master of the Horse, took a cudgel and beat the young lawyer to the purpose.'

By one o'clock next morning, the Temple fire – the last assault of the Great Fire of London – was over. Many of the lawyers' chambers, in Whitefriars, Serjeant's Inn and part of the Inner Temple were completely destroyed; with most of them empty during the Long Vacation, the contents were also lost. Money, law books, deeds and important documents went up in the flames, and Clarendon reported that 'the Eveidences of many Men's Estates' had been burnt. Pale-faced, red-eyed and utterly exhausted, the Duke, who had not been in bed for more than two or three hours since Sunday, rode thankfully back to the Palace to sleep the clock round.

Another man who went home weary on Wednesday night was John Evelyn, who had led a team of fire-fighters all day in the Fetter Lane area, and had been successful in stopping the flames from reaching Holborn from the south. As he rode down to the river bank, to cross over to Southwark and on to Deptford, he passed warehouses, still burning, that threw off such a heat no one could approach nearer than a hundred yards. This reminded him of his pamphlet, *Fumifugium*, published two years before, in which he had complained of the smoke in London's air, and warned of the dangers of having so many fires and ovens and furnaces so close to wooden houses.

'The Coal and Wood wharfes, and magazines of Oyle, rosine, chandler, etc., did infinite mischief,' he wrote afterwards, 'so as the invective [his pamphlet] I but a little while before dedicated to his Majestie and publish'd, giving warning of what might probably be the issue of suffering those shops to be in the Citty, was lookt on as prophetic.'

Evelyn saw thousands of Londoners in the open ground all round the City, in Moorfields, in Highgate, and, across the river south of Southwark, in St George's Fields. 'Some under tents, others in miserable Hutts and Hovells, without a rag, or any necessary utensils, bed or board, who from delicatnesse, riches and easy accommodations in stately and well furnish'd houses, were now reduced to extreamest misery and poverty.'

Two days later, Evelyn rode back to the ruins of the City, passing through 'with extraordinary difficulty, clambring over mountaines of yet smoking rubbish, and frequently mistaking where I was, the ground under my feet so hott, as made me not onely sweate, but even burnt the soles of my shoes'. Standing by the shattered shell of St Paul's, he saw Inigo Jones' portico 'rent into pieces, flakes of vast stone split in sunder, and nothing remaining intire but the inscription in the Architrave which shewing by whom it was built, had not one letter of it defac'd: which I could not but take notice of'.

The Commissioner for Sick Seamen was astonished to see that great stones had been calcined by the heat, so that 'all the ornament Columns, friezes, Capitols and projectures of massie Portland stone flew off, even to the very roof, where a Sheete of Leade covering no lesse than 6 akers being totally mealted, the ruines of the Vaulted roofe, falling brake into St Faithes'.

As Evelyn walked on, dark clouds of smoke, carrying with them nauseating smells, arose from stores still burning in cellars, until he could only liken the scene to Hell on earth. 'The people who now walked about the ruines appear'd like men in some dismal desert or in some great Citty lay'd waste by an impetuous and cruel enemy.' The stench – part of which was probably from 'some poore Creatures' bodys' – nearly made him ill.

He noticed 'vast hinges, barrs and gates of Prisons' which had been melted down by the terrific heat, and in places this heat was still so fierce that Evelyn was unable to walk through what had been the narrower streets, and had to keep to the widest. Even so, 'the ground and aire, smoake and fiery vapour, continu'd so intense' that his hair was almost singed and his feet 'insufferably surbated'. Often he could not tell where he was, until the sight of a distinctive tower or shell of a well-known building enabled him to take his bearings.

Leaving the City to climb the hill towards Islington, Evelyn saw 'two hundred thousand people of all ranks and degrees, dispersed and laying along by their heapes of what they could save from the Incendium, deploring their losse, and though ready to perish for hunger and destitution, not asking one Penny for relief, which to me appeared a stranger sight than any I had yet beheld'.

The King acted quickly to help these homeless thousands, fearing the consequences of either real or imagined indifference to their plight. He issued a proclamation to the Mayors, constables and magistrates of towns and villages about the City ordering them to make available all their spare accommodation for the refugees, and to turn over churches, chapels, schools and public buildings to receive their goods.

Army tents were sent out to the fields north of London, and soon great encampments of people under canvas and in hastily-constructed shacks began to pick up the threads of their lives. Some courageously returned to their burnt-out homes, and built crude sheds of brick and timber, or took shelter in cellars and vaults. Emergency markets were set up among the ruins, and food rushed in from the country.

'It can hardly be conceived how great a supply of all kinds was brought from all places with four and twenty hours,' wrote Chancellor Clarendon.

The villagers around London went some way towards redeeming their cruelty to Londoners during the Plague by receiving thousands after the Fire with 'a marvellous charity'. Clarendon thought it miraculous that, apart from the new encampments in which everyone had some shelter, all the fields, which had been covered with homeless people, were practically empty again by the end of the week.

Two Surveyors, Jonas Moore and Ralph Gatrix, who charted the devastated area, gave a report on the damage. 'Upon the 2nd of September, 1666,' they wrote, 'the Fire began in London at one Farryner's house, a baker, in Pudding-lane, between the hours of one and two in the morning, and continued burning until the 6th of September following: consuming three hundred and 73 acres within the wall of the City of London, and 63 acres, three roods without the walls.

'There remains 75 acres three roods yet standing within the walls unburnt. Eighty-nine parish churches, besides chapels, burnt: eleven parishes within the walls yet standing. Houses burnt, 13,200.'

Five-sixths of the area within the walls had been destroyed; and ninety per cent of the City's living accommodation lay in ruins, and nearly 200,000 people were homeless.

'It is observed, and is true,' wrote Pepys, 'that in the late fire of London, the fire burned just as many Parish Churches as there were hours from the beginning to the end of the fire; and, next, that there were just as many churches left standing as there were taverns left standing in the rest of the City that was not burned, being, I think, thirteen in all of each: which is pretty to observe.'

Among the ruins of one of the churches, a stone was found bearing a Latin inscription which read: 'When these letters shall be read, woe on London, for they shall be read by the light of a fire.'

All the finest of the City's public and private buildings were destroyed. The great City Companies owned sixty Halls, described as 'magnificent structures and palaces'; after the Fire, only eight remained undamaged. Many people, whose fortunes had depended upon rents from properties in the City, were ruined.

On September 26th, Lady Mary Verney wrote to a correspondent: 'You know it was all my sone had to depend on and my girls...ther is bot one house left of eighteen pounds a yeare of all that nomber' (which she owned). The wife of Dr Denton, the King's Physician, similarly lost her entire income. 'Now she hath had a little time to recollect herselfe, she cryes all day long,' wrote her husband sadly. 'All in my power cannot make it good to her.'

London's merchants and traders fared little better. It was impossible to make even a rough estimate of their losses, but a calculation attributed to Wren includes an item: 'Wine, tobacco, sugar, plums etc., of which the City was at that time very full – £1,500,000', and another: 'Wares, household-stuff, monies and movable goods lost and spoilt – £2,000,000.' One City Alderman, Sir Robert Jefferson, lost £20,000 worth of tobacco when his warehouses were destroyed. The value of the dwelling houses destroyed was computed at £3,900,000, about £300 each. Only 1,800 were left standing out of an original total of 15,000 in the City; 400 streets had simply ceased to exist. Not all were rebuilt and so only approximate sites can be given for them.

'The dolefullest sight of all,' wrote a clergyman afterwards, was to see what 'a ruinous confused place the City was, by Chimneys and Steeples only standing in the midst of Cellars, and heaps of Rubbish; so that it was hard to know where the streets had been... No man that seeth not such a thing, can have a right apprehension of the dreadfullness of it.'

The loss of St Paul's alone was written down as £2 million, more than half the figure estimated for 13,200 houses. For two years after the fire, efforts were made to patch up the old cathedral, but these attempts were unsuccessful; and the demolition of the old structure and the rebuilding of St Paul's as it is today was a slow business. It took thirty-four years.

The total London loss in the Great Fire was estimated at about £10 million, but it was probably far more. To calculate the main heads of damage was one thing; to assess the losses of small traders and householders, quite another. The cost of the war had already overtaxed the national economy; the Fire dealt it a mortal blow. Thousands of Londoners went hungry during the long hard winter that followed, and there were constant riots and disorders which troops were called in to quell. Naval ratings and other seamen had to beg for their pay. After several unsuccessful attempts to get it peacefully, they rioted at Wapping and other places; these demonstrations were suppressed by force.

Despite the enormous material loss due to the Fire, only four people were known for certain to have been burned to death.

The Hall of the Parish Clerks' Company was destroyed early on, and with it went the printing press; thus no Bill of Mortality was published until September 20th. A composite Bill for the three weeks from August 28th to September 18th was then issued and out of a total of 704 deaths (104 still from plague) were these headings:

'4 – Burnt at several places
5 – Drowned at several places
6 – Frighted
7 – Kild by several accidents'

How many people died as an indirect result is unknown, but shock and exposure must have killed some of the sick people and women in labour when they hastily retreated to the fields.

The first person to die was, of course, Farynor's maid, very early on Sunday morning. The other three to lose their lives were all old people. During the burning of St Paul's, an old woman was trapped in the cathedral, where she had sought sanctuary from the fire outside; her blackened corpse was later found by the east wall. An elderly man was overcome by fumes when he entered the building to retrieve a blanket he had left there. An obstinate old watchmaker, Paul Lowell, who lived in Shoe Lane, vowed that he would remain in his home even if it fell down on top of him. It did, but he had kept his word; his bones and his keys to his front door were found among the rubble in the cellar.

Throughout the winter that followed, looters and thieves lurked among the ruins, digging for valuables; at night they rushed out to rob and sometimes murder passers-by.

Pepys went in great fear of them, noting on February 13th, 1667, 'a foul evening…and, which is now my common practice, going over the ruins in the night, I rid with my sword drawn in the coach'. Vincent found the desolated City a ghostly place at night, with nettles growing up in the streets, owls screeching from ruined towers and gangs of footpads prowling about looking for travellers to attack.

Now that Londoners had had time to adjust themselves to the calamity, they demanded to know how the Fire began. The official account in the *London Gazette* announced that it was 'an unhappy chance, or the heavy Hand of God upon us for our sins'. Evelyn piously agreed, and thought the disaster 'what we highly deserved for our prodigious ingratitude, burning lusts, dissolute court, profane and abominable lives'.

The King announced that henceforth September 2nd would be regarded as a 'Day of Humiliation' so that they could reflect on their 'manifold iniquities'.

But not all Londoners were content with this explanation of Divine retribution, and fed by a multitude of stories and pamphlets attributing the catastrophe to a Papish plot, they yearned for vengeance. The authorities were thus forced to embark on a lengthy and abortive investigation which satisfied no one and proved nothing.

CHAPTER FIFTEEN

A Scapegoat is Hanged

Robert Hubert, the 25-year-old son of a Rouen watchmaker, was hanged at Tyburn in the middle of October for starting the Fire of London – although it later transpired that he was not even in England when the Fire began.

Sir Henry Keeling, the Lord Chief Justice, not a notably lenient man, thought that Hubert's contradictory stories cast doubt on his guilt, but nevertheless sentenced him to death.

After Hubert's conviction, several Members of Parliament felt that the case had been inadequately investigated, but in the words of a contemporary, Sir John Hawles, 'the Commons resolving to examine Hubert...next day he was hang'd before the House sate, and so could tell no further tales'.

Robert Hubert, who had at one time worked as a watchmaker in London, was arrested at Romford in Essex. He had apparently fled from the capital. This was not in itself suspicious, for foreigners were being roughly treated in many parts of London just because they were foreigners. He immediately announced, however, that when the City was on fire, he had thrown a fireball near the King's Palace in Westminster in an attempt to spread it. He was prompted to do this, he claimed, by another Frenchman named Piedlou. This admission, unasked and unexpected, sent him to Southwark Jail for further questioning. At Southwark, Hubert changed his story completely, and the account he then gave cost him his life.

He explained that in June, he and Stephen Piedlou left France for Sweden. Later, they took ship for England, and arrived in the Thames in a Swedish vessel a few days before the Fire. They remained aboard ship until the night of Saturday, September 2nd, when Piedlou suggested going ashore. They did so and walked together for some time along the river bank. When they came to Pudding Lane, Piedlou turned up the narrow, unlit street and stopped outside a house. He then took three fireballs from his pockets, and handed one to Hubert, telling him to set the house on fire with it.

Hubert said he remonstrated with Piedlou, but at his friend's insistence he finally fixed the fireball on the end of a long pole, lit it with a match, and pushed it in through a window. He held the pole until he could see that the room was well ablaze.

This seemed a possible way in which the fire could have started, and Hubert was indicted on the charge that, being 'led away by the instigation of the Devil', he maliciously fired the property of Farynor, the baker, thus causing the burning of the City.

The first doubt about this confession arose fairly soon afterwards. Farynor had been closely questioned about the outbreak several times and, frightened that he might have to take the blame for burning London, he had been at some pains to prove that the fire could not have started accidentally. Yet when he heard Hubert's description of the window through which he claimed he had pushed the fireball, the baker swore that no such window had existed; and his daughter supported him. There had never been any window of that shape on the wall facing the street.

This did not deter the authorities from allowing Hubert's trial to begin at the earliest possible moment – during the October Sessions, held in a temporary courtroom on the site of the Old Bailey. Hubert gave them every assistance, obligingly changing his account by saying that Piedlou and he each put two fireballs through the window; if there was no window, then they had pushed them through 'a hole broken in the wall'. He further embellished his confession by saying that Piedlou was the leader of a gang of twenty-three plotters, some of whom went with them to Pudding Lane that night.

At the trial, Hubert constantly contradicted himself. He claimed that a man in Paris had persuaded him to act as incendiary, and that he had come to England with others to fire London at the time of the Plague. Then they had decided to postpone the attempt, and he returned to Sweden. He stayed there until he came back to carry out their plan on September 2nd.

'Who was it in Paris who suborned you to this action?' asked the Lord Chief Justice. Hubert replied that he did not know, for he had never seen the man before.

'What money did you receive to perform a service of so much hazard?' asked Keeling.

'I received but a pistole,' answered the Frenchman, 'but was promised five pistoles more when I should have done my work.'

At this news a rustle of incredulity was heard in the shabby room. The Continental gold coin known as a pistole was worth less than the English sovereign – about 18s. Even in those days of low wages it seemed hard to believe that a man would spend a whole year plotting in three different countries for a total eventual reward of possibly £4 10s.

The prosecution's case rested upon Hubert's admissions, and also upon some strange evidence about character. This was given by one Monsieur Graves, a French merchant living in St Mary Axe. He testified that he had known Hubert since he was a child of four, and that the young man had always been of 'mischievous inclination'.

He had also visited Hubert in prison, and, in the hope of gaining his confidence, told him he did not believe for a moment that he would have done such a thing. According to Graves, Hubert replied: 'Yes, sir, I am guilty of it, and have been brought to it by the instigation of M. Piedlou, but not out of any malice to the English nation, but from a desire of reward which he promised me upon my return to France.' Graves added that he knew Piedlou to be 'a very Debased Person, apt to any Wicked Design'.

The Lord Chief Justice was aware that inquiries had shown Hubert to be 'distracted' for some years past, and at times he had also suffered from 'a dead Palsey'. As he admitted to the King later, 'all his discourse is so disjointed that I cannot believe him guilty'.

Keeling therefore decided to discover whether a simple practical test would shed any light on the case. Turning to the prisoner, he asked: 'Do you know the place where you first put fire?'

'I know it very well,' replied Hubert, 'and will show it to anyone.'

Keeling at once ordered John Lowman, Keeper of the White Lion Prison (the Surrey county jail), to take Hubert under guard to the Thames-side, and have him point out the spot where he claimed to have used the fireball. The court was then adjourned. Hubert led the Keeper to Tower Hill, where the party stopped in front of acres of debris. Here and there a blackened burnt-out shell of a building rose from the rubble. Lowman asked the Frenchman to show him the exact place where he fired the house. Hubert replied that it was near London Bridge, so they marched down to Thames Street, but before they reached the bridge, Hubert pointed up Pudding Lane to his right and said simply: 'It was up there.'

This surprised Lowman, for the district was so desolated that even those who had lived there for years found it difficult to recognize streets or even the ruins of their own houses. Then, at the entrance to Pudding Lane, the cautious Keeper stopped again and told Hubert to go and find the exact spot.

'He went along the bricks and rubbish, and made a stand,' Lowman reported to the Lord Chief Justice. 'Then I did ask one Robert Penny, a wine porter, which was the baker's house, and he told me that was the house where Robert Hubert stood.'

Lowman made this inquiry out of Hubert's hearing, and then he went up to him and stood with his back to the ruins of the bakery. Pointing to various other ruins, he asked which house it was that the prisoner had fired. Hubert turned without hesitation, pointed at the mass of sooty bricks and tiles, all that remained of Farynor's home, and replied: 'This was the house that was first fired.'

Hubert was lame in one leg, so Lowman hired a horse, set him on it, and again the little party began to go through the maze of ruins. Every time he repeated his question, Hubert returned to the site in Pudding Lane and insisted: 'That was the house.' He also gave an accurate and detailed description of the house before it was burnt; he described the exact shape of the yard behind it, and the type and position of doors and windows. In view of Farynor's insistence that no such window as he had originally described existed in this house, this seemed very strange.

When Lowman's testimony about the experiment was put before the jury, they convicted Hubert, and he was immediately hanged. Afterwards it was discovered that although of feeble mind he was completely innocent. He had indeed come to England in a Swedish ship, but his captain, Laurens Petersen, swore on oath that Hubert had not disembarked until September 4th – two days after the Fire began. Thus it was physically impossible for him to have started it; he wasn't even there.

Lord Clarendon afterwards declared that 'neither the judges nor any present at the trial did believe him guilty, but that he was a poor distracted wretch weary of his life, and chose to part with it in this way'.

Was this so – or was the dim-witted Hubert a scapegoat for someone else – someone who primed him with words and rehearsed his journey to a house he had probably never seen before? Otherwise, how could Hubert be so sure of the exact site of the baker's house when even people who had lived near for years had no idea where it had stood? How could he describe the house so meticulously after only one hurried visit for a criminal purpose after dark? Why did he make such a blunder about the vital window in his first statement?

These questions were never asked, but if they had been, they might have showed that someone prompted this 'mopish, besotted fellow', as Pepys called him, to confess to a crime he did not commit.

The matter of Hubert's religious belief added a final touch of mystery to the whole business. He was a Huguenot, a strong Protestant, yet he died as a Catholic, receiving the last rites of that Church, and absolution for his sins. The fact that he died apparently a Papist was enough to convince many people that a Catholic plot to burn London had been proved beyond doubt. This intensified the wave of hatred against Catholics, and a Parliamentary Committee was appointed to inquire into the cause of the Fire. Seventy Members of Parliament, under the chairmanship of Sir Robert Brook, a senior Member, sat for months sifting a mass of testimonies and reached no conclusion.

Two days after it held its first session, the House of Commons and the House of Lords presented a petition to the King calling upon him to banish from the realm all Jesuits and Catholic priests within one month; to enforce rigorously existing laws against Catholics; and to disarm anyone who declined to take the Oaths of Allegiance and Supremacy. The King, whose position *vis-à-vis* Parliament was delicate, as he frequently was forced to ask the House for money, had little choice but to give his assent.

The Commons then set up another Committee to inquire into information touching 'the insolency of Popish priests and Jesuits, and the increase of Popery'. They urged that all Members of Parliament should receive the Sacrament; any who refused should be summarily thrown into jail.

The Brook Committee began its investigation on September 26th, and produced an interim report to the House on January 22nd in the following year. Several different versions of the Report were published. The official one was called 'A True and

Faithful Account of the Several Informations etc.', but some others were neither true nor faithful; they included matter not given in the Parliamentary document. One version, which Pepys read and found 'very plain' evidence of a plot, was ordered to be burnt by the public hangman in Westminster Palace Yard, and numbers of copies were confiscated. No one was charged with any offence whatsoever as a result of this Report, and Robert Hubert remained the sole victim for many years afterwards.

The Brook Committee took evidence from Farynor several times, and he convinced them that the fire in Pudding Lane was not an accident. He insisted, so their Report stated, 'that it was impossible any Fire should happen in his House by accident, for he had after 12 of the Clock gone through every Room thereof, and found no Fire, but in one Chimney, where the Room was paved with Bricks, which Fire he diligently raked up in the Embers'.

Was it not possible that a draught through a window or door had disturbed the coals? asked one of the committee.

'No,' replied the baker firmly. 'It was absolutely set fire on purpose.'

Later Farynor added some other facts in his anxiety to exonerate himself. These Sir Robert Viner, one of the committee, passed on to Pepys, who wrote: 'The baker and his daughter did swear again and again, that their oven was drawn by ten o'clock at night: that having occasion to light a candle about twelve, there was not so much fire in the bakehouse as to light a match for a candle, so that they were fain to go into another place to light it: that about 2 in the morning they felt themselves almost choked with smoke, and rising, did find the fire coming up stairs; so they rose to save themselves; but at that time, the bavins [faggots] were not on fire in the yard.

'So that they are, as they swear, in absolute ignorance how this fire should come; which is a strange thing, that so horrid an effect should have so mean and uncertain a beginning.'

Farynor's accounts did not agree with all the other reports. One contemporary letter claimed that 'the baker's boy, having placed some twigs in the oven to dry, about midnight on Saturday they caught fire, setting the whole house ablaze'. Another witness reported that the brushwood had been placed beside the oven ready to rekindle it, and that some sides of bacon hung near by. Edward Chamberlayne, in his book *The Present State of England*, published five years later, blamed the fire upon 'the drunkenness and supine negligence of the Baker'.

Having dealt with Farynor, the Committee then listened to people who were sure that the fire was the result of a plot. A servant, Elizabeth Styles, said that five months before it began, when she resisted 'the importunate advances of a French serving-man', he told her: 'You English maids will like the Frenchmen better when there is not a house left between Temple Bar and London Bridge.'

She replied: 'I hope my eyes will never see that.'

He retorted: 'This will come to pass between June and October.'

Then there was the report of a Mr Light of Ratcliffe, that in February 1665, Mr Richard Langhorne, a barrister and a 'zealous Papist' of the Middle Temple, told him: 'You expect great things in '66, and think that Rome will be destroyed, but what if it be London?'

A statement from a Mr Kitley of Barking in Essex, claimed that on August 13th, a Mrs Yazley, a Catholic from Ilford, visited him. 'They say the next Thursday will be the hottest day that ever was in England,' she said, as a point of conversation.

'I hope the hottest season of the Year is now past,' replied Kitley's mother, but Mrs Yazley went on: 'I know not whether it will be the hottest for weather or action.'

When Mrs Yazley paid another visit after the Fire of London, Kitley remembered this earlier conversation. 'I have often thought of your hot Thursday,' he said meaningly.

'It was not, indeed, upon the Thursday, but it happened upon the Sunday was Sennight after,' she replied. [1]

Examined by the committee, Mrs Yazley denied she had ever said anything about hot weather or hot action.

Letters from the Continent which were thought to have anticipated the fire were also examined. A man in Heidelberg wrote to a London merchant that news of the burning of the English capital had been 'constantly expected and discoursed of among the Jesuits for these fifteen years last past, as to happen this year'. Samuel Thurton, 'a Leicestershire gentleman', testified that he had received an anonymous letter warning him to come to London and look after his property in Southwark, as 'the suburbs will shortly be destroyed'.

Perhaps the strangest witness was Edward Taylor, a boy aged ten, who seemed to have a strong desire to kill his father, his mother and various other relatives. He swore that on the night of Saturday, September 2nd, he went with his father and his uncle, a Dutchman, to Pudding Lane, where they threw two fireballs in at an open window.

They went out again on successive days and did the same in Thomas Street, Fleet Street and the Old Exchange.

The boy claimed that his uncle gave his father £7 for this work, and that on another occasion he accompanied his father and mother, who were wearing black silk hoods, to fire 'a great house' at Acton. His 'confession' was actually submitted to the Lord Chief Justice for investigation.

Lord Clarendon was not greatly impressed by all this. 'Many who were produced as if their testimony would remove all doubts, made such senseless relations of what they had been told, without knowing the conditions of the persons who told them, or where to find them, that it was a hard matter to forbear smiling at their evidence,' he wrote later.

Clarendon quoted the case of the King's firework-maker, one Belland, a Frenchman, whose house and small factory were in Marylebone. Shortly before the fire, Belland collected large quantities of pasteboard, which he needed 'to make fireworks for the King's pleasure'. To acquaintances who wondered at his large production, Belland was supposed to have replied: 'If you should see the quantity that I have made elsewhere by other men, you would wonder indeed!'

A week before the Great Fire, Belland called on the stationer who supplied him with the material, and was apparently agitated because four gross of pasteboard had not been delivered to him as agreed. They were promised for the following Tuesday. He retorted that by then he would have no use for them.

A curious bystander asked him: 'What is the reason of your haste? Have you any show suddenly before the King?' At this Belland was said to have grown red in the face. He was then asked what kind of fireworks he was making.

'I make all sorts,' he replied. 'Some that will fly up in a pure body of flame, higher than the top of St Paul's, and waver in the air.'

'Mr Belland, when you make your show, shall I see it?' asked this bystander.

'Yes, I promise you,' replied Belland, and gave him his hand on it.

The sight of St Paul's throwing sheets of flame into the sky on September 4th was enough to send the stationer and Belland's questioner scurrying off in search of the firework-maker. They discovered that fearing the anger of the mob, he had wisely taken refuge in the King's Palace.

The Committee heard many garbled accounts of suspicious actions seen during the fire – men throwing fireballs, dropping bits of burning material through windows, walking about with gunpowder hidden in lanterns, and so forth. There were also stories of a Frenchman caught by the mob who 'confessed' that he was one of 300 incendiaries engaged upon firing the City, and of a woman, driven hysterical by her accusers, who agreed with every accusation they made.

Some, of course, had a ready explanation for the release of people who clearly had no knowledge of how the fire began, and who had only been arrested on suspicion. They hinted that the Court was engaged in a conspiracy to shield the plotters; after all, the Queen Mother and the Duke of York were both Papists.

So the questions and the answers went on, week after week, month after month, until some committee members had difficulty in keeping awake. Sir Richard Brown, a gentleman who had not been very successful in fighting the fire at Smithfield, provided one moment of excitement when he ordered his lackeys to carry in several large bundles which were tipped out on the floor in front of the chairman. They contained knives, daggers, poignards, and the knight announced that they had been found among the rubbish of a burned house, formerly occupied by a Catholic; but after a few more weeks of boredom, the Committee even forgot to mention this matter when drawing up their Report.

One of the witnesses examined by the Members of Parliament on October 25th was William Lilly, compiler of *Lilly's Almanac*. He was asked whether he knew anything of the cause of the Fire 'because in a book of yours long since printed, you hinted some such thing by one of your hieroglyphics'. This book was called *Monarchy or No Monarchy in England*, published well before the Great Plague. In it, Lilly had included some enigmatical woodcuts; one illustrated a maritime city burning, and another showed three corpses lying on the ground in winding sheets, while two men dug graves near some long sheds.

'Through my art,' Lilly said modestly, 'I discovered there *would* be a Plague and a Fire.' He had, however, been unable to fix any precise timing of these disasters. As for the idea of a plot being behind the Fire, he commented: 'Since the Fire, I have taken pains in the search thereof, but cannot give myself any the least satisfaction therein – I concluded that it was only the finger of God.'

Roger L'Estrange had been Licenser of the Almanacs in 1665, when he was also producing the *Intelligencer*, and he afterwards admitted that 'most of them did foretell the Fire of London, but I caused it to be put out'.

His censorship was supposed to have been through fear in case such prophecies might encourage fanatics to try and prove them accurate. This did not stop L'Estrange himself from writing a pamphlet later, in which he claimed that the Fire was a Jesuit conspiracy. The Papists, with the aid of other 'unsanctified villians and jades', had flung into the houses 700 of 'those little hand grenades called by way of a joke, and secrecy, Tewksbury Mustard-Balls, now better known by the name of Jesuit's Fireballs'.

The interest of the Parliamentary Committee in William Lilly was not difficult to understand. During the April Sessions at the Old Bailey, a number of former officers and soldiers of Cromwell's Army, led by Colonel John Rathbone, had been indicted for a conspiracy to murder the King and fire the City of London.

The day chosen for their attempt was September 3rd, 1666 – just one day after the actual Fire of London broke out. The plotters revealed that they chose this day through reading *Lilly's Almanac*. It was said to be a date when 'the ruling planet' forecast 'the downfall of Monarchy'. Their plan was to surprise the Tower by crossing its moat in boats at night. They would then let down the portcullis to stop any outside assistance and kill the Lieutenant of the Tower.

An assassination attempt upon Lord Albemarle was also planned, and arrangements had been made, by bribing ostlers, to surprise the Horse Guards in the Inns where they were quartered. Had the plot been successful, a Republic would have been declared, and as the *London Gazette* expressed it, 'the better to effect this hellish design, the City was to have been fired'.

Rathbone and seven others were convicted of High Treason and executed, their bodies afterwards being mutilated and put on show as a warning to others.

Twelve years after the Fire, Titus Oates, a clergyman who had not received the preferment he felt was his due, decided to expose 'a Popish plot' which, in fact, did not exist. He swore to the magistrate, that Richard Strang, Provincial of the Jesuits, had told him that the Jesuits caused the Great Fire. Strang was supposed to have said that the conspirators used to meet in the Green Dragon tavern at Puddle Dock in the guise of Fifth Monarchy Men (fanatical anti-Royalists). Rathbone and his men were thus persuaded to take part, but learning that the authorities had heard of the plot, the Jesuits decided against carrying on with it and left Rathbone and his Republicans to be discovered.

They organized a further plot in June 1666, which resulted in the firing of the City by several score Irish and French.

Oates also said that Strang told him the Jesuits had employed additional gangs of looters, who plundered £14,000 worth of valuables during the disaster.

One result of the 'plot' Oates swore to be true was the execution of Richard Langhorne, the Catholic barrister whose remark had figured in the Brook Report. Langhorne protested his innocence to the last. Oates received a pension of £1,200 a year and lived in style near the King's Palace at Whitehall until King Charles' death. When the Catholic Duke of York came to the throne as James II, Oates was tried and convicted of perjury, and condemned to life imprisonment 'to stand in the pillories four times and to be whipped'.

Thirteen years after the Fire, it was said that Rathbone and his fellow conspirators had been 'mere tools' of the Papists. This claim was made by one Captain William Bedloe, a pamphleteer, who published a tract in 1679 called: *A Narrative and Impartial Discovery of the Horrid Popish Plot*. Bedloe claimed to have gained the confidence of the Jesuits, and so was admitted to their secret councils. Every fire that had occurred in the City in 1678–9 he attributed to a Jesuit gang under a Father Gifford, particularly the serious fires at Wapping and Limehouse in 1678, which destroyed large amounts of property. Dedicating his epistle to London's citizens ruined in the Great Fire, he laid the entire blame upon 'the general Disturbers of the Peace and Happiness of Europe, and Pests of Human Society, I mean those subtle, active and most cruel Engineers of the Roman hierarchy'. It was later discovered that Bedloe's pamphlet was also a fake.

The House of Commons received the Brook Report in January. It contained no recommendations whatsoever.

Three weeks later, Parliament was again prorogued, and although the Committee said they had only submitted an interim Report, they never produced anything more substantial. Their chairman, Sir Robert Brook, was drowned in an accident on a French ferry, and as a contemporary drily observed: 'The business drowned with him.'

The Privy Council concluded that nothing had been found to argue the disaster to have been anything else but 'the hand of God upon us, a great wind, and the season so very dry'.

The Monument, designed by Wren and built at a cost of £15,000 in Fish Street Hill to commemorate the Great Fire, claims in an inscription that London rose from its ashes in only three years. Such a feat would have been impossible, and in fact the new London took many years to complete. Work on some buildings went on until nearly the end of the century; St Paul's was not completed until 1710.

Nevertheless, the resurrection of the capital was an amazing achievement. No fire insurance existed, and thus each individual citizen had to make good his own loss. Rebuilding was therefore sporadic, and accomplished whenever the owners could raise enough money. But they worked hard, spent liberally, and built about 10,000 houses in less than eight years. One man wagered that he would have a new home built from the foundations to the roof in forty-eight hours; he won the bet.

Dr Woodward, a professor of Gresham College, remarked in a letter to Wren that 'the Fire of London, however disastrous it might have been to the inhabitants, has proved infinitely beneficial to their posterity'. He was right. The old Restoration London, with its evil-smelling drains, verminous wooden houses and congested streets had been swept away for ever; the new city that arose was considered by many at that time to be one of the finest and healthiest in the world.

The provisions of the Rebuilding Act of 1667 were clearly designed to lessen fire risks and to improve sanitation. Streets were widened, and the old open sewers went out of fashion. Wooden houses were prohibited, and regulations decreed that buildings must be in brick or stone. Gables overhanging the narrow streets and alleys were forbidden, and the size and type of construction of the houses were controlled. Anyone who did not follow these regulations had his house promptly pulled down for his disobedience.

Thomas Delaune, who published his book *The Present State of London* in 1681, said that the results were that London's buildings had become 'more beautiful, more commodious and more solid' – in his opinion, the three great virtues of all edifices. The streets were not only wider and straighter, but for the first time were provided with pavements of smooth-hewn stones and many more massy posts to protect the pedestrians from traffic.

Brick buildings were also a great success. 'Whereas before they dwelt in low, dark wooden houses, they now live in lofty, lightsome, uniform and very stately brick buildings,' said Delaune. He thought that the public halls, new taverns and mansion houses of the noblemen and rich merchants were fit to receive 'the greatest Monarchs in Europe'.

The King did much to foster the rebuilding of London, but the City chose a strange way to honour him for his interest. Sir Robert Viner, who became Lord Mayor, decided that a suitable equestrian statue of Charles II should be built on the site of the new Stocks Market, where Mansion House now stands.

He did not want to spend more on this than was absolutely necessary, however. He heard that a statue of John Sobieski, the King of Poland, had been ordered by the Polish Ambassador in England to commemorate a victory over the Turks, but somehow it had never been collected from Tower Dock. Sir Robert examined it; the statue showed Sobieski astride a noble charger, with a prostrate Turk under his horse's feet: an admirable and traditional pose. Viner bought the statue very cheaply, and arranged to have it converted to show Charles II as the horseman. The vanquished enemy would be Oliver Cromwell.

A new head of the King was carved for the horseman, and the statue was set up in 1675, but somehow nobody gave orders for the Turk's turban-style head-dress to be removed from 'Cromwell'. Thus the niggardliness of the City Fathers was exposed for all to see. The sculpture was the subject of many lampoons until it was removed fifty years later.

The Monument, built to 'preserve the memory' of the Great Fire, reflected the bitter religious controversies of that time.

In 1681, after Titus Oates had given his evidence, a new inscription was carved upon it: 'This pillar was set up in perpetual remembrance of the most dreadful burning of this Protestant city, begun and carried on by the treachery and malice of the Popish faction, in the beginning of September, in the year of our Lord 1666, in order to the carrying on their horrid plot for extirpating the Protestant religion and old English liberty, and introducing Popery and slavery.'

When the Duke of York, a Catholic, came to the throne four years later, he had these words erased.

When William of Orange became King in 1689, the words were cut into the stone once more, for he was a Protestant. Only in the nineteenth century was the inscription permanently removed.

After the Great Fire, Anthony Wood wrote rather gloomily: 'All astrologers did use to say Rome should have an end and Antichrist should come, 1666, but the prophecie fell upon London.' Wood, like many of his contemporaries, could not realise that out of these two catastrophes of Plague and Fire, much good would emerge. A new London grew with wider streets and gracious buildings; and more important, a new, friendly spirit grew with it, tried by adversity and purged by despair.

This remarkable change of heart and mind and attitude came to full and splendid flower, an astonishment and an example to the world, in the City's next time of trial 275 years later: the aerial bombardments of 1940.

1. That is, seven nights after, or a week on Sunday.

A SELECTIVE BIBLIOGRAPHY

The author would like to thank Mrs Joan St George Sanders, and Speakers' and Writers' Research, with Miss Mary Cosh and Mr John Barrows for their help in research

A Collection of Very Valuable and Scarce Pieces, relating to the last Plague in the year 1665, 1721.

Additional MSS, British Museum MSS Department.

Archaelogia, Letters of John Allin, 1857.

A True and Faithful Account of the several Informations exhibited to the Honourable Committee appointed by Parliament, 1667.

Antiquarian Repertory, edited Francis Grose and Thomas Astle, 1807.

AUSTIN, WILLIAM, *Anatomy of the Pestilence*, 1665.

BAXTER, RICHARD, *Reliquiae Baxterianae*, 1696.

BEAVENS, REV. ALFRED B., *The Aldermen of the City of London*, 2 Vols., 1908.

BELL, JOHN, *London's Remembrancer*, 166?.

BELL, WALTER G., *The Great Fire of London*, 19??; *The Great Plague in London*, 1924.

Bloody Almanack, The, 1666.

BEVERIDGE, BISHOP WILLIAM, *Sermons*, Vol. II, London, 1720.

BEDLOE, CAPTAIN WILLIAM, *A Narrative and Impartial Discovery of the Horrid Popish Plot*, etc., 1679.

BOGHURST, WILLIAM, *Loimographia*, 1666. Published by the Epidemiological Society of London, 1894.

BOYLE, ROBERT, *The General History of the Air*, 1692.

BROOK, IRIS, *English Costume of the Seventeenth Century*, 1934.

251

BROWNE, J, *Practical Treatise of the Plague*, 1720.

BRYANT, SIR ARTHUR, *King Charles II*, 1931; *The England of Charles II*, 1934.

BURNET, BISHOP GILBERT, *History of My Own Time*, 1724.

BLUNDELL, WILLIAM, *A Cavalier's Notebook*, 1880; *Cavalier – Letters of W B to his friends, 1620–98*, 1933.

City Remembrancer, edited Gideon Harvey, 1769.

CHAMBERLAYNE, EDWARD, *Angliae Notitia*, or *The Present State of England*, Vols. I and II, 1669, 1671.

CALAMY, DR BENJAMIN, *Sermons*, 1685.

Calendar of State Papers (including Royal Proclamations), 1664–7.

CLARENDON, EDWARD HYDE, EARL, *History of the Reign of King Charles II*, 1757.

COBBETT, WILLIAM, *Collection of State Trials*.

COLLEGE OF PHYSICIANS, *Certain Necessary Directions for the cure of the Plague*, etc., 1665.

CREIGHTON, DR CHARLES, *History of Epidemics in Britain*, 1891.

CROFTON, ZACHARY, *A Defence Against the Dread of Death*, 1665.

DEFOE, DANIEL, *Journal of the Plague Year*, 1722.

DELAUNE, THOMAS, *The Present State of London*, 1681.

Dictionary of National Biography.

DIEMERBROOKE, I, *Tractatus de Peste*, 1646.

DRUMMOND, J C, *The Englishman's Food*, 1957.

DRYDEN, JOHN, 'Annus Mirabilis', 1667.

DUGDALE, SIR WILLIAM, *History of St Paul's*, 1658.

ECHARD, ARCHDEACON LAURENCE, *Account of the Burning of London*, 1721; *The History of England*, 1707–18.

EDLIN, RICHARD, *Prae-Nuncius Sydereus*, 1664.

Encyclopaedia Britannica.

EVELYN, JOHN, Diary; *Fumifugium*, 1661.

GADBURY, JOHN, *London's Deliverance Predicted*, 1665.

GARENCIERES, THEOPHILUS, *A Mite Cast into the Treasury of the City of London*, 1665.

Gentleman's Magazine, 1769.

Golgotha, or *A Looking-Glass for London*, by J.V., 1665.

GRAUNT, JOHN, *Observations upon the Bills of Mortality*, 1665; *Reflections on the Weekly Bills of Mortality*, 1721.

Guildhall Library papers.

GUMBLE, DR THOMAS, *Life of General Monck*, 1671.

Harmsworth Encyclopaedia.

HARPER, CHARLES G, *Half Hours with the Highwaymen.*

HARVEY, DR GIDEON, *A Discourse on the Plague.*

HECHT, J JEAN, *The Domestic Servant Class in 18th Century England*, 1956.

His Majestie's Declaration to His City of London upon occasion of the late Calamity by the lamentable Fire, 1666.

HODGES, DR NATHANIEL, *Loimologia*, 1672; Letter from Dr Hodges to a Person of Quality, May, 1666.

HOLE, CHRISTINA, *English Home Life*, 1947.

House of Commons Journal, Vol. 7, 1651–9.

Intelligencer and Newes, edited Roger L'Estrange, 1663–5.

Journey Book of England – Derbyshire, 1840.

KITCHIN, GEORGE, *Sir Roger L'Estrange*, 1913.

LANG, JANE, *The Rebuilding of St Paul's after the Great Fire of London*, 1956.

L'ESTRANGE, ROGER, *A Compendious History*, 1680.

LILLY, WILLIAM, *History of his Life and Times*, 1715; *Monarchy or No Monarchy in England*, 1651; *England's Propheticall Merline*, 1644; *Collection of Ancient and Modern Prophecies*, 1645; and other works.

London's Dreadful Visitation. Bills of Mortality published by Parish Clerks' Company, London, 1664–6.

London Gazette, 1666–7.

MALCOLM, J L, *Londinium Redivivum*, or *The Ancient and Modern Description of London* (collection of letters), 1807.

MAITLAND, WILLIAM, *History of London*, 1739.

Mayoral Proclamations (preserved in British Museum and at the Guildhall).

MEAD, DR RICHARD, *A Discourse on the Plague*, 1744.

MEIKLEJOHN, J M D, *A New History of England and Great Britain*, 1905; *A General History*, 1901.

MYERS, P V N, *Nature*, February 7, 1884.

Notes and queries, Series 1 to 15.

OLDMIXON, J, *History on England*, 1730.

Observations Both Historical and Moral upon the Burning of London, by Rege Sincera – 1667. (Harleian Miscellany, Vol. VII, 1810.)

Oxford Gazette, 1665–6.

PATRICK, BISHOP SIMON, *Autobiography* – Oxford, 1839.

PEPYS, SAMUEL, *Diary*.

Pepysiana.

Plague's Approved Physitian (The), anon. – 1665.

REDDAWAY, T F, *The Rebuilding of London after the Great Fire*, 1940.

Rugge's *Diurnal*.

SANDYS, W, Letter to Viscount Scudamore.

SEYMOUR, ROBERT, *A Survey of the Cities of London and Westminster*, etc., 1734.

Shutting up Infected Houses, anon., 1665.

STOUGHTON, REV. J, *History of Religion in England*, 1881.

STRAUS, R *Carriage and Coaches*, 1912.

TASWELL, REV. WILLIAM, *Autobiography*.

THOMSON, DR GEORGE, *Loimologia*, 1665; *Loimotomia*, or *The Pest Anatomized*, 1666.

THRUPP, SYLVIA, *The Worshipful Company of Bakers*.

TREVELYAN, G M, *English Social History*.

VERNEY, M M, *Memoirs of the Verney Family*, 1925.

VINCENT, DR THOMAS, *God's Terrible Voice in the City*, 1667.

WOOD, ANTHONY, *Life and Times of Anthony Wood*, 1892.

WOOD, WILLIAM, *The History and Antiquities of Eyam*, 1842; *History of Eyam*, 1859.

JAMES LEASOR

BOARDING PARTY

Filmed as *The Sea Wolves*, this is the story of the undercover exploits of a territorial unit. The Germans had a secret transmitter on one of their ships in the neutral harbour of Goa. Its purpose was to guide the U-boats against Allied shipping in the Indian Ocean. There seemed no way for the British to infringe Goa's Portuguese neutrality by force. But the transmitter had to be silenced. Then it was remembered that 1,400 miles away in Calcutta was a source of possible help. A group of civilian bankers, merchants and solicitors were the remains of an old territorial unit called 'The Calcutta Light Horse'. With a foreword by Earl Mountbatten of Burma.

'One of the most decisive actions in World War II was fought by fourteen out-of-condition middle-aged men sailing in a steam barge…' – *Daily Mirror*

'A gem of World War II history' – *New York Times Book Review*

'If ever there was a ready-made film script…here it is' – *Oxford Mail*

JAMES LEASOR

GREEN BEACH

In 1942 radar expert Jack Nissenthall volunteered for a suicidal mission to join a combat team who were making a surprise landing at Dieppe in occupied France. His assignment was to penetrate a German radar station on a cliff above 'Green Beach'. Because Nissenthall knew the secrets of British and US radar technology, he was awarded a personal bodyguard of sharp-shooters. Their orders were to protect him, but in the event of possible capture to kill him. His choice was to succeed or die. The story of what happened to him and his bodyguards in nine hours under fire is one of World War II's most terrifying true stories of personal heroism.

'*Green Beach* has blown the lid off one of the Second World War's best-kept secrets' – *Daily Express*

'If I had been aware of the orders given to the escort to shoot him rather than let him be captured, I would have cancelled them immediately' – *Lord Mountbatten*

'*Green Beach* is a vivid, moving and at times nerve-racking reconstruction of an act of outstanding but horrific heroism' – *Sunday Express*

JAMES LEASOR

THE MARINE FROM MANDALAY

This is the true story of a Royal Marine wounded by shrapnel in Mandalay who undergoes a long solitary march to flee the Japanese and finds his way back through India to Britain. On his way he has many encounters and adventures and helps British and Indian refugees.

THE MILLIONTH CHANCE

The R101 airship was thought to be the model for the future, an amazing design that was 'as safe as houses...except for the millionth chance'. On the night of 4 October 1930 that chance in a million came up, however. James Leasor brilliantly reconstructs the conception and crash of this huge ship of the air with compassion for the forty-seven dead – and only six survivors.

'The sense of fatality grows with every page... Gripping'
– *Evening Standard*

JAMES LEASOR

THE ONE THAT GOT AWAY

Franz von Werra was a Luftwaffe pilot shot down in the Battle of Britain. *The One that Got Away* tells the full and exciting story of his two daring escapes in England and his third and successful escape: a leap from the window of a prisoners' train in Canada. Enduring snow and frostbite, he crossed into the then neutral United States. This book is based on von Werra's own dictated account of his adventures and makes for a compelling read.

WHO KILLED SIR HARRY OAKES?

James Leasor cleverly reconstructs events surrounding a brutal and unusual murder. It is 1943 and Sir Harry Oakes lies horrifically murdered at his Bahamian mansion. Although a self-made multi-millionaire, Sir Harry is an unlikely victim – there are no suggestions of jealousy or passion. Leasor makes the daring suggestion that Sir Harry Oakes' murder, the burning of the liner *Normandie* in New York Harbour in 1942 and the Allied landings in Sicily are all somehow connected.

'The story has all the right ingredients – rich occupants of a West Indian tax haven, corruption, drugs, the Mafia, and a weak character as governor' – *Daily Mail*

Printed in Great Britain
by Amazon